AF560661

MEDICAL TOURISM IN INDIA

Management and Promotion

MEDICAL TOURISM IN INDIA

Management and Promotion

DR. R. KUMAR
MBBS, MS Ex PGI
Eye Specialist, Health Columnist and
Medical Tourism Advisor,
Chandigarh

Foreword by

DR. RAJ BAHADUR
Professor of Orthopedics and Director Principal,
Government Medical College and Hospital,
Sector 32, Chandigarh

DEEP & DEEP PUBLICATIONS PVT. LTD.
F-159, Rajouri Garden, New Delhi-110027

MEDICAL TOURISM IN INDIA

MANAGEMENT AND PROMOTION

ISBN 978-81-8450-085-1

Typeset by S.S. COMPOSERS
3190, Mohindra Park, Shakur Basti, Delhi-110034.

Printed in India at MAYUR ENTERPRISES,
WZ Plot No. 3, Gujjar Market, Tihar Village, New Delhi-110018.

Published by DEEP & DEEP PUBLICATIONS PVT. LTD.
F-159, Rajouri Garden, New Delhi-110027.
Phones: 25435369, 25440916
E-mail: ddpbooks@yahoo.co.in • ddpubs@gmail.com
Showroom:
2/13, Ansari Road, Daryaganj, New Delhi-110002 • Telefax: 23245122

Contents

	Foreword	vii
	Preface	xi
1.	Perspectives of Tourism: The Height of Credibility	1
2.	What is Medical Tourism?	29
3.	Growth of the Medical Tourism Industry in Asia	49
4.	Realities of India as a Health Tourism Destination	72
5.	India's Islands of Medical and Surgical Excellence	87
6.	How to Promote Medical Tourism in India?	108
7.	Common Surgical Interventions Sought by Foreign Patients	127
8.	How much can you Save by your World-Class Treatment in India?	153
9.	Foreign Medical Tourists: Some Illustrative Examples	168
10.	Kerala the God's own Paradise	183

11.	Medical Tourism and Healthcare Services	206
12.	Medical Tourism as a Distortion of Priorities	214
	Appendices	222
	Bibliography	325
	Index	332

Foreword

I am delighted to see this title 'Medical Tourism in India: Management and Promotion' written by Dr. R. Kumar an eminent ophthalmologist and medical tourism advisor at Chandigarh. I know that Dr. Kumar has written several books on public health and prevention of disease in the last 30 years. Dr. Kumar has added another feather in his cap by penning this unique book that will benefit not only the healthcare and tourism sectors in India, but also the patients all over the world. Medical tourism is an in thing and would benefit the country in several ways. His efforts to promote healthcare and medical tourism at Chandigarh and adjoining states need to be lauded.

Every year thousand of visitors are coming to India from around the world for various types of surgeries related to heart. Bone or liver or eye and others. India can give Thailand and other Asian countries a stiff competition in healthcare services for overseas patients with cost of surgery lower by over 30% and in fact cheapest in entire Southeast Asia. The medical tourism market in India has been pegged to grow to around Rs.. 100 billions by 2012, as per McKinsey-CII study. The notion that catering to the needs of foreigners will be at the cost of poor Indian patients appears misplaced. In fact these are private facilities and are created as a business venture by the Indian industry for a niche market. The government is earnestly making efforts to set up a good public health system, which can be facilitated by the revenue earned from taxes and royalty from the private sector. If India makes medical tourism a success, it will spur more investment in healthcare, greater research and development in medical; field and reversal of brain drain.

The two principal views on medical tourism are:

(i) Medical tourism will be a boon for the country, since it will improve healthcare for the countrymen and make India an economic superpower in the long run through the route of medical tourism. It is an engine of all-round development of the country.

(ii) Ban medical tourism completely, since it will lead to escalation in the cost of medical treatment for the natives, in the private hospitals and deterioration of already overburdened public hospitals. Governments should have no role in promoting healthcare tourism since it negatively impacts the people they are supposed to represent.

The entrepreneurs and hospitals argue that a high-paying Western clientele can subsidize the cost of providing services for the local population. There are 47 millions uninsured Americans; there are 120 millions Americans who are underinsured. Healthcare costs in the United States are prohibitive. In Europe and Canada, the wait list for elective surgery is too long. The private healthcare system in those countries is so expensive that many have little option but to seek medical services from low-cost Asian countries such as India. The cost for heart bypass in India is just 7.7 per cent of the cost in the U.S. The costs for other surgeries including spinal surgery are about 10 per cent of that in the U.S. Even after adding first class airfare and five star hotel facilities, Westerners are better off seeking medical services in India. Obviously. Indian hospitals are ready to exploit such opportunities and the massive cost differentials. Numerous state-of-the-art hospitals are popping up in major Indian cities to service foreign clientele. Apollo group is in the forefront of health tourism as well as healthcare to the countrymen. Many more are needed. India has the potential to become the world leader in medical tourism

The country offers a unique mix of modern medical treatment at world class hospitals along with indigenous systems such as yoga, ayurveda and meditation techniques.

Ambika Soni, the minister of Tourism, stated recently that the capacity of medical tourism to earn foreign exchange is even greater than the IT sector. Setting up of a chain of Medicare cities in different parts of the country would take care of the medical and surgical needs of the people of India and offer spare capacities to the foreign medical tourists. Chandigarh is taking giant strides to create more hospitals and improve existing hospitals.

Chandigarh

DR. RAJ BAHADUR
Professor of Orthopedics and
Director Principal,
Government Medical College
and Hospital,
Sector 32, Chandigarh

Preface

In recognition of the importance of the tourism sector and its contribution to the economy, the Government of India has drawn a National Tourism Policy to reinforce the country's tourism infrastructure. The Government has undertaken an integrated and imaginative marketing strategy of India's tourism products through its *Incredible India* Campaign, which has been so successful that it has received many international accolades. In fact, India recorded 23.5% growth in international tourist arrivals and 33% in foreign exchange earnings in 2004. It is growing, ever since. At the end of year 2007, it was estimated that more than 2 lacs of health tourists came to India for medical treatment.

Indian healthcare is now known for its safety, trust, compassion and excellence. When it comes to blending of healthcare with spirtual well-being India has no rivals. In fact, healthcare is the latest reason to visit India. Patients from 55 countries come to Indian hospitals. It is well known for heart surgery, joint surgeries, eye surgeries and others. India is one of the best places for the medical treatment. Every year thousand of visitors are coming to India from around the world just for the medical check up and various types of surgeries related to Bone or liver or eye and others. India is giving Thailand stiff competition in healthcare services for overseas patients with cost of surgery lower by over 30% and in fact cheapest in entire Southeast Asia. Medical tourism is fast emerging as a big opportunity for India with its low cost advantage, high quality healthcare providers and an English-speaking populace. The medical tourism market in India has been pegged to grow to around Rs. 100 billions by 2012, as per McKinsay-CII study as reported in *Times of India*, dated Sept. 15, 2007. The notion that catering to the needs of foreigners or rich Indian patients will be at the cost of poor Indian citizens appears misplaced. In fact, these are private facilities and are created as a business venture by the Indian industry for a niche market. The government can set-up a good public health system, which can be facilitated by the revenue earned from taxes and royalty from the private sector. If India makes medical tourism a success, it will spur more investment in healthcare, greater research and development in medical field and reversal of brain drain. This will also promote Indian pharmaceuticals and also make India a hub of International conventions.

Health tourism has become a recurrent form of vacationing, and covers a broad range of medical services. It mingles free time, amusing and recreation together with wellness and healthcare packages. The thought of the health holiday is to offer you a chance to get away from your daily habitual and come into a dissimilar calming neighbouring. Here you can take pleasure in being close to the beach and the mountains. At the same time you are able to accept a compass reading that will assist you advance your life in terms of your health and general well-being. It is like reconstruction and cleans up process on all levels—physical, psychological and expressive. However, a nice blend of top-class medical expertise at attractive prices is helping a rising number of Indian corporate hospitals attract foreign patients, including from developed nations such as the UK and the US. The things are going to change radically in favour of India, particularly in view of the high eminence expertise of medical professionals, backed by the fast improving tools and nursing amenities, and above all, the cost-effectiveness of the pack up.

The two principal views on medical tourism that have emerged in the ongoing debate are:

(i) Medical tourism will be a boon for the country, since it will improve healthcare for the countrymen and make India an economic superpower in the long-run through the route of medical tourism. It is an engine of all-round development of the country.

(ii) Ban medical tourism completely, since it will lead to escalation in the cost of medical treatment for the natives, in the private hospitals and deterioration of already overburdened public hospitals. Governments should have no role in promoting healthcare tourism since it negatively impacts the people they are supposed to represent.

However, the seemingly divergent views have no discrepancy, since improvement in healthcare infrastructure for foreign medical tourists will lead to improved healthcare for the countrymen as well.

The entrepreneurs and hospitals argue that a high-paying Western clientele can subsidize the cost of providing services for the local population. There are 47 million uninsured Americans; there are 120 million Americans who are underinsured. Healthcare costs in the United States are prohibitive. Even in Europe and Canada, the wait list for elective surgery is too long. The private healthcare system in those countries is so expensive that many have little option but to seek medical services from low-cost Asian countries such as India. The cost for heart bypass in India is just 7.7 per cent of the cost in the US. The costs for other surgeries including spinal surgery are about 10 per cent of that in the US. Even after adding first class airfare and five star hotel facilities, Westerners are better off seeking medical services in India. Obviously, Indian hospitals are ready to exploit such opportunities and the massive cost differentials. Numerous state-of-the-art hospitals are popping up in major Indian cities to service foreign clientele. Many more are needed. If we have to follow Thailand model, we have to provide adequate healthcare to our own people first of all. That entails massive investment in healthcare infrastructure with public-private partnership (PPP). Once that is achieved it will lead to all round development and prosperity of the country.

Potential to become the world leader

With internationally recognized healthcare professionals, holistic medicinal services and low cost of treatment, India has the potential to attract over one million "health tourists" (equal to Thailand) every year, according to the Confederation of Indian Industry (CII). The country offers a unique mix of modern medical treatment at world class hospitals along with indigenous systems such as yoga, ayurveda and meditation techniques. This, along with the presence of top medical experts and the cost advantage can help earn $5 billion every year. While a heart surgery costs $100,000 in the US, it costs $6,000 in India. Similarly, a bone marrow transplant costs $26,000 here compared to $250,000 in the US. A study by CII-McKinsey estimates that the country could earn Rs. 5,000-10,000 crore by 2012. Ambika Soni, the Minister of Tourism, stated recently that the capacity of medical tourism to earn foreign exchange is greater than even the IT sector.

Citing the example of Thailand, CII stresses that India should aggressively publicize its medical services in association with the tourism authorities. Several Indian state governments have realized the potential of this 'industry' and have been actively promoting it. Visitors, especially from the West and the Middle East find Indian hospitals a very affordable and viable option. Karnataka, Andhra, Tamil Nadu, Maharashtra and Gujarat are in the forefront of medical tourism promotion. Kerala is God's own health paradise. However, the country would have to improve its healthcare infrastructure, connectivity between major cities and streamline visa procedures for medical visitors. Accreditation of Indian hospitals is also essential for attracting such tourists. Apart from receiving patients from those parts of the globe that have poor medical facilities viz. SAARC countries, India has been getting some medical visitors from the West for a variety of reasons, including the long waiting period for treatment in Government hospitals in those countries.

According to senior Government officials, the marketing of medical facilities to a global audience have already started. Our National Health Policy recognizes the treatment of international patients as an export, which allows private hospitals treating such patients to enjoy benefits such as lower import duties, increase in the rate of depreciation (from 25 per cent to 40 per cent) for life-saving medical equipment, and several other tax sops.

There are plenty of challenges that need to be addressed for India to become the world's preferred healthcare destination. The first is to improve healthcare for the countrymen. Prominent among others is the need for proper accreditation and the putting in place of requisite standardization systems. A tripartite synergy between hospitals, tour operators and the government would need to be created. There might be need for a separate regulatory authority viz. National medical tourism authority. Standardization of a price band for graded hospitals and a quality assurance model should be taken up immediately to take medical tourism ahead. Most basic of all is huge investment in the healthcare infrastructure that is required to provide adequate facilities to our own people as well as the visiting patients. Stark contrasts are no surprise in urban India, and in the healthcare sector, the difference between what is available—world-class techniques and service, at a price—and what the common man is missing in terms of even basic facilities in the healthcare system, is sizable. Private sector healthcare centers are gleaming islands of excellence, all too often surrounded by seas of medical neglect and overcrowding in the public health sector. See Appendix 4 for aspects of 'Globalization of medical tourism'.

Look at the possibility of the public hospitals being technologically upgraded to world-class standards with the additional source of income from foreign medical visitors. So the beneficiary of such growth will be the country's desperately overburdened public health system, say industry associations such as CII and FICCI.

Medical Tourism can piggy ride religious tourism

The government is contemplating to develop religious tourism in this region, by connecting Sri Anandpur Sahib, Chamkaur Sahib, Fatehgarh Sahib, Takht Sri Damdama Sahib and Sri Harmandir Sahib. Another circuit of shrines from Naina Devi, Maisarkhana, Durgiana Temple and Vaishno Devi may also be developed. However, potential of synergy between religious tourism and medical tourism is immense, that remains unidentified and untapped. Most of our pilgrimage centers viz. Golden temple at Amritsar, Nadha

Sahib and Mansa Devi shrines at Panchkula, Anandpur Sahib/Naina Devi complex in HP are a few of the examples in the north, which can be connected internationally by the existing airports at Amritsar and Chandigarh respectively. Similarly, well known religious places in the south/west like Triputi/Shirdi have neither the dearth of land nor money required to construct world class hospitals/medical education institutions. In fact, with the two kinds of tourism combined together have greater potential to earn revenue for the nation than any other. Many NRIs can also join hands in supporting this nation-building venture. Massive investment in healthcare through this route can mitigate the sufferings of our own people as well attract patients from all over the world. This does not entail any financial burden on the state budget or adversely affect the existing healthcare structure either in the private sector or public sector. In fact, it will lead to overall improvement in healthcare and other areas.

Hospital industry is booming

The hospital boom in India was fueled by India's growing middle-class who demanded access to quality healthcare. Now, the country known for exporting doctors is trying hard to import patients as well as get back its trained medical manpower. The most important player is the Apollo Group, the largest hospital group in India, and the third largest in the world. Many more are ready to jump in the fray. It makes sense to establish India as a world destination for healthcare, since it will lead to enhanced image of the country in the comity of nations, besides earning precious foreign exchange.

But why should foreigners come here despite the familiar images of the country (teeming, dusty streets, infections and poverty)? Anne Bell, a patient from UK who had a baby and says she's glad she was here, and not in England: "There's been no pressure to go home after the delivery. We've been welcomed to stay as long as we want. They're looking after the baby. They're looking after me, giving me enough time to get settled and get confident enough to go back home. Often in the UK, you might be out of the hospital within five hours if you've had a normal delivery." And in the UK, she wouldn't have had a private room and a private bath. Not to mention massages, and yoga, too. And the doctors? Indian doctors are known worldwide, they speak English, and they're often the very same doctors you may have had in Europe or America, where many of them practiced before returning to India.

Stephanie Sedlmayr couldn't afford to spend the tens of thousands of dollars it would take to get the hip surgery she needed. And she didn't have insurance, either. So she flew from Vero Beach, Fla., to the Apollo Hospital in Chennai. She'd never been to India before, but she already knew quite a bit about Indian doctors. Sedlmayr, says her friends questioned her decision. "Hardly anybody said, 'Oh, great idea.'" But she didn't just come here to save money; she came for an operation she couldn't get at home. It's called hip resurfacing, and it has changed people's lives. It hasn't been approved yet by the FDA, but in India, orthopedic surgeons have performed thousands of them. They showed in India 60 Minutes the difference between a hip resurfacing and hip replacement, which is the standard operation performed in the United States. They say the patients usually recover faster because this procedure is far less radical and doesn't involve cutting the thighbone. Instead, surgeon fits a metal cap over the end, which fits into a metal socket in the hip. The result is that patients end up with enough mobility to do virtually anything. "So patients, you know, play football, basketball, whatever you want. Not a problem," says an Indian surgeon.

Reversal of brain drain

Dr. Praveen Khilnani, a pediatric intensive care specialist, worked at several American Hospitals. Dr. Vikas Kohli is a pediatric cardiologist who worked at hospitals in New York and Miami. They both wanted to come back to India despite the fact that medical care costs much less here, partly because doctors make much less. They wanted to come back, they say, because they felt their expertise was needed here in India much more than in America.

Would you export rice when.......?

Those who are against medical tourism in India argue:

World Health Organization (WHO) identifies India as a country, having the greatest shortage of doctors. India is short of one million of hospital beds. In comparison, the US has 2.56 per 1000 (India 0.60) and most Western nations have at least four times higher density of doctors than India. India has a large number of patients with tuberculosis, malaria, AIDS/HIV, leprosy, and other infectious diseases. India has low public healthcare spending, i.e. only 0.9% of GDP as per 2001 census. Latest figure of 1.39% of GDP of centre and states combined; is also abysmally low. In India, more than 75 per cent of the healthcare spending is in the private sector. The percentage of out-of-pocket spending on private healthcare is a whopping 97 per cent. In the US, it is just 24.5 per cent and in most European countries it is even lower. Private cost of healthcare services in India may rise with the advent of medical tourism, since this will amplify the gap between the demand and the supply. Since doctors' reputations attract patients, there will be a bidding war for well-known doctors. All this can be expected to increase the cost of healthcare services for the local population. Is it then in the best interests of the nation? Should India allow export of essential food grains for enormous profits, when the local population is starving? You need to accept a ban on medical tourism given the abysmal healthcare access? The entrepreneurs, the medical profession, and all the enablers such as industry associations and State governments need to tread carefully.

Further, foreign clientele will expect more than the required resources since the long-term risks involved are higher. Thus, hospitals and doctors will spend disproportionately more resources for foreign (or wealthy) patients. It is hard to conceive how resources can be allocated for poor patients under severe deficit. Is this is a case for socially responsible governance?

As of now the country is considered as a new kid on the block as compared to other Asian countries like Thailand, Singapore, Malaysia, Philippines, and South Korea, etc. Various Metro Cities and other cities like Chandigarh should explore the possibility of setting up "Medi-Cities" with a cluster of superspecialty hospitals; providing world class services at third world prices. In fact this means only improving country's infrastructure in healthcare for the benefit of its own people. Then the foreign medical tourists will like to avail the services automatically.

When the mix is just right, with support from the government in the form of incentives and tax breaks, international healthcare accreditation standards in place, breakthroughs in insurance coverage for overseas patients, and savvy promotion of India as a tourism-plus-medical destination, the numbers will fall into place.

R. KUMAR

Perspectives of Tourism

The Height of Credibility

India is an incredible mix of vibrant colour, exotic wildlife, mesmerizing landscapes, rich heritage, diverse cultures, beautiful women and spicy curries. This and much more was showcased at Internationale Tourismus Bourse (ITB) at Berlin with a high degree of credibility.

Namaste, Berlin mein aapka swagat hai," the lady in immaculately starched Lufthansa uniform at the Berlin Tegel airport was definitely Indian. Clearly, the German capital sported an incredible new colour for one week and the makeover was the talk of the town. India was the partner country at this year's (2007) fair, where more than 10,000 organizations and companies competed with one another in a

1,60,000 sq. m. sized exhibition area, exuded of the country's new-found confidence in the global tourism market. India recorded 4.5 million tourist arrivals in 2006. ITB, between March 7 and 11, 2007 was not about numbers. It was about showcasing a region that always promised big. And the best! "ITB Berlin announced India's arrival on the big stage," said Amitabh Kant, the then joint secretary at the Ministry of Tourism, adding: "Indian companies did business worth $1.45 billion and were successful in selling India as a 365-day destination to the world. We needed to market India on a world stage and it doesn't get any bigger than ITB." The number of trade visitors broke the 100,000 barrier for the first time this year. The figures look even more impressive, and promising, considering that this year; more than 43% of the trade visitors came from abroad. In all, a total of 177,154 visitors came to the sprawling Funkturm Exhibition Grounds in the heart of the city in the five days while the fair was on. And amidst all this, India was the cynosure of all eyes.

"As a principal destination for business travelers and tourists, India has now established a firm place in world tourism. Due to its political stability, strong economy and an increasingly favourable business and investment climate, the growth prospects are much higher." Forty-five of the country's best chefs from Maurya Sheraton, Taj, Oberoi and Hyatt were flown down for a 29-course meal with an assortment of dishes from all over the country, complete with desserts and beverages. The designer Ritu Kumar set the ball rolling at the opening ceremony on March 6, 2007 with her impressive 'Tree of Life' show: a five-part audio-visual sequence that presented India at its best. The show, which has already wowed audiences in Singapore, Hong Kong and at the World Economic Forum, Davos, opened with Rajasthan, moving on to Khadi with motifs like paisley and handicrafts like chikankari, and concluding with showcasing tensile strength of zardozi. German carrier Lufthansa even had an exclusive stall; complete with the Indian crew and food it serves on its long-haul flights from the six destinations it flies out of India. Says the airline's vice-president, marketing and sales: "we are closer to India than any other international airline. Even in our in-flight entertainment, if we give the best of Hollywood, we also have the very best of Bollywood for our consumers. All this because we have enjoyed our long association with India—between 2003 and 2006, with 45 weekly flights from six Indian destinations, we have only doubled our capacity from the country." Says Kant: "More than 6 million people witnessed the extravaganza. We carried with us all the exponents that make India the hottest tourist destination, and the cultural diversity of the country found its voice in the performance of 75 folk artists who accentuated the Indian flavour." Says tourism minister Ambika Soni: "The fact that ITB invited India to be the partner country is a reflection of the rising interest of global travelers towards India." The ITB opened up fresh demands for new products and new areas like Madhya Pradesh, Tamil Nadu, Uttaranchal. Chandigarh, a small territory in the global context was well represented at this fair. This fair has been successful in making the world talk about India. The only dampener was the Pacific Asia Travel Association (PATA) report on the state of tourism in India. Clogged and cracking airports, ageing air traffic control, chronic shortage of hotels and a slow-moving bureaucracy, it said, was cramping India's growth as a world tourism powerhouse. This, when seen in the backdrop of the 13% growth achieved by the tourism industry in the country, with tourist arrivals touching only 4.5 million in 2006 as compared to the 842 million arrivals worldwide, only speaks of a giant in his slumber for long.

What makes India different from any other destination is the myriad of experiences that it offers. This is one land where the ancient and the modern co-exist. India has literally everything that a visitor wants to experience and offers people a complete holiday both physical and mental. This is perhaps the reason why we have

so many repeat visitors. To quote Mark Twain, "India is the cradle of the human race, the birthplace of human speech, the mother of history, the grandmother of legend and the great grandmother of tradition. Our most valuable and most instructive materials in the history of man are treasured up in India." India—the land to travel to, a haven of tourism delights, a civilization to tour through. Tourists come to India for its wealth of sights, cultural exuberance, diversity of terrain and in search of that special something, an extra punch that only India promises and delivers. Teeming with over a billion people who voice over a million concerns in fifteen hundred different languages, India is where people live with variety, thrive on diversity and are too familiar with largeness to let it boggle them. Mud huts and mansions face off across city streets. Lurid luxury and limp living are inhabitants of the same lane. From the smoky mangroves of the Sunderbans to the steaming Thar Desert, sizzling cities like Mumbai and Delhi to the scintillating villages of Khajuraho and Hampi, from the heights of the Himalayas to the deep blue waters around the Andamans, India is a travel haven—a tour package that frustrates and delights, as demanding as it is rewarding.

Incredible India campaign

'Incredible India' marked the first time when India Tourism mounted a concerted, focused and centralised effort to increase what until then was an abysmal tourist inflow. The results are there for everyone to see. According to Nandan; a director in the ministry of tourism, actual arrivals have gone up 25 per cent up last year whereas there has been a 36 per cent increase in forex earnings year on year basis. In fact, foreign tourist arrivals grew 17.3 per cent in February from a year earlier as the sector posted strong growth for the second month after the tsunami. The country recorded 372,269 foreign visitors in the past month against 317,498 a year earlier, while foreign exchange earnings rose 28.8 per cent to $570.53 million. "Before the campaign, India was perceived to be having a very limited tourism product that included the Golden Triangle, Goa, Kerala and Himalayas, etc. However, we are now focusing a lot on the country's diversity which has begun to pay rich dividends," says Nandan. "We are offering a lot more: the colour of India, the food, the flavours, the people, various cultures and the like . . ." "We want to showcase the complete variety that India has to offer: from historical places to the modern India, all that is our strength," she adds. A mix of niche marketing promotions for special interest groups are also in the offing, be it adventure tourism, spiritual tourism, medical tourism, flora and fauna or beaches of India. Hence, a Buddhist Circuit Trail is being seen as a niche effort to woo a larger number of tourists from South-East Asia, China and Japan.

Still a drop in the ocean

Despite all the hype, tourism figures for India, as compared to the world show that Indian tourism is a drop in the ocean, i.e. 0.52% of global tourists. *The Tribune*, dated Oct. 20th, 2007 carried the following data.

Andhra Pradesh accounted for 24.20 per cent of the total 461.16 million domestic travellers. The temple town of Timpati, which draws millions of pilgrims from across the country and abroad, continues to play a major role in the state emerging as a leading tourist destination.

Tirupati, the abode of Lord Venkateswara, attracts about 20 million visitors every year and is one of the most popular religious places in the world. Significantly, AP attracted nearly five times more tourists than Rajasthan, a state which has greater international visibility because of its palaces and exotic locales. Uttar Pradesh, which attracted 22.9 per cent of total domestic tourists, Tamil Nadu (12.7 per cent), Karnataka (7.8 per cent) and Rajasthan (5.1 per cent) are among the top five states.

Surprisingly, Goa, Kerala and Delhi could not make it to the top 10 list. As far as attracting foreign tourists is concerned. Delhi leads the list, accounting for 17.30 per cent of the total 4.45 million tourists last year. It was followed by Maharashtra (14.5 per cent), Uttar Pradesh (11.6 per cent), Rajasthan (10.7 per cent) and Tamil Nadu (9.1 per cent).

AP had to be content with a share of 5.90 per cent. India had hosted 4.45 million foreign tourists last year, an increase of 13.5 per cent from the previous year.

This was just 0.52 per cent of the total global tourist arrivals. With 79.10 million foreign tourists, France was the most visited country in 2006. There was a three-fold increase in the number of domestic tourists in India, from 6.6 per cent in 2005 to 18.1 per cent in 2006.

In terms of numbers, the people traveling within the country increased from 390.47 million in 2005 to 461.16 million in 2006.

The ancient civilization

Nearly five thousand years back flourished India's first major civilizations along the Indus River valley. The twin cities of Mohenjodaro and Harappa now in Pakistan were ruled by priests and held the rudiments of Hinduism. These civilizations are known to possess a sophisticated lifestyle, a highly developed sense of aesthetics, an astonishing knowledge of town planning and an undecipherable script language. The Indus civilization at one point of time extended nearly a million square kilometers across the Indus river valley. It existed at the same time as the ancient civilizations of Egypt and Sumer but far outlasted them. Surviving for nearly a thousand years the Indus valley civilization fell to tectonic upheavals in about 1700 BC, which caused a series of floods.

The coming of the Aryans around 1500 BC, gave the final blow to the collapsing Indus Valley civilization. At the dawn of Vedic ages the Aryans came in from the North and spread through large parts of India bringing with them their culture and religious beliefs. The Four Vedas or the important books of Hinduism were compiled in this period. In 567 B.C. the founder of the Buddhist Religion Gautama Buddha was born. During this time lived Mahavira, who founded the Jain Religion. The Indian subcontinent is full of caves and monuments devoted to these religions and are worth a visit.

Two hundred years later, in the 4th century B.C., Emperor Ashoka, one of the greatest King of Indian history, led the Mauryan Empire to take over almost all of what is now modern India. This great leader embraced Buddhism and built the group of monuments at Sanchi (a UNESCO world heritage site). The Ashoka pillar at Sarnath has been adopted by India as its national emblem and the Dharma Chakra on the Ashoka Pillar adorns the National Flag. They were followed by the Guptas in the north, while in the south part of India several different Hindu empires, the Cholas, the Pandyas and the Cheras spread and grew, trading with Europe and other parts of Asia till the end of the 1100s. Christianity entered India at about the same time from Europe. Legend has it that St. Thomas the Apostle arrived in India in 52 A.D. Even earlier than that people of the Jewish religion arrived on India's shores. In approximately the 7th century A.D. a group of Zoroastrians, or Parsees, landed in Gujarat and became a part of the large mix of religions in India today, each of which adds its important and distinctive flavour. In the 15th century Guru Nanak laid the foundation of the Sikh religion in Punjab. In 1192, Mohammed Ghori, a ruler from Afghanistan, came into India and captured several places in the north including Delhi. When he went home he left one of his generals in charge who became the first Sultan of Delhi. During this time Islam was introduced into a major part of Northern India. It may be mentioned that even before that, just after the period of the prophet, Islam was brought to the western coast of India by Arab traders and flourished in what is now Kerala.

The Delhi Sultanate gradually took control of more and more of North India over the next 200 years, till Timur, who was called "Timur the Lame" or "Tamberlane" came from Turkey in 1398 to attack India. He and his army stole all the valuables that they could carry and left again, and after that the Delhi Sultanate was never so strong again. Soon the Mughals, who were from Iran, came in and took control of the north. In the meantime in the south, in 1336, the Hindu Vijayanagar empire was set-up and became very strong. The Europeans—Portuguese, French, Dutch, Danish and British—started arriving in the early 1600s. All of them held territories in India and made friends and enemies among India's rulers as they got more and more involved, with the Indian politics, but it was the British who eventually controlled most of India and finally made it one of their colonies. India got its independence from Britain in 1947 after a long struggle led mostly by Mahatma Gandhi. In the process of becoming independent, India became, two countries instead of one. In the years since independence India has made huge progress and coped with great problems, and has developed its industry and its agriculture, and has maintained a system of government which makes it the largest democracy in the world.

Religious tourism

India has long been known as a very spiritual, religious heavy area of the world. In India, religion is a way of life. It is an integral part of the entire Indian tradition. For the majority of Indians, religion permeates every aspect of life,

from common-place daily chores to education and politics. Secular India is home to Hinduism, Islam, Christianity, Buddhism, Jainism, Sikhism and other innumerable religious traditions. With devotion and religious fervor in the hearts millions conquer mountains, wade rivers and trek through dense forests to get a glimpse of revered gods and demigods. India's wondrous temples, mosques, synagogues and shrines are fancied by millions the world over. Millions of people from all over the world join us in our journey through a world full of pious thoughts, chants, rituals and faiths. Most people who visit these places donate substantial sums to the coffers of the deity concerned and hope that their wealth will be used for a good cause, e.g. healthcare and relieving the pain and miseries of the people. Once they are satisfied that the cause is good and use is genuine, they can liberally donate. Thus the synergy of religious tourism and medical tourism can be self-financing and lead to all round development.

Hinduism is the dominant faith, practiced by over 80% of the population. Besides Hindus, Muslims are the most prominent religious group and are an integral part of Indian society. In fact India has the second largest population of Muslims in the world after Indonesia. Common practices have crept into most religious faiths in India and many of the festivals that mark each year with music, dance and feasting are shared by all communities. The kind of cosmopolitan existence India has is best reflected in its pilgrim centres. Religion is the heartbeat of the nation and the followers of all the major religious and sects, have lived here for centuries. Their religious and spiritual centres dot the country as much as those of the faiths of Islam and Christianity which came from outside. There is a very long list of temples, mosques and tombs, churches and gurudwaras spread all over the India. In fact, a vacation or holiday can hardly be conceived without a sojourn of pilgrim centers of India.

Religious tourism has emerged as a booming market in India, according to the Delhi-based National Council for Applied Economic Research (NCAER) which shows that of the 230 million tourist trips undertaken in India, the largest proportion is made up of religious pilgrimages. Undertaken by both rural and urban Indians, they outnumber leisure holidays in hill stations, get aways to sea beaches and even trips to metropolitan cities. As many as 23 million people visited Tirupati, a temple town near the southern tip of India to catch a glimpse of a deity known as Lord Balaji. Tirupati's annual list of pilgrims is higher than the total number of travellers visiting Mumbai, Delhi, Bangalore and Kolkata put together. In the northern state of Jammu and Kashmir 17.2 million devotees trek uphill for 15 km to pay respects to goddess Vaishno Devi.

Similarly, most of the NRIs and foreign tourists visiting India do visit one or the other religious place.

If the Char Dham Yatra, along with Ayodhya,

Allahabad, Varanasi, Rishikesh and Haridwar in the North India and other pilgrim centres like Chidambaram, Jagannathpuri and Rameshwaram are important to the Hindus, the shrine of Moinuddin Chisti at Ajmer, Jama Masjid of Delhi and Agra, draw millions of devotees every year. The Golden Temple at Amritsar and Patna Sahib (in Bihar), Bangla Sahib and Sisganj Gurudwaras at Delhi are equally severed by the Sikh Community. The Buddhist pilgrim centres like Rajgriha, Bodhgaya, Nalanda (all in Bihar, and Sarnath in UP are naturally of special interests to the followers of Buddhism. These Buddhist pilgrim centres constitute a very important element of travel and tourism in India. Further the Jain temples of Dilwara and Mt Abu draw thousands of followers, proving once more that a sojourn to pilgrim centres is one of the prominent reason. So much so, that even a small community like Bahai, have their own for travelling in India structure, viz. the Lotus Temple at Delhi, contributing its bit to the tourism in India.

Even, the followers from outside the country travel to India to make a visit of places like Vaishno Devi, Amarnath, Kedarnath, Badrinath, Gangotri and Yamunotri, Brajbhoomi, Rameshwaram—all reflecting the faith and belief of one of the largest religious/religious groups of the world. India is a secular state. Hindu 80%, Muslim 14%, Christian 2.4%, Sikh 2%, Buddhist 0.7%, Jain 0.5%, Zoroastrian and others 0.4% The mosques and shrines of Sufi saints like Moinuddin Chisti and Nizamuddin Aulia, dot the map of and give a boost to tourism in India. The European advent resulted in the erection of number of churches. And the pilgrim centres of Sikhs, relatively young in origin are connected with the life and work of their ten Gurus like Hemkund Sahib, Bangla Sahib (New Delhi), Sisganj (Old Delhi), Nankana Sahib (now in Pakistan) make India a very good religious holiday destination. (See Appendix 3 for more about religious tourism).

Variety of landscapes

India holds virtually every kind of landscape. An abundance of mountain ranges and national parks provide ample opportunity for eco-tourism and trekking, and its sheer size promises something for everyone. From north to south India extends a good 2000 miles (3200 km). Himalayas, the world's highest mountain chain dominate India's northern border. Following the sweeping mountains to the northeast, its borders narrow to a small channel that passes between Nepal, Tibet, Bangladesh, and Bhutan, then spreads out again to meet Burma in the "eastern triangle." Apart from the Arabian Sea, its western border is defined exclusively by Pakistan. North India is the country's largest region begins with Jammu and Kashmir, with terrain varying from arid mountains in the far north to the lake country and forests near Srinagar and Jammu. Moving south along the Indus river, the North becomes flatter and more hospitable, widening into the fertile plains of Punjab and Haryana states to the west and the Himalayan foothills of Uttar Pradesh and the Ganges river valley to the East. Cramped between these two states is the capital city, Delhi. The states of Gujarat, Maharashtra, Goa, and part of the massive, central state of Madhya Pradesh constitute West India. Extending from the Gujarat peninsula down to Goa, the west coast is lined with some of India's best beaches. The land along the coast is typically lush with rainforests. The Western Ghats separate the verdant coast from the Vindya Mountains and the dry Deccan plateau further inland.

India is the home of the sacred River Ganges and the majority of Himalayan foothills, East India begin with the states of Madhya Pradesh, Bihar, Orissa, which comprise the westernmost part of the region. East India also contains an area known as the eastern triangle, which is entirely distinct. This is the last gulp of land that extends beyond Bangladesh, culminating in the Naga Hills along the Burmese border. India reaches its peninsular tip with South India, which begins with the Deccan in the north and ends with Cape Comorin. The states in South India are Karnataka, Andhra Pradesh, Tamil Nadu, and Kerala, a favourite leisure destination. These southern states, together with Maharashtra and Gujarat in the west are in the forefront of Medical Tourism.

Eco-tourism: A mix of glaciers and deserts

Eco-tourism is defined as travel to destinations where the flora, fauna, and cultural heritage are the primary attractions. Responsible Eco-tourism includes programs that minimize the adverse effects of tourism on the natural environment, and enhance the cultural integrity of local people. Therefore, in addition to evaluating environmental and cultural factors, initiatives by hospitality providers to promote recycling, energy efficiency, water reuse, and the creation of economic opportunities for local communities are an integral part of Eco-tourism. Saving the environment around you and preserving the natural luxuries and forest life, that's what eco-tourism is all about. Whether it's about a nature camp or organizing trekking trips towards the unspoilt and inaccessible regions, one should always keep in mind not to create any mishap or disturbance in the life cycle of nature. Eco-tourism accommodates and entertains visitors in a way that is minimally intrusive or destructive to the environment and sustains and supports the native cultures in the locations it is operating in. Responsibility of both travelers and service providers is the genuine meaning for eco-tourism. Eco-tourism also endeavors to encourage and support the diversity of local economies for which the tourism-related income is important. With support from tourists, local services and producers can compete with larger, foreign companies and local families can support themselves. Besides all these, the revenue produced from tourism helps and encourages governments to fund conservation projects and training programs. Eco-tourism is considered the fastest growing market in the tourism industry, according to the World Tourism Organization with an annual growth rate of 5% worldwide and representing 6% of the world gross domestic product, 11.4% of all consumer spending—not a market to be taken lightly.

Blessed with snow-clad peaks, crystal glaciers, rolling meadows and ski slopes, beautiful valleys, meandering and roaring rivers, gushing waterfalls, thick forests rich in wildlife, swampy deltas, long coastlines and magical moonscapes—India has something for everyone. India offers immense climatic diversity and topographical varieties. India has seven principal mountain ranges and the most important amongst them are the Himalayas followed by the Shivaliks, which have the most popular hill resorts. Shimla, Dalhousie, Nainital, Mussorie, Panchmarhi, Mount Abu, and Kodaikanal are some of the favourite hill resorts of international tourists. If you have some time to spare, take a slow toy train up to the hill resort of Shimla, Ooty (Udhagamandalam), Darjeeling or Matheran. There is nothing to match the experience of chugging up the hills, past little hamlets and terraced fields, making your way through tunnels and over breathtaking bridges. Its leisurely pace offers you a panoramic view of changing vistas. The invigorating air and the delights of scenic hill resort provide a welcome respite from the hustle and bustle of the city.

Deserts form the backdrop of many a legend in India, and in the present times, are touted as destinations of tourist interest. The Thar or Great Indian Desert is an arid region (800 km) long and (400 km) wide, in North West of India and East of Pakistan. Largely a desolate region of shifting sand dunes, broken rocks, and scrub vegetation, it receives an annual average rainfall of less than 25 cm. Through the extension of canals fed with Sutlej and Beas waters, irrigation has reclaimed some land for agriculture along the northern and western edges. Nothing can prepare the visitor for the sheer magic and brilliance of the desert cities of Rajasthan. The camel rides on the sand dunes are an unforgettable experience as are the sunsets. These places boast of some very fine reminders of the glorious past—palaces, forts, temples and other elegant monuments of architectural and historical value and unforgettable treat for any visitor. Explore the enigmatic desert of Rajasthan that will mystify your mind with its beauty and vastness. The gateway to the great Indian Thar desert through Jodhpur will enchant you with a vast waste dotted with shifting sand dunes and sparse hamlets with cenotaphs called 'Chattris'. At Jaisalmer in the heart of the desert the majestic golden fort is a memorable sight as is the camel ride at nearby Sam. Equally enchanting are the forts at Bikaner and Madwa, which drifts your mind to the medieval times.

Sea resorts

Thousands of sun-deprived tourists visit India because it incredibly has the most diverse varieties of beaches anywhere in the world. Placid backwaters and lagoons, bays and rough lava-rocked seas, marine estuaries with fish, crashing surf, powdery golden sand or palm fringed shores—Incredible India has them all. The West Coast with the Arabian Sea and the East Coast with the Bay of Bengal offer many a verdant vistas to the traveller. The coasts of India have their own seafood cuisine, relaxing spas, diving and water sports and great places to stay for a balmy holiday. Kovalam undoubtedly is one of India's best sea resorts. The long coastline lined with swaying coconut palm trees dotted with an occasional fishing hamlet is fast developing into one of the world's finest string of beaches. The sea applauds the beach temple in Mahabalipuram, gloriously silhouetted against the spectrum of the seven colours in the sky. Puri, on the East Coast, is surely one of the world's most picturesque beaches. And then there is Digha, a three-hour drive out of Kolkata, a beautiful beach, splendid in its isolation. The beach holiday to beat them all is in the Isles of Andaman and Nicobar and Lakshadeep, where you can see the myriad colours of the flashy fish in the coral reefs from above the green waters.

Now fully developed as an international beach resort, Goa offers the best holiday villages on its beaches. Everything about Goa is spellbinding from the landscape dotted with Portuguese architecture, to the way of life that exudes an irresistible Old World charm. Anjuna or Calangute Beach, and Miramar Bay in Panjim are quieter. Beach vendors sell all manner of kitsch in Anjuna and Calangute. You can rent beach mats and mattresses, sunglasses, and the usual tourist paraphernalia. You can even get all sorts of spaghetti, German bread and Italian food. The beach at Calangute is rocky. At Anjuna the waters are gentle and offer opportunities for boat rides, sea scooter rides, spot-the-dolphins rides, and motorboat rides. Colva and Benaulim are quieter and less crowded than Anjuna. The Fort Aguada beach offers gorgeous views that merit a visit. Sinquerim and

Candolim are also quiet beaches that afford anonymity. Whether it's the isolated horizons of the Konkan Coast or the Arabian Sea; the golden sands or the water drenched seashores, every beach in India makes a picture perfect holiday destination.

Palaces and villas

The rich architectural heritage of the past can be visualized by the wealth of palaces and villas remains surviving in the foothills and the valleys of Western Himalayas, that is Himachal Pradesh, northern Uttar Pradesh, and Jammu and Kashmir. In towering magnificence, the Himalayas stretch along Himachal Pradesh on the northern border of India, with densely forested mountain slopes, undulating foothills, valleys with rivers and the human settlements, which have their typical culture and religious heritage. Palaces and villas of Himachal Pradesh follow the same architectural tradition that is prevalent in and necessary to Himachal Pradesh. Finest among the magnificient edifices that adorn Rajasthan, Samode Palace stands unique in serene splendour. A perfect example of the Rajput-Mughal style of architecture, the stately corridors, fescoed walls, and ethereal audience halls harmoniously refelect the skill of master craftsmen. Recently, this charming palace was transformed into a premier heritage hotel. More than just the exquisite beauty of Samode and the luxury that it offers, are the moments spent discovering life

outside the palace walls, on the camel back-returning to evenings of traditional Rajasthani music, whilst the cuisine completes the feeling that is royal, that is Rajasthan.

The feast and festivals

In a country as diverse and complex as India, it is not surprising to find that people here reflect the rich glories of the past, the culture, traditions and values relative to geographic locations and the numerous distinctive manners, habits and food that will always remain truly Indian.

From the eternal snows of the Himalayas to the cultivated peninsula of far South, from the deserts of the West to the humid deltas of the East, from the dry heat and cold of the Central Plateau to the cool forest foothills, Indian lifestyles clearly glorify the geography. The food, clothing and habits of an Indian differ in accordance to the place of origin.

Indians believe in sharing happiness and sorrow. A festival or a celebration is never constrained to a family or a home. The whole community or neighbourhood is involved in bringing liveliness to an occasion. A lot of festivals like Diwali, Holi, Id, Christmas, Mahaveer Jayanthi are all celebrated by sharing sweets and pleasantries with family, neighbours and friends. An Indian wedding is an occasion that calls for participation of the family and friends. Similarly, neighbours and friends always help out a family in times of need. Observed with enthusiasm and gaiety, festivals are like gems ornamenting the crown of Indian Culture. They are round the year vibrant interludes in the mundane routine of life.

Every season brings along new festivals, each a true celebration of the bounties of the rich traditions followed for time immemorial. That's not all! The birthdays of Gods and Goddesses, saints and prophets, great historical happenings and the advent of the New Year, all find expression in colourful festivities. New attire, dance, music and rituals—all add to their joyful rhythm. It is a time for prayer, for pageantry and procession . . . a time to rejoice, in celebration of life.

The Indian cuisine boasts of an immense variety not restricted to only curry. An authentic Indian curry is an intricate combination of a stir-fried Masala—a mixture of onion, garlic, ginger, and tomatoes; various spices and seasonings with which meat; poultry, vegetables or fish is prepared to produce a stew-type dish. Food in India is wide ranging in variety, taste and flavour. Being so diverse geographically, each region has its own cuisine and style of preparation. Indian cuisine, renowned for its exotic gravies seems complicated for any newcomer. The Mughlai cuisine of North differs sharply from the preparations of the south. The Wazwan style of Kashmir is luxurious but the same can be said about Bengal's Macher Jhol, Rajasthan's Dal Bati, Uttar Pradesh's Kebabs and Punjab's Sarson Ka Saag and Makki di Roti. In India, recipes are handed down from generation. to generation. The unique and strong flavours in Indiàn cuisine are derived from spices, seasonings and nutritious ingredients such as leafy vegetables, grains, fruits, and legumes. Most of the spices used in Indian cooking were originally chosen thousands of years ago for their medicinal qualities and not for flavour. Many of them such as turmeric, cloves and cardamoms are very antiseptic, others like ginger, are carminative and good for the digestion. All curries are made using a wide variety of spices. In Indian cuisine, food is categorized into six tastes—sweet, sour, salty, spicy, bitter and astringent. A well-balanced Indian meal contains all six tastes, not always can this be accomplished. This principle explains the use of numerous spice combinations and depth of flavour in Indian recipes. Side dishes and condiments like chutneys, curries, daals and Indian pickles contribute to and add to the overall flavour and texture of a meal and provide balance needed.

The languages, cultures and dances

18 languages are officially recognized in India of which Sanskrit and Tamil share a long history of more than 5,000 and 3,000 years respectively. The population of people speaking each language varies drastically. For example, Hindi has 250 million speakers, while Andamanese is spoken by relatively fewer people. Tribal or Aboriginal language speaking population in India may be more than some of the European languages. For instance Bhili and Santali both tribal languages have more than 4 million speakers. The vividness can be ascertained by the fact that schools in India teach more than 50 different languages; there are Films in 15

languages, Newspapers in 90 or more languages and radio programmes in 71 languages! Indian languages come from four distinct families, which are: Indo-European, Dravidian, Mon-Khmer, and Sino-Tibetan. Majority of Indian population uses Indo-European and Dravidian languages. The language families divide India geographically too. Indo-European languages dominate the northern and central India while in south India; mainly languages of Dravidian origin are spoken. In eastern India languages of Mon-Khmer group is popular. Sino Tibetan languages are spoken in the northern Himalayas and close to Burmese border. In terms of percentage, 75% of Indian population speaks languages of Indo-European family, 23% speak languages of Dravidian origin and about 2% of the population speaks Mon-Khmer languages and Sino-Tibetan languages.

Natya Shastra

Legend has it that the Devas (Gods) had vanquished the Asuras (Evil) and were relating the happenings to

Brahma, the God of Creation. The Asuras thought this was a renewed attack and retaliated. Brahma intervened—"This is only a performance, henceforth it will only be held on earth". From the purpose of natya, to the architectural format, stage rituals, Rasa, Bhava, Abhinaya, gestic communication, music, types of instruments. Later century works like Abhinaya Darpana, Abhinaya Chandrike, also have great relevance to the dancer today. And Brahma passed on all the information on Dance and Drama to Bharata Muni who compiled it as the Natya Shastra. Temples were raised to the house the Gods and became the focal point for the community. They also became centres of learning and contributed to the advancement of such arts as sculpture, painting, music and dance. Mostly built by Kings, who were also the patrons of arts, encouraging a continuity and enriching rituals of worship, the earliest basis of the classical performing arts. It was from the temple that the Devdasi cult (Temple Dancers who performed for the Lord) began. Once a practice countrywide—the Kulvantalu in Andhra Pradesh, the Maibi in Manipur, the Devdasi in Tamil Nadu and the Mahari in Orissa, all trace their roots to the temple. The countless sculptures of dance poses in the temples, hint at the potency of dance as a path to spiritual exaltation and lays out a complete lexicon of dance techniques.

Conferences, conventions, MICE

India is not just one of the world's oldest civilizations, it is also the world's largest democracy, and has made stupendous progress among developing nations. India's impressive variety of history and culture, from the ancient Gangetic Kingdoms to the present state, harmoniously blend to form a unique atmosphere in over a million square kilometers of scenic sights. A continent-sized country, India possesses an amazing wealth of sights and sounds, tastes and textures. From a bustling cosmopolitan city to the quiet countryside, hill station or a beach resort, India has destinations, which offer a backdrop of unmatched beauty for a business meet. You will find a fascinating amalgam of tradition and culture, beauty and nature, style and splendour, warmth, feelings and courtesies, comfort and convenience virtually everything the modern conference organiser or delegate could expect. Conferences here bring fresh meaning of the concept of combining work with pleasure.

Amidst the countless ways that India can capture world attention as a tourist paradise, there also exists a dynamic business opportunity as a splendid venue for international conferences and conventions of no less than global standards.

India is undoubtedly a unique Conference Destination as it offers cultural and heritage sites, the exotic and mystical, excellent facilities of beach and adventure holidays which can be combined as pre- and post-conference tours. Enchanting India's image as a conference destination is also projected through the chains of Hotels, providing international standards in facilities and services. Exclusive business hotels and exotic resorts, with meeting rooms of distinction, spacious convention facilities, modern business centres and a wide range of conference facilities.

India is in a continual process of upgrading its MICE (Meetings, Incentives, Conferences and Exhibitions) facilities. There are multiple plans on the anvil for more world-class convention centers, airports that contest with the best in the world and efforts to team the famous Indian hospitality with customisation as per a visitor's requirement. You could also offer the credit to the world class incentive programs, her ability to heal spiritually, her unmatched offering as a health destination or continually improved infrastructure facilities that over 3 million foreign tourists thronged her this year generating over US $30 billion as revenue, even as most other preferred hotspots marked a decline in their tourism graphs. The inbound MICE (meetings, incentives, conventions and events) segment is growing at 15 to 20% annually. It is estimated that the total national and international MICE meetings market all over the world is in excess of $270 billion. India ranks 27th in the Global Meetings market.

The Infrastructure

India provides an impressive combination of accommodation and other conference support facilities. To mention a few; Vigyan Bhawan in New Delhi, Centre Point, Renaissance Hotel and Convention Center in Mumbai, the BM Birla Science and Technology Centre in Jaipur, the Jaypee Hotels and International Convention Centre, Agra and the Cochin Convention Centre, Kochi, etc.

India is now an important MICE destination. The Indian sub-continent is emerging as one of the finest Incentive destinations in the world owing to the diverse culture and geography. From the icy Himalayas to the tropical islands and from citadels in the desert to verdant jungles it is a world in itself. With the emergence of exciting new destinations every year one has unparalleled choices for the incentive operator here. The incentive programmes are a combination of old world charm and tradition interlaced with modern cosmopolitan sophistication.

It is estimated that a person traveling to a country for a conference or convention spends anywhere four to eight times more than a normal leisure traveler. They spend more on food, more on business centre services. India is globally connected to a network of over 50 international airlines and several domestic airlines, which provide convenient connectivity within India. Added to this is an elaborate network of surface transportation system. There is an excellent Railway system running through the entire country. All-important cities are connected with state-of-the-art 'Shatabdi and Rajdhani' Express trains. Special trains like Palace on Wheels and Royal Orient Express, comprising of air-conditioned saloons decorated in the old Maharaja Style offer guests a chance to stay on the train and visit colourful Rajasthan and fascinating Gujarat. An excellent network of roads, national and state highways, luxury coaches, Indian and foreign-make vehicles add to the convenience and comfort of surface travel. And, to add to this, India offers an educated manpower base where fluency in English and other official international languages can be expected.

The important conference centres in the country are at New Delhi, greater noida, Mumbai, Agra, Bangalore, Chennai, Cochin, Goa, Hyderabad, Jaipur and Kolkata. Some important hotel chains like the Taj Group, ITC-Welcomgroup, the Oberoi's, Meridien Hotels, Marriott Hotels, etc. also have excellent conference facilities. The exhibition industry has also gained fresh impetus with exhibition centres like Pragati Maidan in New Delhi, the Nehru Centre in Mumbai and the Chennai Trade Centre in Chennai amongst several other options.

Health for All—A distant dream

Epidemics of infectious diseases are problem of not only in underdeveloped world, the new emerging viral infections and HIV/AIDS are major upcoming problems of developed world too. Simultaneously, the non-communicable diseases, i.e. diabetes mellitus, hypertension, coronary artery diseases and obesity were said to be diseases of affluent developed countries, now spreading in big way to underdeveloped world so.

Rapid migration of trained and untrained personnel from one part of the world to another is also posing new dimension to healthcare. Rapid advancement in communication technology and access to information has raised the aspiration of every one to get best healthcare services.

Each and every country has its own pattern of healthcare systems. Most of the European countries, North America including Canada, Australia and New Zealand have excellent primary healthcare services and very strong Health Insurance System well supported by government funding. South East Asian countries (barring Japan and Singapore), i.e. India, China, Pakistan where healthcare system is partially supported by government and free, but very much insufficient for population's need. Spurt of private sector facilities in these areas is remarkable and some of the institutions are at par in technology to western world, but out of reach to population at large. There is complete lack of healthcare system in African and South American countries barring few pockets.

It is a duty of health professionals to promote health as a global human right, global public goods, and for this reason we all must be very dedicated before launching headlong into the globalisation of healthcare. The health professionals should take care that globalisation action benefits to all around the world.

Health tourism

India has been a home of traditional medicine that has been practiced for several thousand years as a part of *Manav Dharam* to give relief to the needy and generally free of cost. With modern diagnostic and treatment facilities, experienced surgeons, one of the largest pharmaceutical industries in the world, and a tradition of caring. India provides word-class surgical and healthcare facilities at a fraction (sometimes as low as 5-10%) of world costs, with comparable success rates and prompt service levels. A National Accreditation Board for Hospitals has been established to monitor safety and hygiene norms. Several modern hospitals have been set-up by surgeons and physicians with decades of experience abroad, viz., USA, UK and Europe. India has the distinction of providing wellness and preventive services through Yoga, Ayurveda and other indigenous services. In the year 2006 over 2 lakhs of foreign medical tourists visited India. It is just the beginning. The potential in health tourism is such that it can even surpass the revenue earned from I.T. sector, as per Union Tourism minister. (See Appendix 1 for a list of prominent hospitals of India.)

MEDICAL VISA

A medical category visa may be issued with the following conditions:

- The Indian Missions/Posts abroad nay scrutinize the medical documents very carefully and satisfy themselves about the bonafide purpose for which a medical treatment visa is being requested.
- Missions may satisfy that the applicant has sought preliminary medical advice from his country of origin/country of residence and he has been advised to go for specialized medical treatment.
- Incase the foreign national desires to go for treatment under Indian System of Medicines, his case may also be considered.
- This type of visa should be granted for seeking medical attendance only in reputed/ecognized specialized hospitals/treatment enters in the country.

  Although not exhaustive, following illustrative list of ailments would be of primary consideration; serious ailments like neurosurgery, ophthalmic disorders, heart related problems, renal disorders, organ transplantation, congenital disorders, gene-therapy, radio-therapy, plastic surgery, joint replacement, etc. The basic idea would be that the mission may satisfy about the need of the foreign national to come to India for medical treatment/ health enhancement.

Validity of visa and extension of visa

The initial period for such a visa may be upto a period of one year or the period of treatment, whichever is less, which can be extended for a further period of upto one year by the State Governments/FRROs on production of medical certificate/advice from the reputed/recognized/specialized hospitals in the country. Any further extension will be granted by the Ministry of Home Affairs only on the recommendations of the State Governments/FRROs supported by appropriate medical documents. Such visas will be valid for maximum three entries during one year.

State Government/FRROs may permit one additional entry in emergent situations, if required.

Visa to attendant/family members

Attendant/family members of the patients coming to India for medical treatment shall be granted miscellaneous visa co-terminus with the 'M Visa' of the patient. Such visas may be granted to the spouse/children or those who have blood relations with the patients. However, not more than two attendants may be allowed at a time for grant of miscellaneous visas. Such visa will be called 'MX visa'. Such foreigners are also required to get themselves registered with the local FRROs/FROs well within 14 days from the date of the arrival.

Registration

Foreigners coming on 'M Visa' will be required to get themselves registered mandatorily well within the period of 14 days from the date of arrival with the concerned FRROs/ FROs.

Registration for Pakistani and Bangladeshi Nationals

It may be clarified that the 'Medical Visa' will be available to all the foreign nationals including China,

Pakistan, Bangladesh and Sri Lanka. However, registration formalities for Pakistani and Bangladeshi nationals will be as per the provisions contained in para 106 in respect of Bangladeshi nationals and para 118 of the Visa Manual in respect of Pakistani nationals. Similarly, entry and departure of these foreign nationals will also be governed as per the existing policy in respect of these nationals.

What is Medical Tourism?

Medical tourism means provision of 'cost effective' private medical care in collaboration with the tourism industry for foreign patients needing surgical and other forms of specialized healthcare. This process is being facilitated by the corporate sector involved in medical care as well as the tourism industry—both private and public. It entails patients going to a different country for either urgent or elective medical procedures—is fast becoming a worldwide, multibillion-dollar industry. The reasons patients travel for treatment vary. Many medical tourists from the United States are seeking treatment at a quarter or sometimes even a 10th of the cost at home. From Canada, it is often people who are frustrated by long waiting times. From Great Britain, the patient can't wait for treatment by the National Health Service (NHS) but also can't afford to see a physician in private practice. For others, becoming a medical tourist is a chance to combine a tropical vacation with elective or plastic surgery. And many more patients are coming from poorer countries, e.g. Bangladesh, Nepal, Pakistan, Bhutan, etc. where treatment may not be available.

Medical tourism is not new

Medical tourism is actually thousands of years old. In

ancient Greece, pilgrims and patients came from all over the Mediterranean to the sanctuary of the healing god, Asklepios, at Epidaurus. In Roman Britain, patients took the waters at a shrine to bathe, a practice that continued for 2000 years. From the 18th century wealthy Europeans traveled to spas from Germany to the Nile. In the 21st century, relatively low-cost jet travel has taken the industry beyond the wealthy and desperate. The most recent trend in privatisation of health services is medical tourism, which is gaining prominence in developing countries. Globalisation has promoted a consumerist culture, thereby promoting goods and services that can feed the aspirations arising from this culture. This has had its effect in the health sector too, with the emergence of a private sector that thrives by servicing a small percentage of the population that has the ability to "buy" medical care at the rates at which the "high end" of the private medical sector provides such care. This has changed the character of the medical care sector, with the entry of the corporate sector. Corporate run institutions are seized with the necessity to maximise profits and expand their coverage. These objectives face a constraint in the form of the relatively small size of the population in developing countries that can afford services offered by such institutions. In this background, corporate interests in the Medical Care sector are looking for opportunities that go beyond the limited domestic "market" for high cost medical care. This is the genesis of the "medical tourism" industry. With global revenues of an estimated $2.8 trillion, the healthcare industry is the world's largest industry. The Indian healthcare industry has the potential to show the same exponential growth that the software and pharmaceutical industries have shown in the past decade. Countries that actively promote medical tourism include Cuba, Costa Rica, Hungary, India, Israel, Jordan, Lithuania, Malaysia and Thailand. Belgium, Poland and Singapore are now entering the field. South Africa specializes in medical safaris—visit the country for a safari, with a stopover for plastic surgery, a nose job and a chance to see lions and elephants.

Need for Medical Tourism

Medical tourism has become a common form of vacationing, and covers a broad spectrum of medical services. It mixes leisure, fun and relaxation together with wellness and healthcare. The idea of the health holiday is to offer you an opportunity to get away from your daily routine and come into a different relaxing surrounding. Here you can enjoy being close to the beach and the mountains. At the same time you are able to receive an orientation that will help you improve your life in terms of your health and general well-being. It is like rejuvenation and clean up process on all levels—physical, mental and emotional. Many people from the developed world come to India for the rejuvenation promised by yoga and Ayurvedic massage, but only a few consider it a destination for hip replacement or brain surgery. However, a nice blend of top-class medical expertise at attractive prices is helping a growing number of Indian corporate hospitals lure foreign patients, including a few from developed nations such as the UK and the US.

As more and more patients from affluent nations with high Medicare costs look for effective options, India is pitted against Thailand, Singapore, Malaysia and some other Asian countries, which have good hospitals, salubrious climate and tourist destinations. While Thailand and Singapore with their advanced medical facilities and built-in medical tourism options have been drawing foreign patients of the order of several lakhs per annum, the rapidly expanding Indian corporate hospital sector has been able to get a few thousands for treatment. But, things are going to change drastically in favour of India, especially in view of the high quality expertise of medical professionals, backed by the fast improving equipment and nursing facilities, and above all, the cost-effectiveness of the package. As Indian corporate hospitals are on par, if not better than the best hospitals in Thailand, Singapore, etc. there is scope for improvement.

Scope for medical tourism

With internationally recognized healthcare professionals, holistic medicinal services and low cost of treatment, India has the potential to attract over one million health tourists every year, according to confederation of Indian industry (CII). The country offers a unique mix of systems such as yoga, ayurveda and meditation and modern medical system. This, along with world-class experts and the cost advantage, can help earn $5 billion every year, a CII release said. While a heart surgery costs $30,000 in the US, it costs $6,000 in India. Similarly, a bone marrow transplant costs $26,000 here compared to $250,000 in the US. If a liver transplant costs in the range of Rs. 60 lakhs-70 lakhs in Europe and double that in the US, a few Indian hospitals, such as Global in Hyderabad, have the wherewithal to do it in around Rs. 15 lakh-20 lakhs. Similarly, if a heart surgery in the US costs about Rs. 20 lakhs, the Chennai-headquartered Apollo Hospitals Group does it in roughly Rs. 2 lakhs. Knee surgery (on both knees) costs 350,000 rupees ($7,700) in India; in Britain this costs £10,000 ($16,950), more than twice as much. Dental, eye and cosmetic surgeries in Western countries cost three to four times as much as in India. Take the rising popularity of "preventive health screening". At one private clinic in London a thorough men's health check-up that includes blood tests, electro-cardiogram tests, chest x-rays, lung tests and abdominal ultrasound costs £345 ($574, €500). By comparison, a comparable check-up at a clinic operated by Delhi-based healthcare company Max Healthcare costs $84. The Indian government predicts that India's $17 billion-a-year health-care industry could grow 13 per cent in each of the next six years, boosted by medical tourism, which industry watchers say is growing at 30 per cent annually. Price advantage is, of course, a major selling point. The cost differential across the board is huge: only a tenth and sometimes even a sixteenth of the cost in the West.

NRIs and tourists from around the world are beginning to realize the potential of modern and traditional Indian medicine. Indian hospitals and medical establishments have also realized the potential of this niche market and have begun to tailor their services for foreign visitors. At a regional level, this nascent industry came to limelight with the arrival of 'Naby Noor' from Pakistan, who came by the Indo-Pak bus service and got a red-carpet treatment at a hospital in Bangalore. Several Indian state governments have realized the potential of this 'industry' and have been actively promoting it. Visitors, especially from the west and the middle-east find Indian hospitals affordable and viable option to grappling with insurance and National medical systems in their native lands. Many prefer to combine their treatments with a visit to the 'exotic east' with their families, however, the country would have to improve its healthcare infrastructure, connectivity between major cities and streamline immigration procedure for medical visitors. Accreditation of Indian hospitals is also essential for attracting such tourists. A viable healthcare, infrastructure for the 'common man' is the first pre-requisite for the Medical Tourism to succeed.

Government corporate sector must join hands

Close on the heels of introducing a medical visa, the Government has started overseas marketing of India as a medical tourism destination. According to senior Government officials, they hope to complete the process of price-banding of hospitals in various cities. Statistics suggest that the medical tourism industry in India is worth $333 million (Rs. 1,450 crore) while a study by CII-McKinsey estimates that the country could earn Rs. 5,000-10,000 crore by 2012. While the trickle of foreigners coming to India for treatment has started, officials are hopeful that this will become a flood once the various initiatives being taken by the Government take-off. Indian Government has introduced the following policy measures to encourage medical tourism.

National Health Policy recognizes the treatment of international patients as an export, which allows private hospitals treating such patients to enjoy benefits such as lower import duties, increase in the rate of depreciation (from 25 per cent to 40 per cent) for life-saving medical equipment, and several other tax sops—

- India's relatively developing medical tourism segment has been anointed by healthcare and tourism industry pundits as the next 'best' thing for the country.
- There are plenty of challenges that need to be addressed for India to become the world's preferred healthcare destination.

- Prominent among them being the need for proper accreditation and requisite standardization systems in place, a tripartite synergy between hospitals, tour operators and respective state governments.
- They spoke about the various challenges impeding the growth of the medical tourism industry and emphasized the need for a synergy between hospitals, state government and international tour operators.
- India will have to project itself as being a holistic medical destination to get an edge over other countries.
- We need to club together a couple of 'pathies' because we have a very strong base of alternative healing therapies like yoga, naturopathy, ayurveda, etc.
- Creating awareness about India's facilities is a must to establish credibility in foreign markets.
- Standardization of a price band for graded hospitals and a quality assurance model should be taken up immediately to take medical tourism ahead.
- The private healthcare industry is quietly facilitating a revolution to enable India to emerge as a health destination.
- STARK contrasts are no surprise in urban India, and in the healthcare sector, the difference between what is available (world-class techniques and service, at a price) and what the common denominator urgently needs is no less so.
- private sector healthcare centres are gleaming "islands of excellence", as the industry calls them, all too often surrounded by seas of medical neglect.
- When the mix is just right (support from the government in the form of incentives and tax breaks, international healthcare accreditation standards in place, breakthroughs in insurance coverage for overseas patients, and savvy promotion of India as a tourism-plus-medical tech

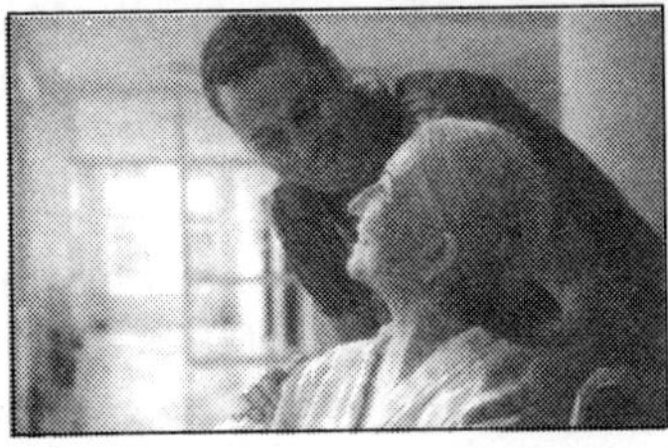

destination) the sector is certain the numbers will fall into place.

- What's more, the beneficiary of such growth will be the country's desperately overburdened public health system, say industry associations such as the Confederation of Indian Industry (CII) and the Federation of Indian Chambers of Commerce and Industry (FICCI), which see medical tourism a mirror of the early years of India's info-tech growth.
- Look at the possibility of the public hospitals being technologically upgraded to world-class standards with this source of income.
- Such optimism apart, India's three-tier public health system—primary health centres (PHC) in villages, district hospitals, and tertiary care hospitals—is increasingly unable to attend to the medical needs of the population.
- There is no doubt that a technology-centric approach to healthcare, such as that promoted by the major private hospitals, will inevitably affect the cost of care to the common man.

India moving ahead

India is considered one of the leading country

promoting medical tourism and now it is moving into a new area of "medical outsourcing," where sub-contractors provide services to the overburdened medical care systems in western countries. India's top-rated education system is not only churning out computer programmers and engineers, but an estimated 20,000 to 30,000 doctors and nurses each year. The largest of the estimated half-dozen medical corporations in India serving medical tourists is Apollo Hospital. Dr. Prathap C. Reddy, the chairman of the company, began negotiations in the spring of 2004 with Britain's National Health Service to work as a sub-contractor, to do operations and medical tests for patients at a fraction of the cost in Britain. Apollo now has 37 hospitals, with about 7000 beds. The company is in partnership in hospitals in Kuwait, Sri Lanka and Nigeria. Apollo has also reacted to criticism by Indian politicians by expanding its services to India's millions of poor.

India will be happy to provide fixed-price treatment packages, integrating all transport, medical and living costs into one price. Plus a vacation at any of India's fabulous destinations. India is hoping to expand its tourist industry—to include visitors with heart conditions and cataracts. The sight of the country's overcrowded public hospitals, open sewers and garbage-littered streets would unsettle most visitors' confidence about public sanitation standards in India. Though the quality of healthcare for the poor in countries like India is undeniably low, private facilities offer advanced technology and procedures on par with hospitals in developed nations.

Vishal Bali, of Wockhardt Hospitals, points out as proof of quality that the US private health insurers Blue Cross and Blue Shield insure patients treated at his group's hospitals. The British health insurer Bupa also insures the costs of treatment at Wockhardt hospitals. Mr. Bali adds that Wockhardt is in talks with Britain's National Health Service about outsourcing the treatment of British patients to India. Early this year Rosemarie—who is into tourism business—encountered a leg ailment which curtailed her active life. She made extensive enquiries with the Turkish hospitals. She wanted to know what exactly was wrong with her leg, what are the corrective procedures available, what are the latest advances in the field, what is the success rate and how long will it take her to bounce back to her active life. Around this time, she happened to read "Stern," a popular German magazine, which had a special feature on India. It featured India's advancement in medical field. She underwent special hip resurfacing surgery, at Workhardt Hospital, Mumbai. Her entire medical experience in India was wonderful.

Ind-US health

If you or a loved one have a health problem that is causing concern about the cost and quality of available care, Ind-US health suggests you consider the excellent, high-quality treatment options available to you in India at a fraction of the cost in a US hospital. Ind-US health's case managers and alliance of physicians in North America are ready to work with you to evaluate your needs and provide the necessary guidance that will help you take advantage of the exceptional care options available to you at one of our partner super-specialty hospitals in India.

At Ind-US health, we strive to make each patient's experience nothing short of an outstanding success. Any patient seeking affordable, high quality medical care can benefit from the Ind-US health system. However, those who may benefit the most are uninsured individuals who may face staggering medical bills for serious procedures. It's notable that half of US bankruptcies are a direct result of catastrophic medical events and their associated costs.

- Patients seeking treatments that are routinely performed in India, but not approved in the US (robot assisted joint replacement as an example).
- Patients that want to take personal accountability for their healthcare decisions, and make the best choice from global, rather than local options.
- Wait-listed patients with chronic pain or disability e.g. Canada.

Advent Medical Services

Advent Medical Services group is a leading medical service provider based in India with accomplished and distinguished physicians and surgeons with a vast experience in variety of disciplines including cardiothoracic surgery cosmetic and plastic surgery, laparoscopic surgery, endoscopic surgery, microsurgery, joint replacements and highly advanced form of ophthalmic and ear surgery. Advent is closely affiliated with world-class medical laboratory and research facilities. The group offers the best of class and personalized medical care in a cost-effective manner. It provides a risk free concept of medical evaluation. After completing the registration, he/she can complete the medical history form which is securely transmitted to expert team of Board Certified physicians and surgeons in India. Team evaluates the patient's medical history and provides a professional opinion and an estimated cost for the treatment.

Every year 1 billion dollars are spent by Nigerians, on Medical Care in US and Europe. This expenditure can be reduced as much as 50% or more, through quality service available in India. The package offers free Preventive Healthcare Program (PHP) for one person accompanying the patient. This package includes Echocardiography; CT scan; Ultrasonography; Treadmill testing; X-ray Hormonal levels, Liver, Kidney and Pulmonary function tests, Blood Urine and Stool investigations or any other relevant investigation.

India's Medical Tourism

The healthcare sector in India has witnessed an enormous growth in infrastructure in the private and voluntary sector. The private sector which was very modest in the early stages has now become a flourishing industry equipped with the most modern state-of-the-art technology at its disposal. It is estimated that 75-80% of healthcare services and investments in India are now provided by the private sector. An added plus had been that India has one of the largest pharmaceutical industries in the world. It is self-sufficient in drug production and exports drugs to more than 180 countries.

- Bone Marrow Transplant
- Brain Surgery
- Cancer Procedures (Oncology)

- Cardiac Care
- Cosmetic Surgery
- Dialysis and Kidney Transplant
- Drug Rehabilitation
- Gynaecology and Obstetrics
- Health Checkups
- Internal/Digestive Procedures
- Joint Replacement Surgery
- Nuclear Medicine
- Neurosurgery and Trauma Surgery
- Preventive Healthcare
- Refractive Surgery
- Osteoporosis
- Spine Related
- Urology
- Vascular Surgery
- Dental jobs

A typical package will consist of:

- Assessment of medical history
- Patient received at the airport/Package inclusive of accompanying person.
- Transfer to a hotel.
- Escorted to the specialty hospital as per appointments for admission.
- Treatment administered.
- Rejuvenation holiday begins.
- Post-treatment check-up.
- Transfer to airport and departure.

Dental care Packages

Following are some of the procedures offered under Dental care packages:

- Veneers
- Filling and Asthetic reconstruction
- Dental Implants
- Bleaching
- Crowns and Bridges

- Cast partial dentures
- Periodontal Surgery
- Oral Surgery
- Pedodontics

Eye Care

India's ophthalmologists offer you custom made solutions for all your eye care problems. From corrective eye disorders to Diabetic retinopathy, Glaucoma, Cornea and Refractive Surgery to Low-stress cataract surgery. The eye surgery techniques have now become so advanced that the cataract surgery can be done in a day. LASIK (Laser Assisted Stromal In-situ Keratomileusis), a method of re-shaping the external surface of the eye to correct low, moderate and high degrees of nearsightedness, astigmatism and far-sightedness is also offered. The cost of such treatment in the UK is Pound 4000 and in the USA $ 5000 as against $ 1200 or less in India for the same treatment with highly experienced Indian doctors. A cataract surgery in the UK costs about Pounds 3000 and in the USA about $11000. In India in one of the best eye hospitals the cost is about Pound 400 or $ 700. This includes all investigations including the A scan on the IOL Master, the best intraocular lenses (Alcon Acrysof and the Allergan Sensar from USA, Pharmacia Tecnis Wavefront IOL from Sweden and also the Acritec from France) hospital stay, surgeon's fee, pre and post-operative treatment as well as follow ups. Chandigarh has a centre of excellence in eye care at Advanced eye centre, PGI. Several private clinics also offer world class services. Dr. Grewal Eye Institute, Chandigarh has earned JCI recognition, recently.

A worldwide market

While, India has attracted patients from Europe, the Middle East and Canada, Thailand has been the goal for Americans. India mainy attracted people who had left the country for the West; Thailand treated western expatriates across Southeast Asia. Many of them worked for western companies and had the advantage of flexible, worldwide medical insurance plans geared specifically at the expatriate and overseas corporate markets. With the growth of medical-related travel and aggressive marketing, Bangkok became a centre for medical tourism. Bangkok's International Medical Centre offers services in 26 languages, recognizes cultural and religious dietary restrictions and has a special wing for Japanese patients. The medical tour companies that serve Thailand often put emphasis on the vacation aspects, offering post-recovery resort stays.

Cuba, for example, first aimed its services at well-off patients from Central and South America and now attracts patients from Canada, Germany and Italy. Malaysia attracts patients from surrounding Southeast Asian countries; Jordan serves patients from the Middle East. Israel caters to both Jewish patients and people from some nearby countries. One Israeli hospital advertises worldwide services, specializing in both male and female infertility, in-vitro fertilization and high-risk pregnancies. South Africa offers package medical holiday deals with stays at either luxury hotels or safaris.

The newest and fastest-growing area of medical tourism is a visit to the dentist, where costs are often not covered by basic insurance and by only some extended insurance policies. India, Thailand and Hungary attract patients who want to combine a filling, extraction or root canal with a vacation.

Facilities Available in India

Indian corporate hospitals excel in cardiology and cardiothoracic surgery, joint replacement, orthopedic surgery, gastroenterology, ophthalmology, transplants and urology to name a few. The various specialties covered are Neurology, Neurosurgery, Oncology, Ophthalmology, Rheumatology, Endocrinology, ENT, Pediatrics, Pediatric Surgery, Pediatric Neurology, Urology, Nephrology, Dermatology, Dentistry, Plastic Surgery, Gynecology, Pulmonology, Psychiatry, General Medicine and General Surgery

The various facilities in India include full body pathology, comprehensive physical and gynecological examinations, dental checkup, eye checkup, diet consultation, audiometry, spirometry, stress and lifestyle management, pap smear, digital Chest X-ray, 12 lead ECG, 2D echo colour doppler, gold standard DXA bone densitometry, body fat analysis, coronary risk markers, cancer risk markers, carotid colour doppler, spiral CT scan and high strength MRI. Each test is carried out by professional M.D. physicians, and is comprehensive yet pain-free.

There is also a gamut of services ranging from General Radiography, Ultra Sonography, Mammography to high end services like Magnetic Resonance Imaging, Digital Subtraction Angiography along with intervention procedures, Nuclear Imaging. The diagnostic facilities offered in India are comprehensive to include Laboratory services, Imaging, Cardiology, Neurology and Pulmonology. The Laboratory services include biochemistry, hematology, microbiology, serology, histopathology, transfusion medicine and RIA.

Procedure Charges in India and US (US $):

Procedure	*Cost (US$)*	
	United States	*India*
Bone Marrow Transplant	2,50,000	69,000
Liver Transplant	3,00,000	69,000
Heart Surgery	30,000	8,000
Orthopedic Surgery	20,000	6,000
Cataract Surgery	2,000	1,250

Here's a brief comparison of the cost of few of the Dental treatment procedures between USA and India

Dental procedure	*Cost in US ($)*		*Cost in India ($)*
	General Dentist	*Top End Dentist*	*Top End Dentist*
Smile designing	-	8,000	1,000
Metal Free Bridge	-	5,500	500
Dental Implants	-	3,500	800
Porcelain Metal Bridge	1,800	3,000	300
Porcelain Metal Crown	600	1,000	80
Tooth impactions	500	2,000	100

Root canal Treatment	600	1,000	100
Tooth whitening	350	800	110
Tooth colored composite fillings	200	500	25
Tooth cleaning	100	300	75

Questions and answers on medical tourism

Q: Is India really a better place to get medical treatment?

Ans.: Yes, Currently India receives patients from over 50 countries across the world. Here are some reasons behind its emergence as the preferred healthcare destination: India has a vast reservoir of skilled doctors. Many of them have proved their mettle in the US and UK and returned to India to work in hospitals here. The caliber of other doctors practicing in India is also of a very high order.

Q: Why should patients come from USA for treatment to India?

A recent film 'Sicko' has indicted the American healthcare system; the insurance and pharma companies are exploiting the American citizens. Those who are not insured cannot afford treatment at home and hence come to India for world class healthcare at a fraction of cost.

Q: *I always thought India was a poor nation of snake charmers and rope tricks. How then can it offer world-class healthcare, that too at minimal costs?*

Ans.: India has all along been a knowledge-oriented nation. However, it never had a chance to showcase its expertise. The revolution in Information Technology changed the rules of the game. And India made complete use of the knowledge base built by its English-speaking engineers to come out and display its immense capabilities.

Ans: And now for the costs. India is a diverse economy where a family of four can live comfortably, without debt, on a monthly income of just $300. As a result, the costs of services and products too have stayed at extremely low levels.

Now, thanks to the world becoming inter-connected and people being more willing to explore other nations, India has emerged as a preferred source of low cost healthcare. An extremely welcome alternative to the prohibitive costs prevalent in the western countries.

Q: I don't know anyone in India. I'm already ill. Then how am I to cope with travel, stay and surgery in India?

Ans.: It's ok if you don't know anybody in India. After all, **Mediescapes India** brings you comprehensive, custom-built schemes for healthcare. This includes:

- Getting second opinions from well-known board certified doctors in India offering all support information on.
- Your ailment.
- Recommended mode of surgery.
- The hospital that will perform the surgery.
- Costs involved.
- Mediescapes India has entered into exclusive affiliate arrangements with a leading hospital in India. This means that you can count on special and personalized attention when you come to India for medical treatment through Mediescapes India.

Q: I just need a second opinion. I don't intend to come to India. Is it possible to get an opinion alone from one of your affiliated hospitals?

Ans.: Yes, of course. Just pay $ 50 and get a second opinion from one of our affiliate hospitals. You are not obligated to have your surgery in India through Mediescapes India just because you have asked for a second opinion.

Q: Do I have to pay any fees or commissions for your services?

Ans.: We do not charge any fees or commissions from people who want to use the services of our healthcare partners.

Q: How do I pay the costs of surgery?

Ans.: You pay the costs of surgery directly to the hospital. The benefits of such a payment are:

Your money is paid directly to the service provider, i.e. the hospital and not to any intermediary

Our healthcare partner have been rich expertise in treating patients from almost all parts of the world. Hence, the Payment systems are well in place in the partner hospital to accept payments from almost any part of the world.

Q: *What are the surgeries offered by your partner hospital and what are the rates?*

Ans.: Click here to find the spectrum of hospitals as well as surgeries/treatments our partner hospitals/clinics offer.

Costs exclude travel, visa and any other incidental costs. Cost only include cost of surgery, boarding and lodging for the package period for the patient and the boarding and lodging expenses of ONE accompanying person.

Q: *I want to get my surgery/medical treatment done in India. How should I go about it?*

Ans.: Here's suggested step-by-step process:

Step I: With your initial medical enquiry sent to us, submit your name, e-mail address, postal address and contact phone numbers.

Step II: Complete the second opinion questionnaire (Medical Quote Request Form) that we send to you by email. Basically this Medical Quote Request Form covers current nature of your ailment/your need for second medical opinion/ various types of Diagnostic reports available with you and other medical records such as CT Scan/ MRI Scans/back home hospital or clinic or your personal doctor's conducted test reports/X-Rays, etc. All these past or current medical history of a patients' information's helps our board certified medical specialists in answering your medical query with full details.

Step III: If further asked by our attending medical specialists/doctors for better understanding your medical conditions then send scanned copies of all your diagnostic reports/pathological reports/MRI/ CT-Scans/OPG Images/Dental Moulds/X-Rays/ Angiograms, etc. to facilitate out specialists second opinion. You can also use our postal address to send CD's or Xerox copies of all reports or use our Telefax or can also use postal mail or courier to send these.

Step IV: Based on all above receive full information from our board certified attending specialist doctor's/ medical consultants advice on your medical treatment approximate cost for rough planning purposes and total duration of your stay required at the hospital with pre-operative and post-operative extra stay requirement, etc. based on your posted surgery/medical treatment in India medical enquiry.

Step V: Also receive full details about cost of your stay at respective treatment city using a hotel or service apartment or guest house from us. Also receive full details about your treating institution/hospital in India with profile of attending doctor's/ specialist and respective department at the Hospital where your medical treatment is suggested for your approval/consent and for planning purposes.

Step VI: Acquire consent of your local physician to fly down to India. Inform us about consent/medical trip making condition.

Step VII: Enter into the required agreements (Pre-Registration/Indemnity or Consent Bond or Agreement) with the hospital in India for your firm medical treatment with them.

Step VIII: Enter into similar agreements (Indemnity Bond) with chosen hotel/service apartment/guest house in India for pre-operative and post-operative stay duration.

Step IX: Pay the surgery/medical treatment full cost/full fees to the hospital directly via us to book OT/ doctors' appointment/ward or room category chosen by you booking, etc.

Step X: Receive details of your date of surgery/medical treatment via email support form us.

Step XI: Proceed for India Medical Visa (given for special medical emergencies). Here you have to carry confirm appointment with your Indian medical specialist/India hospital booking, etc. papers given by us for speedy India visa clearance (we can issue you medial visa recommendation letter)

Step XII: Book tickets to fly to India. Inform us about your international arrival/departure flight timings and flight number, etc.

Step XIII: Fly down to India. receive by our representative. Orientation of your treatment city/hotel or service apartment or guest house stay, etc. are undertaken by us for your familiarization.

Step XIV: Meet the attending specialist/treating doctor at the hospital/treating Institution where you will undergo surgery/your medical treatment and proceed on your specific treatment/medical surgery there.

Step XV: On completion of treatment/medical procedure/ discharge from the hospital with final medical bill clearance and as per post-operative stay requirement suggested by your attending Indian medical specialist/doctor stay at the pre-booked hotel or service apartment or guest house and ones full clearance received from attending medical specialist/doctor is received either fly back home or enjoy a recuperative holidays in India for few weeks or as per opted choice.

Step XVI: Carry medications or prescriptions for generic medicines/drugs recommended by your attending medical specialist/doctor to carry home. Afterwards continue your post-treatment follow-up if any, through email with attending medical specialist/doctor.

Medical Insurance covers in the West for treatment in Indian Hospitals

As per a report published in *Economic Times,* dated December 26, 2007 has been predicted:

"In its Sigma report on Global Trends in Private Medical Insurance, Swiss Re has observed that in view of the significant savings potential, some experts believe that health insurance plans covering medical tourism will eventually become available and revolutionalise healthcare delivery. "The globalisation of healthcare is expected to have a significant impact on the strategy of health insurance companies. A recent study shows that if one-tenth of US patients travel abroad for treatment, savings of $1.4 billion could be realised after taking into account the cost of travel" the report said. The report pointed out that many hospitals in low-cost countries like India are already getting international accreditation such as Joint Committee on Accreditation of Healthcare Organisations and often employmedical and nursing staff with American or European professional certification.

"Medical tourism will lead to an overall improvement in healthcare services. Once the market expands, everybody benefits. Today, there are hospitals working at 110% capacity and the ones who are suffering are the insurance companies," said ICICI Lombard managing director Sandeep Bakhshi.

According to him, what was pushing up costs was that those with health insurance choose to go to a handful of leading hospitals even though there was a capacity available in smaller centres.

"In the short-term, it could result in a shortage of beds in high-end hospitals," said Bajaj Allianz General Insurance CEO Swaraj Krishnan. "But in the longer-term, I expect this to result in more investments in healthcare. This could also result in a reversal of the braindrain, with medical professionals returning to their homeland," he added. He said that the cost of healthcare for Indians is unlikely to go up on account of the influx, as hospitals in any case have a differential tariff for medical tourists.

India, considered one of the leading medical tourism providers, attracted five-lakh foreign medical tourists in 2006. Revenues totalled $350 million and the annual growth rate for such services was 30%," the report said. Although Thailand got less than a third of medical tourists into India, its revenues have been far higher at $1 billion. At present, the obstacle to insurers providing cover for treatment in India is a lack of network with service providers.

3

Growth of the Medical Tourism Industry in Asia

The divide of east and west is becoming hazy. The birth of new technologies, has transformed the globe's vast population into a boundary-less "Global village Community." From a 'consumer' point of view, it is now possible to take advantage of both cheap airfares and often higher standards or more affordable medical treatment in foreign countries, than those available in their own countries. From a patient perspective, the benefits of global healthcare are numerous. Even if cost is not the over-riding factor, the wait for surgeries in some developed nations can be off-putting. Canada and Great Britain have reported a surge in the number of people traveling outside the country to avoid long queues in the National Health Service, which can often be for a year or more for some surgical procedures. The South East Asian countries such as Thailand, Malaysia, Singapore, Korea and Philippines are the popular destinations for medical treatment. India is positioning itself as the primary destination for advanced medical procedures in the world.

Private sector is leading the Growth in Asia

Medical tourism is a promising new industry in Asia,

offering prospects for private hospitals facing saturation in patient growth. It is with a clearer view of the addressable market potential, internal strengths and limitations, as well as the level of external competition, that healthcare providers may best move forward to realize this potential. Healthcare providers may now consider the medical quality of their services, how non-medical services are key to encouraging patient access, and the various marketing options available to them. Thailand's Bumrungrad Hospital was among the first in the region to focus on attracting foreign patients. The Malaysian Government has successfully exerted its leadership to facilitate and encourage hospital industry development, with the formation of National Committee for the Promotion of Health Tourism. The Hong Kong Government is starting to consider to possibility of marketing its Traditional Chinese Medicine (TCM) capabilities to the region, while concerted efforts have similarly been launched by government agencies in Singapore to market its world-class medical capabilities. In countries such as Thailand, the onus remains on the private sector to analyze available opportunities, spearhead sectoral development, and formulate strategies to improve their competitiveness.

With the tightening of immigration rules and security checks, the US has seen a decline in the number of foreign patient visits. More patients, especially those in the Middle-East, are moving towards alternatives like Thailand. Over 100,000 foreign medical tourists visit Malaysia annually, while Singapore and India are also starting to experience positive growth in patient visits as a result of their aggressive marketing initiatives to source countries like Indonesia. However, Thailand leads the Asia-Pacific region. Thailand is able to attract a large volume of patients as it has a variety of existing tourist attractions for recuperating patients, a relatively low cost of living, overseas patients' friendly locals, and a respectable quality of healthcare, in cosmetic surgery.

Industry's best practices

Medical tourists expect the highest possible quality of care, having traveled great distances to seek world-class doctors and hospitals. Many leading hospitals have expounded on this by branching their medical expertise into super-specialization. For instance, some Australian hospitals focus not only on cancer, but perhaps on specific variations of skin cancer. This also builds credibility and buy-in, when the referring doctors are trained in the post-procedural stage to provide a continuum of patient care. Even nursing teams are trained to specialize as oncology nurses, while the cross-fertilization of medical teams such as with dermatologists, radiologists and oncologists ensures that all complications are completely accounted for. Medical quality is also supported by hardware and software investments. Hardware investments include the purchase of cutting-edge technology such as MRI or Gamma Knife machines. Software refers to the intellectual output of the hospitals as demonstrated by the latest medical research.

Non-medical services

Many hospitals offer airport pick-up services for patient convenience. Hospital reception areas are fitted as luxuriously as five-star hotels; Bumrungrad Hospital in Thailand for instance even features a Starbucks café and McDonald's outlet. Bangkok's Piyavate Hospital may even feature SPA facilities that offer a holistic wellness experience. Western-style hospitals such as in the US, UK or Australia feature their own on-site accommodation, both for patients in the aftercare stage, as well as for their relatives. Similarly, many Asian hospitals that do not manage their own accommodations also offer link-ups with different hotels, hostels, etc. Apart from bedside manners, hospital staff members are also being recruited to accommodate to their religious, dietary and cultural needs.

Hospitals that are successfully attracting foreign patients enlarge their geographical footprints with representative offices or agencies in other countries. For example, Cromwell Hospital in the UK has representatives in India and Pakistan, while hospitals in Singapore are also setting up offices such as in Indonesia or the Middle-East. These agents help establish and maintain relationships such as with local hospitals, doctors, embassies, sponsor corporations, or insurers. Participating in different events also facilitates such relationships. For instance, trade shows, exhibitions or training seminars allow healthcare providers to share their medical expertise.

With budget air travel and the Internet providing access to information about cheap or specialist treatment overseas, medical centers across Asia are vying with each other to become regional or even global hubs for healthcare. Singapore is aiming to attract one million foreign patients per year by 2010 while India is gunning to be a top medical tourist destination, benefiting from its huge base of medical professionals and low costs.

However needs can vary widely between the 'essential' healthcare seekers—traveling by necessity, because treatment is not available or unaffordable locally—and the 'premium' medical tourists, who are typically looking for wellness or cosmetic procedures and may want first-class flights and exclusive add-ons. Pacific Healthcare Holdings Patient Relations Manager Alison Lim says, our International Patient Liaison Centre has seen an increase in these "premium" medical tourists seeking high end elective treatments like titanium dental implants, complex cosmetic procedures as well as deluxe health screening. An emerging trend is the bundling of five-star healthcare services with unconventional post-operation treatment. India is providing traditional recuperation forms such as yoga and naturopathy, while Thailand is promoting its ancient Thai herbal remedies to the West, Middle East and Far East. To create awareness and market their medical services, Singapore's Raffles Hospital works with 50 agents in 12 countries. Parkway Group Healthcare has marketing offices in 15 countries including China, India, Bangladesh, Sri Lanka, Vietnam, Brunei, UAE, Britain, Russia, Canada, Indonesia and Malaysia, which last year helped attract over 17,000 indoor patients and 140,000 outpatients.

Top 10 in medical tourism

- Bumrungrad International Hospital in Bangkok
- Buchinger Clinic in Germany
- All India Institute of Medical Sciences in Delhi

- The Fyodorov Clinics in Russia
- A Technology Prescription: Denver Health
- Brigham and Women's Hospital
- Sourasky Medical Center in Tel Aviv
- Hôpital Edouard Herriot in Lyons
- Hospital for Tropical Diseases in London
- Mount Sinai Medical Center

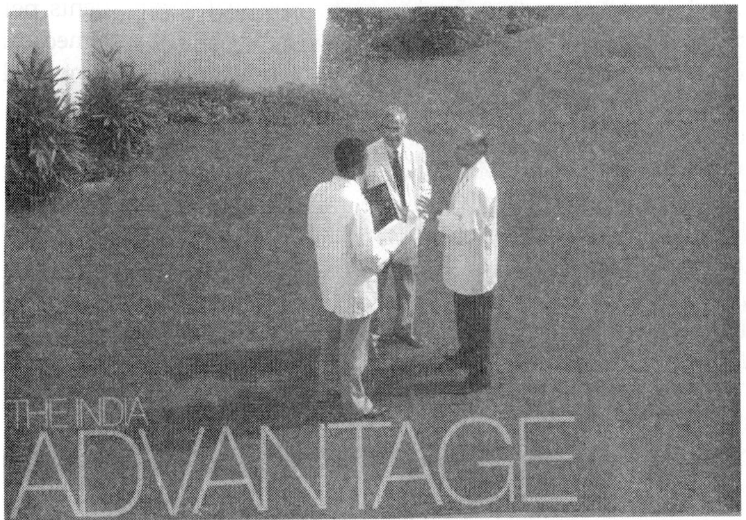

India Story

The medical tourism policy can draw strength from recommendations that the corporate sector has been making in India, and specifically from the "Policy Framework for Reforms in Healthcare", drafted by the Indian prime minister's Advisory Council on Trade and Industry, headed by Mukesh Ambani and Kumaramangalam Birla. Certain other Asian countries have taken Giant strides in promoting medical tourism in their respective countries. However, the current market for medical tourism in India is mainly limited to patients from the Middle East and South Asian economies, besides the NRIs from all over the globe. Analysts say that as many as 150,000 medical tourists came to India in the year 2005 and over 200,000 in the year 2006. Afro-Asian people spend as much as $20 billion a year on healthcare outside their countries—Nigerians alone spend an estimated $1 billion a year. Most of this money is spent in Europe and America, but it is hoped that this would now be increasingly directed to developing countries like India.

The foreign patients come from SAARC region, Afghanistan, Ethiopia, Nigeria, Tanzania, other parts of Africa, CIS countries and the Middle East, especially Oman and Yemen. As per New trends from 2003, patients from the US, UK and Canada, escaping high costs and waiting lists are coming to India. Also from Europe, Australia and New Zealand for procedures not covered by insurance such as cosmetic surgery, obesity treatment, and new techniques like hip resurfacing Around 30 private tertiary hospitals, are situated in Delhi, Mumbai, Bangalore; Chennai, Calcutta, Thiruvananthapuram, Coimbatore and Hyderabad. It Includes hospital groups like Apollo, Wockhardt, Fortis, Max, Escorts. At an Indian medical tourism expo in the UK last year, 25 per cent of visitors were seeking medical treatment in India. India's Apollo is setting up hospitals in joint ventures in Dhaka and Colombo; and clinics in Yemen and Saudi Arabia Parkway Holdings of Singapore in tie-up with Apollo in Calcutta; with Asian Heart Institute and Research Centre in Mumbai; International chain Columbia Asia has a 75-bed multi-speciality hospital in Bangalore.

Indian corporate hospitals have a large pool of doctors, nurses, and paramedics ensuring individual, personalized care for all. The highly skilled personnel, with wide experience and international exposure excel in cardiology and cardio thoracic surgery, joint replacement, orthopedic surgery, gastroenterology, ophthalmology, transplants and urology to name a few. The various specialties covered are Neurology, Neurosurgery, Oncology, Ophthalmology, Rheumatology, Endocrinology, ENT, Pediatrics, Pediatric Surgery, Pediatric Neurology, Urology, Nephrology, Dermatology, Dentistry, Plastic Surgery, Gynecology, Pulmonology, Psychiatry, General Medicine and General Surgery.

Thailand's Bangkok; a shining example

Catch some sun, take in a few golden temples, and get a new hip—a new slogan coined by the Thailand Tourism, to promote medical tourism. It's an increasingly popular itinerary for foreign visitors who are flying into Thailand in ever greater numbers to get quality hospital care at bargain prices, part of a 'medical tourism' boom that is turning into a multi-billion dollar industry in Asia. The kingdom is one of several countries in the region cashing in on its ability to use cheap but highly skilled labour, affordable hospital accommodation and offer specialist treatments. Of a total of one million patients each year at Bumrungrad, nearly 50 percent are foreigners with Americans making up the biggest group, followed by patients from the United Arab Emirates, Bangladesh, Oman, Britain, Japan, Australia, Cambodia and Myanmar. Among Americans, back surgery and hip and knee replacements are the most popular procedures at Bumrungrad, while many Australians seek plastic surgery. Bumrungrad International Hospital offers a full spectrum of services from executive health tests to cardiac packages, cancer therapy, eye surgery, liposuction and other cosmetic options. Bumrungrad has more than 700 internationally-trained and board-certified doctors, and a complete range of healthcare services and facilities.

Five million tourists for medical treatment

According to the Tourism Authority of Thailand (TAT), at least five million tourists come to the country annually for medical treatment. Various plastic surgery clinics could attest that the number of both Thais and foreigners undergoing dental and plastic surgeries, lasik, and other physical enhancement procedures is increasing. Aside from these, Thailand has earned its reputation as an excellent location for spa services. "The growth of spa business is a good sign that tells us that we can respond to customers' needs," Mr. Apichai added pointing to Proud Asia 2008 as an excellent venue where the international community can actually see the advancements that Thailand has taken the field of medical tourism.

"Beauty business will continuously grow as both men and women care about their looks," President of Thai Society of Cosmetic Dermatology and Surgery, Dr. Thada Piamphongsan said, adding that Thailand has more advantages than other countries in Asia when it comes to offering the best quality medical and beauty services but at cheaper rates.

Proud Asia 2008 is definitely not just the usual exhibition event on beauty and healthcare products and services we see here and in other countries. What makes this event extraordinary is the fact that we are going to have a grand showcase of the latest innovations of products and services in the field of medical tourism, spa and wellness. Everybody will be here the expert in medical tourism, the best spa and wellness providers, and the most highly interested buyers. "The event promises to be a big one for both suppliers and buyers and the most important thing is that it will be held right here in Bangkok. This means that the Kingdom will again have the chance to prove to the international community that Thailand has sufficient MICE infrastructure to be the best venue for this kind of trade exhibition and conference. Proud Asia 2008 is a huge event that will help the country achieve its goal of becoming a regional hub for exhibitions and conventions business and Mice market."

Bumrungrad *vs.* Bangkok Hospital

Charles Runckel writes about two leading hospitals in Thailand. Thailand is the world leader for medical tourism, but which hospital within Thailand is best for you? While there are many hospitals in Thailand that cater to medical tourists, these are two full-service facilities that have strong reputations for quality and experience with foreigners. The aspiring medical tourist should consider these two in Bangkok before any other Thai hospitals, even ones with a slightly lower cost, as they are the gold standard for medical tourism not only in Thailand but worldwide.

Background and Location

Bumrungrad Hospital treats 4-5 lakhs foreign patients every year and has made medical tourism its major focus. The monolithic hospital consists of a large tower and several associated buildings adjoining, all conveniently located in downtown Bangkok. The hospital is within walking distance of Bangkok's Skytrain (light rail system) but only barely, and

Bumrungrad Hospital's main building and entrance

Bangkok Hospital's Buildings and one of their entrance

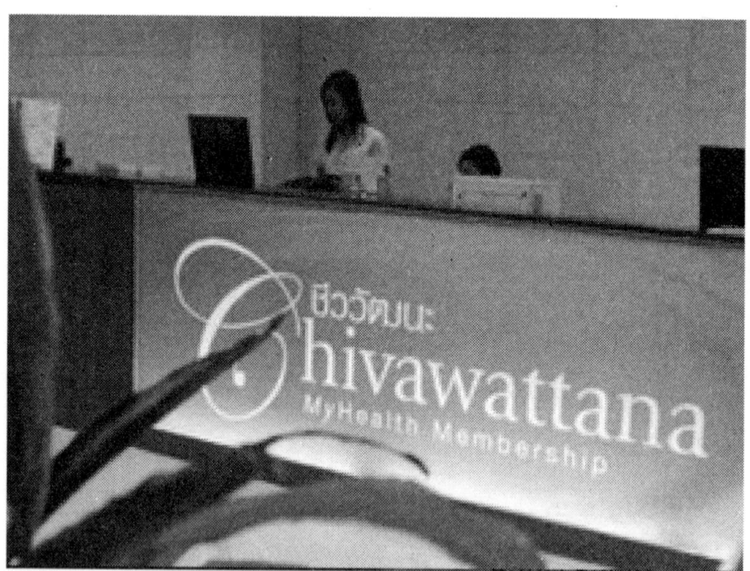

given the heat usual in Thailand most patients are strongly advised to take a taxi. International patients are so much a part of Bumrungrad's focus that they recently broke from their single tower architecture and built a separate International Tower that caters specially to foreigners with a brand new Physical Exam wing and upgraded VIP rooms.

Bangkok Hospital Group is a network of Thai hospitals focused on Bangkok and sprawling into the provinces and even Cambodia, though the portion of this that is most important to foreigners is their Bangkok Hospital Medical Center (BMC) complex. This campus consists of their International Hospital as well as their main General Hospital and a collection of specialty hospitals, including their Heart Hospital, Rehabilitation Center and Dental Clinic. The BMC is a series of adjacent buildings connected by skywalks and, apart from the main General Hospital building, are new having been built in the past five years. The BMC is located near, but not walking distance from, several Skytrain and subways stations, so a taxi is in order in this case as well. While BMC and Bumrungrad treat about the same number of total patients each, a lower proportion of BMC's patients are from overseas and total only 150,000 annually, though these are often for more serious treatments.

Layout and Impressions

Bumrungrad Hospital is, as previously mentioned, monolithic. Visitors enter into the lobby of the main tower at the ground floor, but this and the next floor contain mostly restaurants, coffee shops and the cafeteria. The Hospital portion does not begin until the third floor, where the patient is greeted with a larger lobby and registration area. Elegantly uniformed staff register new patients with digital cameras—both Bumrungrad and BMC are very tech savvy hospitals with test results updated and delivered electronically and pictures of each patient checked at every stage to avoid foul-ups. This registration area is both the point of entry and exit, and next to registration are desks for checkout and a pharmacy.

On every floor of Bumrungrad runs a long, wide hallway with specialty clinics and divisions branching-off, generally four to six per floor. Each has its own lobby, which looks out onto the hall. The older main tower and new international tower are quite different, with the older tower very much feeling like a mature hospital, with traditional waiting areas and layout, while the new wing is decidedly more modern and up-to-date, from the lobbies and hallways to furnishings in patient rooms.

Upon walking into BMC's main building, one is immediately greeted with the registration staff. They are far more eager to register you than those at Bumrungrad, though this has a strong basis in necessity. Upon registration, a patient's schedule will likely initially take them to another building, or several buildings if they have multiple appointments. The BMC staff then ensure that you are taken to the right building or floor of the main structure. There are enclosed walkways between the buildings, however most patients are initially led to the shuttles, which are over-sized gold carts or minivans that scoot patients around the campus.

Each division, clinic or specialty hospital at BMC has its own modular area with it's own independent registration and cashier services (so you don't have to go through the main lobby at all, if you know where you're going). These lobbies, especially in the newer buildings, are considerably more aesthetically appealing and pleasant to wait in than many of Bumrungrad's specialty clinic lobbies, mostly due to their smaller size, more updated furnishings and clever

One of many MRI scanners at the Bangkok Hospital

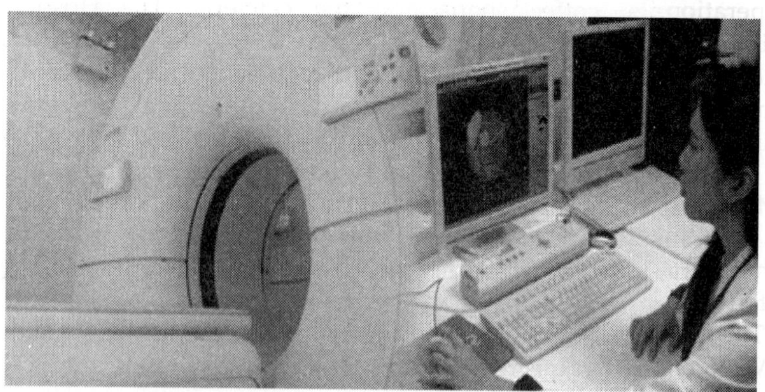

architectural design. Like Bumrungrad, there is a clear difference in ambiance between their older General Hospital building and the new, adjoining specialty centers.

The famed, or infamous, Bangkok Hospital Phuket is renowned as a world leader in sex-change operations, but is also a state-of-the-art hospital for more mundane purposes and nothing beats Phuket's beaches for physical therapy and recuperation after a surgery in Bangkok, which the Phuket Hospital supervises and coordinates.

Unlike many other aspects of a hospital experience, the sheer technical capabilities of a hospital are somewhat easily quantified, and it is in this aspect that Bangkok Hospital most outshines its competitor. BMC has focused a tremendous amount of resources to being on the cutting edge of medical technology, and while Bumrungrad is certainly not unsophisticated, there is general agreement that Bumrungrad is a solid step behind BMC-technologically. BMC's hi-tech drive falls into two general areas: advanced imaging and non-invasive surgery. Their advanced imaging options include at least seven MRI scanners in their main campus alone. Each department receives its own specialized diagnostic equipment, unlike many hospitals which must pool resources, including Digital Mammography and a brand new 128-slice CT scanner currently being installed. It is peerless in South-East Asia, and BMC boasts one of Thailand's only two clinical PET-CT scanners. The non-invasive offerings include state-of-the-art radiation systems such as the Novalis device for brain tumors and robotic laparoscopic surgery for both heart and joint operations (with different robots, of course). Bumrungrad simply does not compete in this field, which gives BMC a decisive advantage in the specific operations these advanced machines enable; reducing risk, discomfort and hospital stay time.

Marketing

Bumrungrad is probably the best-marketed hospital in the world. Their fame is well deserved, but their marketing staff and management have put a tremendous effort in being "The" medical tourist hospital that potential patients in the Western world have heard of, specifically through news reports on ABC and CBS as well as multiple appearances in Newsweek. BMC, in contrast, is more famous within Thailand and elsewhere in Asia and the Middle East. Both hospitals treat approximately the same total number of patients—about 1 million a year—however Bumrungrad began courting foreign patients much earlier than BMC and now draws 400,000 foreign patients a year to BMC's 150,000-250,000. It is worth noting that different hospitals use different metrics to calculate these numbers (visits *vs.* patients) so these comparisons must be taken with a grain of salt, however, it is commonly accepted that Bumrungrad's proportion is higher than BMC's, though not by as much as the disclosed numbers suggest. While BMC's focus for the future includes increasing the proportion of foreign patients, the target countries of both hospitals will likely remain the same with Bumrungrad focusing on the US and BMC focusing on the Middle-East and Asia, affecting the level of marketing in each area.

Part of Bumrungrad's early marketing included aggressive pursuit of international certification, and as a result Bumrungrad correctly claims a number of regional "Firsts" with various international credentialing organizations. In many ways, Bumrungrad was a trendsetter and these certifications were necessary when no one had even heard the term "medical tourism" and there were serious doubts about the quality of a Thai hospital. Today, the first and second tier of Thai hospitals are firmly within international standards and rising acceptance of medical tourism make this less necessary. BMC has, itself, a slew of acronyms attesting to its quality, many of which overlap Bumrungrad's, and comparing certifications should be less important to the potential medical tourist than other aspects of reputation, but for a nervous first time medical tourist Bumrungrad's list of "firsts" can be welcome reassurance.

The savings on one 'major tooth repair' can pay for an economy level 2 week vacation including air.

- Root canal and cap front tooth 14,000thb US$354. AUD$481. EU284.
- Significant dental work (2 teeth) would result saved money in your bank account + the vacation!

- Very simple but necessary dental procedures from cleaning to cosmetic . . . available at significant savings.
- Diagnostics, imaging, lab analysis, physical rehabilitation, cosmetic surgery, dental . . . all 80% off US pricing.

Anonymous violent crime/robbery, common in the West, is all but unknown in Thailand.

- Most "Thailand Citizen US Educated Doctors" return to Thailand after graduation from their US Medical School.
- Plus, access to top Thai specialists within 24 hours is pretty reassuring
    - o . . . no waiting, ever, for anything! + a free tasty lunch!
- The Dell computer system at Bumrungrad is equal to any in the world.
    - o Orthopedic images, blood work, diagnostics, specialist notes . . . all are available across the network.
    - o No carrying film/records to a specialist . . . it's in the system and instantly available.
        - > Doc suggests additional imaging: . . . OK, he orders it, the test is completed and you are back in his office getting his interpretation within 24-48 hours.
        - > Doc orders a CAT scan and it's completed– the next morning and immediately it's in the computer system! . . . !!
- Appointments are coordinated system wide . . . smooth patient flow . . . no bottle necks . . . no waits, respect . . . professional! + smiling happy Healthcare team and bilingual clerical staffing.

In the Chiang Mai/Chiang Rai area some incredible Lanni Thai style house are available for short-term rental . . . quite marvelous houses built from 100% teak. The house above rents for 17, 000 Thb (US$400, Euro 325 per month)

- Grand Imperial Travel of Bangkok offers Executive Medical Tourism Packages!

  - They assist with appointments and suggest hotels/apartments near your medical provider.
  - They pick you up at the airport, provide a cell phone for your stay, provide a personal guide for both tourist outings and medical appointments . . . all for a flat fee.

Bangkok is a wonderful mix of Ancient Far East and Ultra Modern West

Golden Triangle

Beaches

Bangkok

Thailand can provide an "extremely cost effective" Medical Vacation.

- Bumrungrad and Bangkok Hospital compare well to US Med Center Hospitals . . . and far better than rural US hospitals.

Bumrungrad Hospital, is very foreigner friendly. Said to be #1 in Asia! Bangkok Hospital, off New Petchaburi Road, is foreigner friendly and comparable to most western hospitals. Private hospital room is $60 per day. A few extra days in the hospital, no problem. Many Japanese companies send their employees to Thailand for annual physicals as well as long term medial care modalities. The savings on medical fees and the high quality medical care makes the air fare inconsequential.

Dental experiences vary greatly. These clinics offer modern equipment and a full range of 'pain reduction techniques'.

- Asavanant Clinic.
- Bangkok Dental Hospital.
- Siam Family Dental.
- The Dental Hospitals on Suk Soi 55, Suk Soi 49 and Suk Soi 39 as well as the Dental clinics at Chula Hospital and Bumagard Hospital are professionally staffed and equipped well.
- Bumagard Hospital has serviced apartments adjacent to the hospital. . . hospital staffed rehabilitation apartment suites for less than $100 per day.
- Affordable 24/7 out patient nursing $100 per day can provide luxury hotel accommodations, gourmet meals and 24 hour 'private duty assisting provider'.

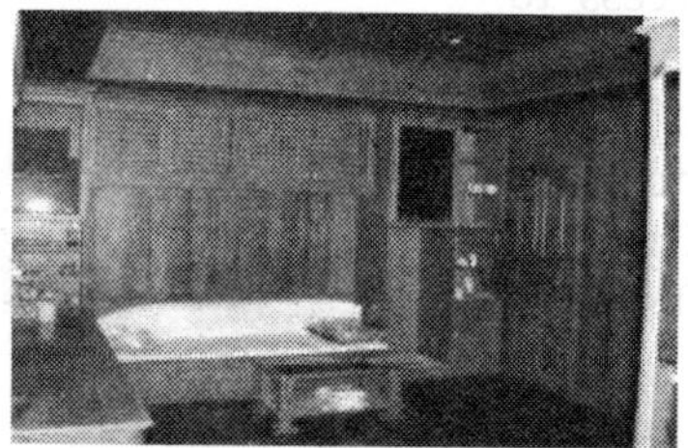

More than 150,000 North Americans and Europeans currently seek medical treatment overseas each year, estimates Josef Woodman, author of the forthcoming "Patients without Borders." For invasive surgeries, preferred destinations include India, Thailand, Singapore and Malaysia. Large hospitals, such as Bumrungrad and the Apollo chain in India, actively court American, European and Middle Eastern patients. Bumrungrad arranges limousines to pick up patients at the airport, and sheiks and princes congregate in the Platinum Lounge of Apollo's Delhi hospital. Abacas International, a leading travel facilitator, reports that medical tourism to Asia could generate billions of dollars.

Businesses are taking notice. At least 40 corporations have signed on to the overseas plan that United Group Programs, a health insurer in Boca Raton, Florida, began offering six months ago. Sending an employee abroad can save 80 percent of the costs of a procedure; a $50,000 angioplasty in the United States costs less than $6,000 in Mohali, Chandigarh, India, according to Global Choice Healthcare, a firm that arranges foreign medical procedures. Walk-in patients see a specialist in 17 minutes on average. Since 75 percent of hospital revenues are paid by patients directly, health and insurance companies have no say in treatment. Low labour costs allow Thai hospitals to employ more staff.

In Australia, Europe and North America, "complementary and alternative medicine" (CAM) is increasingly being used in parallel to modern medicine, particularly for treating and managing chronic disease. Concern about the adverse effects of chemical medicines, a desire for more personalized healthcare and greater public access to health information, fuel this increased use. For the past six years, persons from over two hundred countries with difficult and chronic conditions, i.e. diverticulitis, cancer, and incurable autoimmune diseases such as Systemic Lupus Erythematosis (SLE), Multiple Sclerosis (MS), Lou Gherig is Disease (ALS), have been motivated to explore the options Traditional Chinese Medicine (TCM) offers them at Huai Hua Red Cross Hospital. Since these conditions are chronic and often times incurable, they have led many patients and/or their family members to seek and decipher complex, baffling, and, obscure medical information and to explore options encountered beyond the diagnostic and treatment scope generally available to them. Despite their diverse cultural backgrounds, many persons reach this intersecting destination at the time-honored tradition of TCM and the Huai Hua Red Cross Hospital for Difficult and Chronic conditions.

Medical tourism boom takes Singapore by storm

Singapore makes world headlines for performing complex neurosurgical procedures and delivering cutting-edge medical treatment by the region's leading health specialists. The Republic's reputation for high quality medical facilities and well-trained doctors pulled in more than 370,000 visitors in 2004. The cost of treatments in Singapore, such as a hip replacement, can be less than a third of the price in the United States.

Raffles Hospital, has gained fame in recent years for highly publicized operations to separate conjoined twins, exemplifying the highly skilled expertise available.

The tiny island of Singapore, having a populace of 4.4 million, is fast positioning itself as a medical tourism hub. The authorities are ambitious of serving one million foreign patients annually by 2012 and generate USD 3 billion in revenue.

Parkway hospitals group is Singapore's largest private healthcare group in Asia, owning three tertiary care private hospitals: East Shore, Gleneagles and Mount Elizabeth. The magnificent façade of these hospitals are complemented by equally competent doctors and excellent services with world class equipment.

Incidentally, quite a few patients come from India for liver transplant. Nitin Saxena, who brought his father all the way from Delhi to Gleneagles for a liver transplant, opines unlike Indian hospitals, the services and facilities value for money.

Stem cell transplant is yet another field developing rapidly on the health map of Singapore. The haematology and stem cell transplant centre of Mount Elizabeth Hospital has pioneered stem cell treatment for patients with advanced cancer tumours. Headed by director Dr. Patrick Tan, a world renowned specialist in the field of oncology, cost of treatment here ranges from USD 72,000 to USD 90,000 per person, compared to USD 235,000 for similar treatment in the US. Recently, a 12-year-old girl from Delhi underwent cord blood transplant at the centre. As a mark of hospitality, hospital staff goes to receive patients and their relatives from the airport, make arrangements for their stay and even provide with language whenever required.

The medical tourism boom is just not restricted to Singapore alone. Current trend of economic developments in the Asian region, higher life expectancies, an ageing population and an ever-increasing awareness of the benefits of the quality healthcare have given a shot in the arm to the Asian healthcare industry, taking it to witness an unprecedented growth. Presently, there are only 140,000 hospitals serving an Asian population of 3.5 billion. With Asian population expected to grow to 5.6 billion by 2050, the consumer expenditure on healthcare services and goods will increase from US$90 billion in 1999 to US$188 billion in 2013. Malaysia is targeting the Middle East and China to generate whopping revenue of 2.2 billion by 2010. These emerging markets prove that there's immense potential in the Asian healthcare business, remarked Ms Tan-Hoong Chu Eng, MD, Parkway Promotions Pte Ltd., a subsidiary company of Parkway-Holdings Ltd. the largest private healthcare group in Asia.

Demand for healthcare is rising in the Middle East with millions of dollars spent in establishing specialised hospitals and clinics, expanding existing facilities and adopting world class technology in Bahrain, Kuwait, Yemen, Oman and Qatar. In the UAE, for instance, the government plans to double the bed capacity of public hospitals to achieve a target of one for every 300 people by the end of the decade.

The Philippines Faith healers

The Philippines probably beat other countries to this idea of medical tourism. You may recall how in the 1970s, faith healers like Tony Agpaoa were offering tour packages for people coming in from Europe and Japan who wanted the faith healers' services. Agpaoa even had his own little hotel in Baguio City so that patients didn't have to look for their own accommodations. The faith healing packages eventually went into decline, and last I heard, it was our faith healers who were going to Eastern European countries to do their road-show healing.

Earlier this year, then-secretary of tourism Roberto Pagdanganan announced that the Department of Tourism was teaming up with the Department of Health, specifically the Philippine Institute of Traditional and Alternative Healthcare, to promote medical tourism. At that time, he said only the St. Luke's hospital had been accredited for their program but Asian Hospital, Capitol Medical Center, and Medical City had also applied. Our medical and nursing curricula are certainly tougher than many of our neighbours in Southeast Asia.

Malaysia

Malaysia raked in RM 203.6 million in hospital receipts in 2006 from nearly 300,000 foreign medical patients. Health Ministry parliamentary secretary Datuk Lee Kah Choon said Penang's portion of the takings amounted to RM129.9 million or 63.83 per cent of the total. The other cities involved were Kuala Lumpur, Malacca and Johor Baru. "We are expecting double-digit growth for hospital receipt figures this year," he said after witnessing the signing of a clinical research collaboration between YSP Industries Sdn Bhd and Penang-based Infor Kinetics Sdn Bhd here. Among the types of treatment sought are for heart ailments, cosmetic surgery, and wellness treatment at spas. "Patients include those from Indonesia and Singapore. The government is studying ways to make medical tourism more attractive to invest in." Healthcare tourism in Malaysia took-off in an aggressive manner in 2002 when Tourism Malaysia began promoting it overseas. "This includes tax-relief on the purchase of medical equipment or capital allowance on costs for new buildings," he said, adding that the proposed breaks were to reduce the "burden" on these institutions to enable them to continuously invest in upgrading their services. Important hospitals include Sunway Hospital, Sabang Medical, Gleneagles and KPJ chain. The Health Ministry is pursuing international accreditation for two Kuala Lumpur hospitals to boost medical tourism.

KPJ Healthcare is currently the largest commercial health and medical care provider in Malaysia and is one of the major players in Southeast Asia.

With over 5000 staff, the company operates several of Malaysia's most advanced and respected medical facilities. Among them are the Ampang Puteri hospital with 230 beds, and Damansara Specialist Centre (155 beds) and the Tawakal hospital (147 beds).

Last year, KPJ served about 145,000 inpatients and 1.4 million outpatients and recorded a turnover of approximately RM831 million.

The Group also holds the distinction of being the first home-grown healthcare company to be listed on the Main Board of the Kuala Lumpur Stock Exchange. It was listed in late 1994.

Apart from its medical centres, the company also administers its Puteri Nursing College, Lablink—a laboratory and pathology facility-and manages its own procurement and planning facility through Pharmaserv Alliances Sdn Bhd (PASB).

With its philosophy of "Think Global, Act Local", KPJ is looking to enjoy the same success as a regional player as it has in Malayia.

To date, KPJ's international operations include hospitals in Bangladesh (United Hospitals Thaka) and Indonesia (Rumuh Sakit Salasih and Rumah Sakit Permata.

—(*New Skaits Times*, Oct. 2007)

Several other countries in Asia and other continents are also working for medical tourism.

Realities of India as a Health Tourism Destination

India's tertiary healthcare sector is on the road to global fame. It is an ironic outcome of economic reforms that in spite of failures in public health, India is increasingly seen as an attractive international healthcare destination. That potential is based, in part, on the low cost of care in international price terms, competent medical personnel and absence of long waiting times for procedures, says a CII report. Stories of foreign nationals undergoing complicated surgery in the country are frequently featured in the media. 25 millions NRI visit the home country at least once a year and take consultations and treatment from the clinics of their choice. Those who come now are not just from other developing countries, but also from the United Kingdom, Europe and North America. Tanzania and Iraq have a Memorandum of Understanding with the Madras Medical Mission.

Salient features of Indian healthcare:

(i) Five star facilities and international quality treatment.

(ii) Well qualified and experienced superspecialists.

(iii) Latest equipment, e.g. Robotic Cardiae Surgeries, 64 Slice CT Scan, Linear Accelrator.
(iv) Strict blood safety.
(v) Tele-medicine, Viedeo-conferencing, etc.
(vi) English speaking populace.

De-stressing and health-building

The CII-McKinsey report says that the modern system can offer treatment in specialties such as cardiac, liver, renal and orthopedic procedures, while Indian systems of medicine could attract patients from even the developed world to treat "lifestyle diseases" such as stress and rheumatism. Many visitors who come for such de-stressing and health-building treatment may also choose to visit tourist spots. Such tourism potential holds the key to Kerala's plans. The Ayurveda State had declared 2006 the year of medical tourism and is actively supporting its well-known traditional medicine and tourism sectors, as they reach out to more potential visitors.

Karnataka, which gets about 8,000 patients a year and forecasts an annual growth rate of 25 per cent, will promote a massive health park near it's city near a new international airport in Bangalore. Famous Hrudalaya and Bangalore Health City already exist, under the command of Dr. Devi Shatty. Non-resident Indians have formed a medical tourism company in Vadodara and international property developers are venturing into the healthcare sector to participate in the construction boom. In Maharashtra, the State Government has set-up Medical Tourism Council that has members from Association of Hospitals and FICCI. In New Delhi. Naresh Trehan, executive director of the Escorts Heart Institute and Research Centre (now with Apollo) has proposed a Medi City on the outskirts of the capital to develop a 1,500-bed healthcare centre of international standards with 20 super specialties. It will incorporate traditional medicine too and have such facilities as hotels, serviced apartments, clinical and biotechnology laboratories. The corporate healthcare sector views such support as critical, considering that it is competing with Thailand, Singapore, Malaysia and South Korea for a bigger share of Asia's medical tourism market.

Accreditation benefits

Joint Commission International (JCI), a benchmarking body lists Indraprastha Apollo, New Delhi, and Wockhardt, Mumbai, as accredited hospitals. Accreditation apparently brings immediate benefits. "There has been a steady increase in the number of patients, particularly from the U.K. and US. The numbers have been increasing after accreditation, particularly from the US," says Vishal Bali, chief executive officer of Wockhardt. (See Appendix 5 for more on JCI accreditation and other aspects of medical tourism promotion).

It is also important to have systems that meet the criteria of insurance companies. Says cardiac surgeon V.V. Bashi of MIOT Hospital, Chennai: "Our medical standards are world class, but if we have to get more patients from the US and other developed countries, we must match their hospital documentation standards. This is really important because the insurance companies must cover all the risks in the event of an adverse treatment outcome."

Synergy between Government and private care

The perceived potential of medical tourism is apparent in the fact that even the Ministry of Tourism (MoT) has included healthcare in its campaigns. CII on its part has provided a list of hospitals to the ministry, which has come out with a special medical tourism brochure under its Incredible India campaign. It, together with CII, plans to develop a strategy to market these services overseas as well. While these efforts validate the health tourism phenomenon, there is still a very fragmented approach by the stakeholders viz. tour operators, health institutes and tourism boards—barring Kerala. Kerala tourism board has proved to be a pioneer by taking its international patients, health facilities and its oldest stronghold—tourism, seriously. It has formed a forum with about eight major health institutions and has applied to NABH for accreditation and is considering looking at an international accreditation as well. However, there seems to be a lack of synergy between healthcare professionals and travel agents with the former preferring to restrict their roles to getting patients to their hospitals, instead of exploring the tourism potential as well. Even Dr. Trehan insists that healthcare is serious business and "we do not want to make it cheap". Similarly, Chennai-based Apollo Hospitals restricted itself to a marketing tie-up with the Tamil Nadu Tourism Development Corporation, where tourists were given coupons for master health check-ups. But visiting international patients or relatives were not being offered composite packages by the tourism board or the hospital.

In Malaysia, a strong contender for medical tourism, the holiday packages offered vary depending upon the choice of treatment desired and are planned keeping in mind the patient's state of health and amount of post-operative recuperation. In order to create the perfect healthcare package, the hospital sends strict guidelines regarding recuperation and permissible postoperative activities for each procedure. Based on this, the tour operator creates holiday packages for each individual procedure with suitable itineraries and sends it back to the hospital for approval. After careful scrutiny, the hospital selects a final holiday package which is the safest and most advantageous for the particular treatment.

India's next big story

As the concept of medical tourism continues to gain momentum in India, the Ministry of Health and Family Welfare, following a meeting with the Ministry of Tourism, has stated that a NABH has to be set-up for maintaining international standards in our medical facilities. The intricacies discussed include price banding, hospital accreditation, quality control, categorization and selection of hospitals, etc. Minister of Health and Family Welfare Dr. Anbumani Ramadoss said that the government has cleared medical visa and there is tremendous potential for tourism as well as for the health sector, with India specially being cheapest destination for medical care of highest standards. He also emphasized on modern diagnostics with Indian systems of medicinal care, which has been accepted as an effective system of healthcare worldwide.

Dr. Ramdoss said that some measures like fast track clearance for medical patients at the airport are in the offing in coordination with other Ministries that would be of great help to foreign tourists coming to India for medical treatment. In this regard, the Minister also mentioned development of appropriate health packages for traditional therapies like yoga, meditation, ayurveda and other traditional systems of medicine, which would not only attract high-end tourists from European and Middle East countries but also give a boost within the country.

Some people might ask, "What if something goes wrong during the surgery?" Well, here you have the reputation of the hospital and the surgeon at stake. They know that they must offer you outstanding, high-quality service. Otherwise, word will spread via the internet and elsewhere, and tourists won't come to visit their hospital. Things can go wrong, but they can go wrong anywhere. Something like one percent of all people undergoing gastric bypass surgery die on the operating table. That's going to happen in any country, anywhere you are. And whether or not there's medical insurance and malpractice insurance in effect at the time of your surgery doesn't affect your outcome. All it does is it gives people a chance to sue when they don't get the outcome they want.

The specialty hospitals excelling in the medical tourism are:

- Escorts/Fortis Heart Institute and Research Centre Limited, Delhi
- All India Institute of Medical Sciences, Delhi and PGI, Chandigarh
- Manipal Heart Foundation, Bangalore and Narayan Hrudalaya
- B.M. Birla Heart Research Centre, Kolkata
- Breach Candy Hospital, Mumbai
- Wockhardt Hospitals, five in number
- Christian Medical College, Vellore
- Asian Heart Institute, Mumbai
- PD Hinduja National Hospital and Medical Research Centre, Mumbai
- Jaslok Hospital, Mumbai
- Apollo Hospital, Delhi
- Apollo Cancer Hospital, Chennai

Apollo has been a forerunner in medical tourism in India and attracts patients from Southeast Asia, Africa, and the Middle East. The group has tied up with hospitals in Mauritius, Tanzania, Bangladesh and Yemen besides running a hospital in Sri Lanka, and managing a hospital in Dubai. Another corporate group running a chain of hospitals, Escorts, claims it has doubled its number of overseas patients—from 675 in 2000 to nearly 1,200 in 2005. Recently, the Ruby Hospital in Kolkata signed a contract with the British insurance company, BUPA.

Benefits in India

(i) Cost Benefit

Many of the Indian hospitals, serving international patients, have state-of-the-art infrastructure, highly educated doctors and top-notch services but the figure on that price tag is a fraction of what it would be in developed countries.

(ii) Timeliness

Another advantage is the possibility of getting immediate medical attention. There are no waiting lists or delays to contend with, due to insurance issues or unavailability of doctors, etc.

(iii) Quality Healthcare

Indian doctors and paramedics are well trained and are one of the best in the world. Many professionals, at most of the lead hospitals in the country, have been trained abroad prior to working in India.

(iv) Personalized Care

It is relatively easy to find quality personalized care for critically ill or aged patients.

(v) Technological Sophistication

State-of-the-art equipment and infrastructure is the order of the day at most of the top corporate hospitals.

(vi) Facilitation by Government

The Government of India has recognized the economic potential of medical tourism. It has facilitated travel by introducing a special visa category known as 'medical visa' for patients as well as introduced tax incentives for hospitals.

(vii) Ease of Travel and Communication

Travel in India has become easier and much faster due to introduction of private airlines. Access to Internet in India is considered to be one of the cheapest in the world and communication facilities are well established. Travel agencies have a great online presence and can offer you package deals that include travel costs, boarding as well as treatment costs.

(viii) Easy availability of medicine and drugs

Certified drugs and medicines are easily available in India, at comparatively lesser prices.

(ix) Modern and Traditional

This is India's USP. Modern medical aid as well as traditional therapy, such as ayurveda, yoga, naturopathy, etc. is available at different locations across the country including Bangalore.

(x) Tourism Potential

People who come for relatively simple, but important procedures, can consider packing in some travel too, with their doctor's permission! This is an added advantage. Every part of the country is rich in history and diverse in geography.

Quest MedTourism

Quest MedTourism facilitates uninsured and underinsured North American patients seeking affordable medical treatments along with an opportunity to explore mystic Asia and near by tourist locations. We help our clients with completion of their travelling documents, departure from their home country, arrangements at the airport, hotel accommodation and assist them choosing the best, cost effective medical procedures at various hospitals across India along with can exhilarating vacation package. Healing begins when the mind and body are relaxed. Let us help you start the healing process. Medical Treatment-India. com (MTI) is an Indian Company, established to help people with Medical needs, schedule Medical Treatment and Travel Arrangements in India. Some of the Medical Treatment Packages offered by MTI are Open Heart Surgery, PTCA (Percutaneous Transluminal Coronary Angioplasty), Total Knee Replacement, Total Hip Replacement, Cervical Spinal Decompression, Bone Marrow Transplant, Spinal Fusion, Spinal Tumor, Craniotomy-Arterio, Micro Vascular Decompression, Excision of Brain Tumor, Breast Reduction, Breast Augmentation, Face Lift, Whipples, Lap Hernia Repair, Nephrectomy, PCNL, Hysterectomy, LSCS with Tubectomy and Kidney Transplant to name a few. Prerana Health-Care Services (PHS) is another managed care service organization providing innovative services towards healthcare requirements. Delhi-based Beachcomber Tours and Travel that has a tie-up with 'doctors' working in hospitals in and around Delhi. It helps international patients fix appointments with these doctors and facilitate the entire travel, stay and treatment process, besides arranging tours for relatives and patients, including yoga, and ayurvedic treatments. Kerala-based Great Indian Tour Company has however opted for a more professional approach, thanks to its tie-up with one of the most reputed hospitals, Kerala Institute of Medical Sciences. The travel company also helps smoothen the entire process for the patients by acting as a facilitator between the hospital and the patients, besides suggesting holiday destinations.

Some treatment's may not be available in their home country like Hip Resurfacing, less radical than Hip Replacement, but not yet approved by the US Food and Drug Administration, can be availed over here through Medical Treatment India. India also offers a unique variety of Rejuvenation services like Yoga, Meditation, Ayurveda, Allopathy, Homoeopathy and other systems of medicines. What makes us a favourable destination is the ease and affordability of international travel, favourable currency exchange rates in the global economy, rapidly improving technology and standards of care.

NABH

India seems to have made its mark on the world travel map. Overseas holidayers and travelers have put India in the big league, ranking it as the fourth most attractive and satisfying holiday destination in the world. It stands ahead of several developed and traditional hot spots like US, France, Singapore, Thailand and South Africa. Thanks to CII's proactive role in recognizing the pressing need for standardization in healthcare. CII has therefore constituted the National Accreditation Board for Hospitals and Healthcare Providers (NABH) in January 2006 as a constituent board of Quality Council of India (QCI), set-up with the cooperation of Ministry of Health and Family Welfare, Government of India and Indian Health Industry. According to NABH, there are about 100 standards to be obtained and over 500 measurable objects. The entire procedure of accreditation is a three-cycle process, beginning with the hospitals seeking a pre-assessment procedure. Accreditation of a hospital would be valid for two years, after which it would have to undergo another assessment. They would have to score 70 per cent on the scoring card to get accreditation. The rest of the 30 per cent would have to be covered over the two-year period. Dr. Naresh Trehan, formerly ED of Escorts Heart Institute and now at Apollo hospital, New Delhi and chairman of CII National Committee on healthcare, reasons that the glaring deficiency in healthcare standards in the country has resulted in the birth of NABH, which would lend the much required credibility to these hospitals. "We have invited hospitals to get themselves accredited and have received about 50 applications. It is a process and the general standards of delivery will improve in the next couple of years. It is just a matter of time before patients start looking for accredited hospitals," he observes. This in turn will enthuse hospitals, interested in luring international patients, to equip themselves with accreditation. CII has also come out with a price band, in consultation with 16 states, for specialties such as cardiology, minimally invasive surgery, orthopedics and oncology. Veering towards a more sticky issue of insurance, insurance companies are now tying up with Indian hospitals so that international patients can get their expenses covered. What we need is for the medical fraternity as well as the insurance companies to apply for standard accreditation. CII has already started interacting with insurance companies towards this cause and it won't be too long before these companies start recognizing NABH accreditation. Although a standard for accreditation has been set in place by the NABH, there is no mandate that forces hospitals to apply for it if they want to join the health tourism fray.

An Indian enterprise

Health Tourism India is a professionally managed, diversified enterprise engaged in four core segments of life-Healthcare, Biotechnology, Information technology and Education. www.health-tourism-india.com is part of the healthcare division of Health Tourism India, registered with Government of India as a limited company. Health Tourism India is being managed by a group of medical professionals with an experience of 18 years in the Indian Healthcare industry. At Health Tourism India, our commitment is to deliver high quality services always; our belief in values and dedication towards achieving the best is reflected in our work and client satisfaction. At Health Tourism India we commit and dedicate ourselves to our core values of always extending smiling services to the humanity with respect to every individual and the entire existence.

The hospitals are selected on a number of parameters including experience in specific healthcare segments, panel of doctors, certifications, infrastructural base and past records. Our panel of consultants and surgeons are highly trained and experts in their fields. Most of the doctors have graduated from top US and UK universities and have vast experience in the critical surgeries and procedures they perform. They offer assistance at every stage including pre-travel arrangements and pre- and

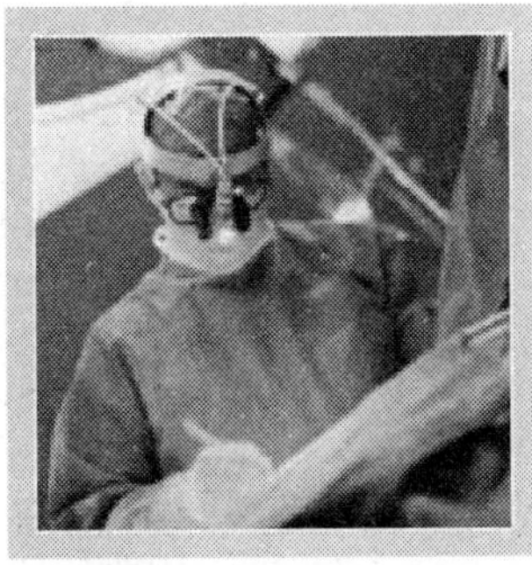

post-medical treatment support, including passport and visa assistance, itinerary planning, selection of hospital and surgeons, treatment procedure, suitable accommodation, sight seeing of various tourist destinations and finally the much-awaited homecoming.

A large percentage of the overseas public does not have financial access to major medical procedures. These procedures can be a quality of life procedure such as orthopedic, dental cosmetic or a life saving procedure such as cardiac or oncology.

Some of the services offered are:

- Suggesting Hospitals/Clinics as per treatment required/budget.
- World-class Treatment by UK/USA trained Doctors in India.
- Fixation of appointment with Chief Doctors on top priority prior to arrival.
- Arranging consultations with doctors.
- Assisting in planning treatment/check up with appointment fixing and travel scheduling.
- No waiting time for surgical procedures.
- Packages offered only for Medical Treatment till discharge from hospital.
- Coordinating all appointments.
- Nurses/Guide.
- Online assistance to the Patients.

Optional Services

- Stay arrangements, pre-hospitalization and post-hospitalization.
- Arranging accommodation for family members and attendants.
- Package Tours can be organised at very reasonable cost to various places of interest in places like, Delhi, Chennai, Bangalore, Hyderabad, Mumbai, Agra, etc.
- Can fix-up guides/escorts to accompany if willing.
- All these optional services can be availed, if desired, at nominal service fees.

- Post-treatment medical check-up before departure
- Airport transfers.

A new trend of healthcare tourism overseas is Corporate or Institutional medical tourism where corporations are coming up with employee healthcare benefits strategies that would save on corporate medical treatment costs; particularly the corporate are concerned about the rising cost of business health insurance that comes with high premiums to cover surgical interventions and hospitalization expenses for their employees. The corporate surgery treatment abroad and wellness plans provide an easy alternative to save the costs incurred on employee healthcare and this also keeps the employees happy when they enjoy a family vacation overseas, in privacy, comfort and relaxed setting with the experience of the world-class, advanced healthcare treatments.

United health group spreads its wings to India

United Health Group began investing in India in 2002 through the acquisition of a health management and administration company, today called United Healthcare India. In 2006, United Health Group's commitment to India grew substantially with the start-up of United Health Group Information Services headquartered in Gurgaon. United Health Group employee strength in India will exceed 2100 by the end of 2007 in these two entities. A key strategic location, United Health Group Information Services, Gurgaon is the largest international location outside America for the enterprise. They provide expertise in software development, healthcare claims adjudication, and biopharmaceutical services.

United Healthcare India, headquartered in Mumbai, provides health plan management and administration services. It also provides medical provider management and underwriting solutions to the life insurance industry in India. Its network of healthcare providers spans 600 cities across India, and includes 1100 multi-specialty hospitals and over 1500 diagnostic centers.

The type of work handled by the IT team in Gurgaon includes:

- Healthcare claims processing systems architecture, development and maintenance targeted at optimally matching claim detail, benefit eligibility and contractual structures.
- Provider systems that enable contract creation and management between hundreds of thousands of doctors, hospitals and United Health Group.
- Eligibility and billing systems that allow customized consumer benefits configuration, billing schemes, and eligibility and benefit matching to patient and provider needs.
- Consumer, employer and other portals providing real-time access to health claim status, care quality information, physician or hospital proximity to consumers and other critical information.
- Data warehouse and healthcare analytics experience with one of the largest, production data warehouses in the world.
- Commercial software product development for many of our Ingenix solutions.
- Testing Center of Excellence with an emphasis in cross application testing utilizing automated, white box, black box and smoke testing methods.
- Customer Relationship Management (CRM) systems innovation, development and maintenance.

The Healthcare business services

The Healthcare Business Services team at United Health Group is at the forefront of knowledge and expertise in providing services to the members, healthcare providers and other key constituents in the healthcare lifecycle. Presently, these are provided through five distinct disciplines:

1. Claim Adjudication

Manual Claim Adjudication for multiple healthcare specialties, places of service, benefit and plan types inclusive of both core medical and ancillary care services

2. Network Intelligence

Reimbursement analysis for competitive markets and efficiency ratings in delivery of healthcare services.

3. Member Benefit Analysis

Analysis of member benefit details and policy changes in support of member usability and access and the efficiency of the claim adjudication cycle.

4. Member Benefit Creation and Database Management

Workflow focused on detailed creation of multiple benefit types for the member community and management of changes to same.

5. Back-end Rule Setting

Setting proper rule structures to the end of driving higher efficiency and accuracy in the automatic and manual adjudication processes.

Destination Bangalore/Chandigarh

Chandigarh and Bangalore were planned and set-up as new modern cities after independence. Chandigarh has become a hub of medical tourism for the domestic patients of northern India. Now it is in the forefront of planning facilities in the private sector to attract medical tourists from abroad. The concept of a Medical city, with a cluster of hospitals in every discipline is being explored. Mohali, a town adjacent to Chandigarh and a part of tri-city (Chandigarh, Panchkula, Mohali) has several good hospitals. Besides fortis, which has received JCI approval, there are several other good hospitals, viz. Silveroak, Grecian, Shivalik, Prime Heart Institute, etc. According to S. Harpal Singh, Chairman, Fortis Group, "Fortis will emerge as a key player in the medical tourism market in the north. The Mohali hospital is receiving several patients from abroad, mostly from SAARC, CIS, Middle-East and East African countries. Western market still needs to be tapped. (See Appendix 6, Bedside India (Bruce Stokes), study on the Fortis hospitals in Delhi). Chandigarh Administration has conceived a project 'Chandigarh Medi City' and is now in the process of setting it up.

Bangalore has professional experts, technological sophistication and healthcare services that easily match the best in the world. Bangalore has a pleasant weather all through the year. Some of the lead institutes and private hospitals in Bangalore with regular patients from abroad include: Hosmat, Recoup, Soukya, Narayana Hrudalaya, NIMHANS, Wockhardt, Advanced fertility centre, Sagar Apollo, Kidwai Memorial Institute of Oncology, Sri Jayadeva Institute of Cardiology, St. John's Hospital, St. Martha's, Victoria Hospital and Sri Sathya Sai Institute of Higher Medical Sciences, Mallya Hospital, Manipal Hospital and The Bangalore Hospital.

Popular specializations for medical consultation, treatments and surgeries in Bangalore include Cardiology, Orthopedics, Nephrology, Neurology, Neurosurgery, Dentistry, Oncology, Infertility, Gynecology, Homoeopathy, Ayurveda, Naturopathy, etc.

Wockhardt's hospital in Bangalore, which has a Harvard Medical International tie-up, gets half of its foreign patients (about 900), from the U.K. The media reported the story of one such patient with coronary heart disease, 73-year old George Marshall last year. This violin repairer from Bradford was operated upon at the hospital for a quarter of what he would have paid for private care in the UK, including the airfare. When he arrived in India, he was initially shocked by the traffic chaos and urban squalor, but it appeared to be a better decision than having to suffer a long delay for bypass surgery in a state-supported National Health Service hospital. Another 35 per cent of Wockhardt's patients come to Bangalore from the US and the rest from the European Union and South East Asia. Another heart care institution in Bangalore, Narayana Hrudayalaya, has a record of 15,000 surgeries performed on patients from 25 foreign countries, half of them children.

The biggest disincentive to medical tourism, the hospitals say, is the insensitive handling of visa issuance to those who come for treatment.

5

India's Islands of Medical and Surgical Excellence

A patient comes to India where he undergoes surgical treatment and recuperatrates in a resort having world class facilities. The whole thing would save him a lot of money and he will get to discover India at the same time. A number of private hospitals in India offer packages designed to attract foreign patients, with airport-to-hospital bed transfer service, Internet access, and other facilities. Some packages include add-ons, such as a yoga holiday or a trip to the world-famous Taj Mahal.

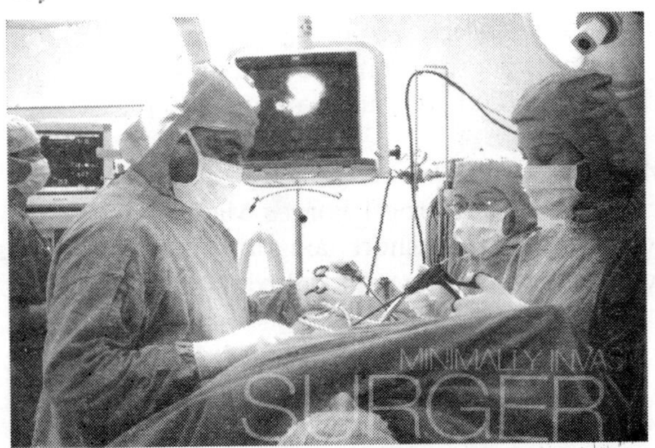

However, the sight of the country's overcrowded public hospitals, open sewers and garbage-littered streets can unsettle visitors' confidence about sanitation standards in India. Private healthcare providers argue that foreigners can be sheltered from such nastiness. "In a corporate hospital, once the door is closed you could be in a hospital in America." Vishal Bali, President of Wockhardt Hospitals, points out as proof of quality that the US private health insurers Blue Cross and Blue Shield insure patients treated at his group's hospitals. The British health insurer Bupa also insures the costs of treatment at Wockhardt hospitals. We have already mentioned about the excellence of Fortis hospital group in the north.

Some other Indian Hospitals of repute are:

AIIMS, New Delhi

A public sector hospital; source of trained manpower and research.

Apollo Hosptials Group

Most well organized and with JCI accreditation

B.M. Birla Heart Research Centre

A specialized hospital dedicated exclusively to the diagnosis, treatment and research related to cardiovascular diseases. It has established itself as India's most advanced heart center.

Christian Medical College, Vellore

Occupies a prominent place among medical institutions in India as a 1700-bed multi-campus complex.

Tata Memorial Cancer Hospital

Located at Dr. Ernest Borges Marg, Parel, in the Central District of Mumbai, a short taxi ride from the local stations, the hospital has private and deluxe rooms.

Apollo Cancer Hospital

The first hospital in the country to be awarded the ISO 9002 certificate.

Indraprastha Medical Corporation

India's first corporate hospital and the third largest corporate hospital outside the USA.

Institute Cardiovascular Diseases

Has gained a reputation for being one of the most advanced centers in the world.

Escorts Hospital and Research Centre

One of the most frequented hospital for heart ailments.

Nehru Hospital, PGI, Chandigarh

A centre of excellence for trained manpower and research.

Sahaj Dental Clinic

Experience Mystic India with World Class Dental Treatment.

Inspiration Kerala

Kerala tour operator, offering ayurveda packages.

Advent Medical Services

Medical service provider with vast experience in medical field.

Prerana Healthcare Services

A managed care service organization.

Hinduja Hospital

Indian National Hospital and Medical esearch Centre

MediEscapes India

Indian Medical Tourism operator which offers world class medical treatments

Care and Cure Medi-Tours

Facilitate ailing patients in neighbouring countries to Chennai (India).

Longfield Management

World Class Economical Healthcare.

Dr. Agarwal Vasan's Eye Hospital

One of the leading eye hospitals in Tamilnadu.

Dr. Grewal's Eye Institute, Chandigarh

It has recently been approved by JCI.

India aims to replicate the Thai model, which is still the first Asian destination for International Patients. A case study done by CII has revealed that Thailand with a population of 60 millions has been successful in attracting 5 million health tourists last year because of the development of world-class infrastructure. It was possible due to aggressive international marketing in conjunction with tourism authority. It has also been integrated with traditional medicine.

Government should encourage medical tourism by increasing air connectivity linking major cities like Delhi, Chennai, Bangalore, Hyderabad, Chandigarh and Kolkata, and create health support infrastructure. Setting up of a chain of world class hospitals, i.e. Medi city model of healthcare will not only attract medical tourists from all over the world but also solve the problem of healthcare of the Indian people.

CII study

Medical tourism industry in India would bring in revenues worth USD 25 billion by 2020. One of the best-managed healthcare groups in India with about 6,000 beds, has revenue of about USD 125 million. going with these numbers, the assumption based on crude mathematical projection is that, it would require about 60,000 beds, to reach USD 1.25 billion revenue and 12,00,000 beds to obtain a revenue of USD 25 billion exclusively from healthcare services.

In 2003, about 2,726,000 tourists visited India and the revenue from the same was USD 3.5 billion. Well, if that many relatives of patients (about 3 million) travel to India, we could manage another USD 3.5 billion from tourism services.

Currently, the bulk of the patients come to India from neighbouring countries such as Bangladesh, Pakistan, other Asian countries, Africa and the Middle East. A segment of patients sponsored by the governments in their respective countries such as Middle East and Africa come to India; relatively a cost-effective option compared to Europe or the US. Unsponsored patients from these countries look at India as value for money option *vis-a-vis* Europe and US. Moreover, post 9/11 there has been a dramatic drop in patients from Middle East to the US. The market segment that the healthcare industry is targeting is the patient population from Europe and the US. There are several patients of Indian origin residing in UK and US, who are already using the services of hospitals in India, when they are on vacation, etc. Apart from this we have the widely-publicized cases of patients from the US and Australia. We may want to recognize that a strategy which works for attracting patients from Bangladesh may not work for patients from Britain, since the expectations and drivers are different. What is a good reason for an average senior citizen in the US to fly 18-20 hours to get his hip replaced? Can he even travel with hips in such bad shape? Obviously if he is not covered by insurance and cannot afford the same in US he has to look at options. What if this can be done in Mexico or Costa Rica at comparable rate and a shorter flight? Would a patient be willing to trust his heart, kidneys, hips and face if there is an iota of doubt regarding the quality of care? This segment of high yielding procedures is where the Indian medical tourism market is looking forward to for better profits.

The Apollo Hospitals Group

The Apollo Hospitals Group's hospitals are Located at Delhi, Chennai, Hyderabad, Madurai, etc. Its history of accomplishments, with its unique ability of resource management and able deployment of technology and knowledge to the service of its patients, justifies its recognition in India and abroad. India could earn more than $1 billion annually and create 40 million new jobs by sub-contracting work from the British National Health Service, says Apollo Hospitals. This includes surgery for hip and knee replacements and coronary bypass that would slash waiting times dramatically, reducing the queues of British patients waiting to see their doctors, Dr. Reddy said.

Apollo group alone has so far treated 95,000 international patients, many of whom are of Indian origin. Reddy cited two recent cases of UK nationals who opted for private healthcare at the Apollo network. One of them—Cyril Parry, a 50-year-old man from Birmingham—successfully underwent hip replacement surgery at Apollo, Chennai. The other—Buckingham Palace employee Elaine Ackrill—was also treated at the Chennai Apollo for cancer of the uterine cervix. Apollo was represented at a London meeting that was also attended by a UK government health adviser and private healthcare providers from South Africa, Australia, India and the UK. The Apollo team offered a medical tourism package that would cut waiting times for surgery in the UK. "They have a one million waiting list for all kinds of things, especially orthopaedic surgery," explained an Apollo spokesman.

In Apollo hospital group, about 100 beds are usually occupied by foreign patients, mostly from the Middle East, Africa and countries of South Asia. Indeed, demand for medical tourism is most likely to come from among the 25 m-strong Indian diaspora, says Deep Kalra, chief executive officer of travel agency makemytrip.com. NRIs would combine regular visits to India and save time and money by undergoing non-emergency procedures such as eye operations, dental work, cosmetic surgery and knee surgery.

For follow-ups of the medical tourists, Apollo has set the telemedicine centres, where through video-conferencing patients get in touch with their patients, informs Anjali. Last year in November, the group opened a telemedicine centre at the Om Hospital in Nepal. Incidentally, Apollo opened its first international Apollo Health and Lifestyle Ltd. (AHLL) clinic at Doha in 2005. Apollo is looking to branch in South-east Asia, West Asia, Africa, UK and USA through this model, informs Mr Jalan. Talking about challenges; competition from Singapore and Thailand. However, the cost in India is one-fifth of Singapore and half of Thailand. The cardiac success rate here is more than 98.6 per cent. "We are planning to work with insurance providers and healthcare providers abroad in the UK and the US", they add. Patient break-up at Apollo from various countries is as follows: US and other countries—10.5 per cent, Maldives—46 per cent, Nepal—16.6 per cent, Oman—10.1 per cent, Sri Lanka—22 per cent, Bangladesh—27 per cent.

- Among the few providers of quaternary care for complicated medical conditions.
- Touched the lives of over 10 million patients till date.
- Over 4,00,000 Preventive Health checks done.
- Has the largest and the most sophisticated sleep laboratories in the World.
- Pioneered procedures like Total Hip and knee replacements, and the Birmingham Hip Resurfacing technique.
- Has performed over 750,000 major surgeries and over 10,00,000 minor surgical procedures till date.
- Has performed over 49,000 cardiac surgeries at a 98.5% success rate.
- Has performed over 2,00,000 angiograms, 16,200 angoplasties (PTCA) and 3500 mitral balloon valvuoplasities.
- First heart transplant patient is alive, 7 years after the operation.
- Has performed over 9400 renal transplants.
- 130 Bone Marrow Transplants performed at high success rates.
- Over 30 Liver transplants done (Live and cadaver)
- Has over 4000 specialists and super specialists, 3000 medical officers spanning 53 clinical departments in patient care.

International Affiliations

- Apollo Hospitals is recognized as a training centre by the National Board of Examination in India for post-graduate training in 16 medical departments.
- The Department of Radiology at Apollo is

recognized by the Royal College of Radiologists, United Kingdom for training for fellowship examinations like FRCR.

- Recognized as a centre for conducting research work leading to Ph.D. of the Anna University, Chennai, in medical physics and digital signal processing.
- Apollo Hospitals is recognized by the Royal College of Physicians and Surgeons in Edinburgh for training post-graduates in radiology, surgery and trauma care.
- Apollo Hospitals is the only International training organization for the American Heart Association Technical support from Texas Heart institute and Minneapolis Heart Institute for Cardiology and Cardio Thoracic surgery.
- Apollo Hospitals has exchange programs with the Hospitals in the US and Europe.
- Apollo Hospitals have an association with Mayo Clinic and Cleveland Heart Institute, USA.
- Apollo Hospitals is also associated with Johns Hopkins University.

Apollo launches Asia's first health city: Hyderabad,Tuesday, 12 June, 2007

Going beyond the realm of curative care it offers, the health city is an integrated facility offering solutions across the healthcare space including preventive care, holistic medicine, research, information technology and education. Spread over 33 acres at Apollo Hospital in Jubilee Hills here, the health city encompasses a 300-bedded multi-speciality hospital with over 50 specialties and super specialties along with 10 centres of excellence. Centres of excellence for heart diseases, cancer, orthopaedics and joint diseases, emergency, renal diseases, neurosciences, eye, minimally invasive surgery, trauma and cosmetic surgery are coming up in the integrated facility.

The Apollo Group plans to apply for a special economic zone (SEZ) status to the health city. "It is not a medical city where you treat only the illness. The Apollo

Health City takes care of totality of wellness," Prathap C Reddy, Chairman, Apollo Hospitals Group, told media hours before the formal launch of the city. He said Rs. 1000 crore were already spent in creating the existing infrastructure for the health city while another Rs. 150-Rs. 250 crore would be invested in setting up research institutes over the next six months. "Once Britain dominated the healthcare space, then US and now India is emerging as the global healthcare destination and Hyderabad with the Apollo Health City will lead the way for that," he said. He pointed out that research and technology had always been the thrust of Apollo. Apollo Health City has a variety of initiatives including medical BPO services for offshore customers (health street), online education for medical professionals (Medvarsity) and telemedicine services. The health city has already tied up with Tata Consultancy Service (TCS) for hospital information system. The system connects all Apollo Hospitals and 100 telemedicine centres in India and in Dubai, Kuwait, Doha, Nigeria, Dhaka and Sri Lanka. "We plan to connect 52 African countries through telemedicine," he said. Reddy said Apollo Group was focussing on research in key areas like cardiology, oncology, diabetes and neuro sciences. Apollo has joined hands with Johns Hopkins Medicine International, US, to undertake a collaborative study on cardiovascular diseases in India. "We want to find out why Asians are more prone to heart diseases," he said. He said Apollo created many benchmarks since its inception. "We have performed more than 59,000 heart surgeries with a success rate of 99.6 per cent," he said. Apollo Health City is equipped to create a global talent pool of medical professionals. It will have institutes of PG education for doctors, nursing school and college, hospital administration, medical informatics, emergency medicine and paramedics. The focus at the health city will be on holistic health and facility will offer alternative forms of medicine, the benefits of which have been demonstrated across the world.

One of Asia's largest healthcare groups, Apollo runs 41 hospitals in India and abroad. It has an annual turnover of Rs. 600 crore.

Escorts Heart Institute and Research, Delhi

Dr. Naresh Trehan (now moved to Apollo), worked as a heart surgeon in Manhattan from 1968 until 1988, and then returned to India to start the Escorts Hospital Group in India. He says the success of the operations performed and the care dispensed at his hospital have established the institute's credibility: "Now we do over 4000 heart operations a year, and the mortality, which is an index of how well things are, is 0.8% which is even better than most places in the world. The other thing that we measure is infection rate. Ours is 0.3% as compared to the world average of 1%."

Escorts is steadily consolidating its presence in healthcare, which is likely to emerge as the largest service sector industry. Currently, Escorts is operating three large hospitals in New Delhi, Faridabad and Amritsar. Together with 11 heart command centres and associate hospitals, Escorts is managing nearly 900 beds. Escorts excellence in providing healthcare services has received due recognition. Escorts Heart Institute and Research Centre (EHIRC), New Delhi, has been ranked as the best cardiac hospital in India by an Outlook survey and has been given the highest grade by CRISIL—an acknowledgement of the quality of delivered patient care. EHIRC is a leader in the fields of cardiac surgery, interventional cardiology and cardiac diagnostics. The Institute has introduced innovative techniques of minimally invasive and robotic surgery. The Institute's latest addition of state-of-the-art Cardiac Scan Centre providing a combined power of CV-MRI and Smart Score CT Scanner to diagnose coronary artery disease at its very early stage. This facility is the first of its kind outside America. State-of-the-art infrastructure and equipment has made this set-up technically the largest and the best dedicated cardiac hospital in the world. The 332-bed Institute has nine operating rooms and carries out nearly 15,000 procedures every year.

NM Excellence, Mumbai

NM Excellence was formed from one man's vision to provide a healthier future for 'the citizens of Mumbai. Established in 2001 by Dr. Nilesh Shah, this modern and sophisticated preventive health checkup centre aims to revolutionize the way healthcare is perceived and practiced in India. Backed by over two decades of diagnostic experience under the banner of NM Medical, NM Excellence employs the latest, top-of-the-line imagining modalities, operated by qualified and professional doctors, with a friendly and efficient staff to make a client's experience as memorable as possible. Having viewed the vast range of diseases that can be prevented if detected early enough through its diagnostic experience, NM Excellence philosophizes that a preventive health checkup in today's day and age is an absolute must. NM Excellence is one of Mumbai's foremost preventive healthcare centers boasting of top-of-the-line diagnostic equipment, highly qualified doctors, a well-trained service staff, and a professional yet warm environment that makes one feel at home immediately. Health Plan for NRI's and Foreigners

The Plan Price starts from US$ 225+ and includes the following:

Pathology Tests

Complete haemogram, test for diabetes, test for liver disease, test for kidney disease, test for heart disease.

Diagnostic Tests

Digital Chest X-ray, ECG, Sonography, Stress Test, 2D Echo, Spirometry, Dexa Bone Densitometry, Body Fat Analysis, Mammography, Transvaginal Sonography.

Consultations

Physical Examination by Physician, Dental Checkup, Eye Checkup, Diet Consultation, Gynecological Checkup, Pap-Smear

PD Hinduja National Hospital and Medical Research Centre, Mumbai

An ultramodern hospital on the busiest artery in Central Mumbai, PD Hinduja National Hospital and Medical Research Centre was established by the Hinduja Foundation in collaboration with Massachusetts General Hospital (MGH), Boston. The fulfilment of Founder Parmanand Deepchand Hinduja's dream, the 351-bed hospital offers comprehensive services covering the gamut from diagnosis and investigation to therapy, surgery and post-operative care. As a tertiary care hospital, the services offered are comprehensive covering investigation and diagnosis to therapy, surgery and post-operative care. According to Dr. Gustad B. Daver, director,

professional services, Hinduja Hospital, "A good set-up in a hospital like pre-operative evaluation, an extensive lab set-up and operation theatre facilities, good post-operative, intensive care and radiological facilities will be of major help to boost health tourism." Besides this, "a proper civic infrastructure needs to be in place like airports and good roads. There should be proper visa facilities and preferential treatment at immigration," opines Verma. Experts cite that medical insurance, alternate wellness concepts and BPO in diagnostics are other upcoming businesses, which will give a boost to medical tourism in the coming years. Apollo's business began to grow in the 1990s, with the liberalization of the Indian economy.

The inpatient services are complemented with a day centre, out-patient facilities and an exclusive center for health check for executives. Hinduja Hospital was the first multi-disciplinary tertiary care hospital to have been awarded the prestigious ISO 9002 Certification from KEMA of Netherlands for Quality Management System

The Hinduja Foundation's quest for upgradation of healthcare facilities in India has prompted it to join hands with the 45,000 member American Association of Physicians of Indian origin (AAPI), with the objective of bringing to India well qualified and experienced doctors from USA to upgrade the expertise of HNH doctors, provide quality medical care and continuing medical education; to ensure co-operation in research and pursue joint projects in the fields of: Coronary artery disease, Osteoporosis and Asthma; and to provide consultancy, technology and treatment support to AAPI dispensaries in India on case to case basis Hinduja Hospital has a fully automated Laboratory Medicine Department. The Laboratory offers over 500 different types of tests, some of which are exclusive. It also offers an emergency/Stat menu of tests with a very short-turn around time. The department participates in International Quality control programme conducted by the College of American Pathologists, WHO and National Quality Control Programme where it has achieved and maintained a high ranking consistently for a number of years. Imaging forms a key part of the diagnostic facility at the hospital.

The hospital keeps upgrading its technology by acquiring new state-of-the-art diagnostic and therapeutic equipment. Hinduja Hospital was the first in India to acquire the Gamma Knife-gold standard in Radio surgery, a non-invasive neurosurgical tool. The hospital was also the first to acquire the Holmium Laser in the country thus replacing the surgeon's scalpel. The Oncology Services are wholistic and complete with installation of the Linear Accelerator with Multileaf Collimator (MLC) and Micro MLC. The hospital is the first centre in India to have installed the sophisticated state of the art GE-LCA Digital Subtraction Angiography System. In keeping with the quest for continuos improvement in quality and technological advancement, the hospital has recently commissioned the Bone Mineral Densitometer (DEXA), an addition to the Imaging department.

L.V. Prasad Eye Institute, Hyderabad

In October 1987, L.V. Prasad Eye Institute began the work of realizing its mission to achieve excellence, equity and efficiency in eye care. In addition to treating patients dealing with a wide range of vision problems, LVPEI began to conduct research into eye diseases and vision-threatening conditions, train eye care workers, product development and rehabilitate those with incurable visual disability. The focus, right from the start, has been on providing eye-care services to underprivileged populations in the developing world.

Set-up as a not-for-profit trust, LVPEI has now come a long way in its journey towards realizing these goals. However, our changing world continues to throw up new challenges and new threats to health, and LVPEI too continues to search for ways in which these challenges can be overcome, in the field of eye health. In partnership with international health organizations such as the World Health Organisation and the International Agency for the Prevention of Blindness, LVPEI designs and implements innovative eye health programmes that reach people in the most remote rural areas. 'While the range of our research and training activities is international, our focus is on bringing this quality of care to the poorest segments of India and the developing world. Our successes include the establishment of rural eye health centers that provide high-quality eye care at the lowest possible cost, or at no cost to those to whom such care would otherwise be inaccessible. In fact, it is this same model that operates successfully in our nodal center in Hyderabad, Andhra Pradesh', said one hospital official. At the L.V. Prasad Eye Hospital, nearly 50 percent of our patients are treated free of cost. The Eye Hospital forms the nucleus of the Institute's activities. Designed along the lines of the finest eye hospitals in the world. Patients with a wide range of eye disorders are treated which is staffed by a world-class team of dedicated doctors representing all ophthalmic sub-specialties and a highly competent support staff. The Hospital's comprehensive facilities also include the in-house expertise of physicians, microbiologists, pathologists and biochemists trained to apply their knowledge and skills to eye care.

India's most-favoured healthcare destination

Around Rs. 2,000 crore has already been invested in the Bangalore city's healthcare and medical infrastructure. It houses four medical colleges (two more are coming up), three super-speciality hospitals, development bases of medical equipment manufacturers like GE Medical, Siemens and Philips, research outfits of Novo Nordisk (diabetic) and AstraZeneca (TB), in addition to a large number of pharma and biotech companies. Increased direct air connectivity brings in patients, mostly suffering from heart ailments, from countries like Bangladesh, the UAE, Nepal, Sri Lanka and Malaysia to Bangalore. A by-pass surgery that costs Rs. 5 lakh in Malaysia costs only Rs. 90,000 in Bangalore. The Karnataka government, in association with the Confederation of Indian Industry (CII), is currently creating a blueprint for a competitive hospital infrastructure in the city. "Bangalore has the potential to become the world's third largest healthcare hub after Phoenix (Arizona) and Florida," says D.A. Prasanna, CEO, Wipro Healthcare and Life Science. Prasanna heads the recently formed 50-member CII Committee for Healthcare with trade body, government, academia and healthcare industry representatives. According to him, the panel is in the process of locating potential niches in healthcare. "All these will enhance medical infrastructure of the city to be on par with global standards."

Vishal Bali, Wockhardt President and Head, CII Task Force on Health, feels Bangalore definitely is the leading healthcare destination in the entire Asian sub-continent. "We have competitive technology, clinical expertise and a clear focus on patients' satisfaction." Wockhardt is the only hospital in the country to have a tie-up with the Harvard Medical School. "We are trying to create Bangalore as a healthcare hub through international partnerships and expertise sharing. We are trying to bring in global medical and clinical practices and expertise," Bali adds. Here's what Narayana Hrudayala founder Devi Shetty has to say: "The basic requirement for healthcare is super-specialty professionals, and Bangalore has a large pool of them." According to him, even reputed doctors from the US, Europe and West Asia are willing to relocate to Bangalore as the hospitals are capable of matching their salaries. Setting up hospital infrastructure in Bangalore is cost-effective reasons, said Dr. Shetty. For instance, a hospital which costs Rs. 100 crore in Bangalore will cost Rs. 500 crore in Mumbai. Novo Nordisk. India Managing Director Dr. Anil Kapur says Bangalore, which is already an IT hub, is fast becoming a biotechnology base. Though the biotech-based pharma industry is still in a nascent stage in the city, it can easily capitalize on the existing medical infrastructure to become a leading player in terms of patient-record systems, drug research and telemedicine. Dr. S. Anand Kumar, Director, Research Foundation of AstraZeneca, says Bangalore had an excellent environment for drug discovery, but needs a marketing push.

Destination Bangalore

Some of the lead institutes and private hospitals in Bangalore with regular patients from abroad include: Hosmat, Recoup, Soukya, Manipal, Narayana Hrudalaya, NIMHANS, Wockhardt, Advanced fertility centre, Sagar Apollo, Kidwai Memorial Institute of Oncology, Sri Jayadeva Institute of Cardiology, St. John's Hospital, St. Martha's, Victoria Hospital and Sri Sathya Sai Institute of Higher Medical Sciences,

Mallya Hospital, Manipal Hospital and The Bangalore Hospital.

Popular specializations for medical consultation, treatments and surgeries in Bangalore include Cardiology, Orthopedics, Nephrology, Neurology, Neurosurgery, Dentistry, Oncology, Infertility, Gynecology, Homoeopathy, Ayurveda, Naturopathy, etc.

Kovai Medical Centre and Hospital Ltd.

Spread over a campus of around 20 acres, Kovai Medical Center and Hospital Ltd. (KMCH) is a 400-bed multi-disciplinary super-specialty corporate hospital located in Coimbatore. The hospital is equipped with most modern equipments like CT Scanner, Angiography equipment, Operating Microscope, Mammography, Colour Doppler, etc. The hospital has over 30 Medical Departments and 11 Operation Theatres. The hospital is fully equipped and has developed expertise to conduct Super Specialty procedures like Coronary Bypass surgeries, Coronary Angioplasty, Stent Implantation, Laparoscopic and Vascular Surgeries, Hip and Knee replacements, Kidney transplants, and complex Neuro-surgeries. The hospital is recognized to carry out Renal transplants, Corneal transplants and Heart transplants by Tamil Nadu Government.

Satellite Centres

The hospital has two satellite medical centers located at Ramnagar in Coimbatore and Perundurai, Distt. Erode. The satellite centre at Coimbatore is a 10 bed hospital with facilities like 24 hours Accident and Emergency Services, 24 hours pharmacy, Laboratory, X-Ray and ECG Services, Obstetrics and Gynecology, Pediatrics, Dermatology, General Consultation, Physiotherapy Centre and Dental Hospital. The other satellite centre located at Perundurai is a 50 bed hospital with facilities like 24 hours Accident and Emergency Services, Laboratory, Radiology and pharmacy services, General Medicine, Chest Clinic, Obstetrics and Gynecology, Pediatrics, Dermatology, General Consultation, and Physiotherapy Centre.

Financials

The latest financials of the company are given in Table on next page. The company is scaling up its capacity through an expansion project and through acquisitions. The company is currently expanding its capacity by 200 beds at its existing campus at Coimbatore. The specialty block is under construction and is expected to start operations from June 2008. The expansion programme will also improve certain infrastructure facilities like captive power generation, centralized air-conditioning system, pneumatic pipe line system for transporting materials and a state of the art IT Infrastructure for managing the Hospital operations. The company is also making substantial investments to upgrade the diagnostic treatment facilities to cover specialty departments in the Hospital like Cardiology, General Surgery, Orthopedics, and Intensive Care, etc. The company has recently entered into a Memorandum of Understanding (MOU) with Idhayam Hospitals Erode Ltd. located at Erode to acquire 100% stake in the company. The agreed purchase consideration is Rs. 925 Lacs, which involves discharge of unsecured loans, one time settlement with the Lenders, Cost of Medical Equipments and payment to the shareholders. Idhayam Hospital has a 50-bedded Hospital at Erode, which is exclusively for Cardio-thoracic patients.

Kovai Medical owns a 400-bed hospital and two Satellite Centres located in Southern part of the country. The company is aggressively scaling up its capacity—both through organic and inorganic route. For the current FY, the expected revenues of the company are Rs. 70-72 crores with a PAT of Rs. 7.0 crores. With its existing market cap of Rs. 60 crores, the valuations of the company look attractive, when compared with the peer group.

The new hospital acquired by the company is capable of adding Rs. 8-10 crores to the topline of the company in a year. Therefore, assuming a growth of 20% from the existing operations and addition from Idhayam Hospital, the company can target revenues of Rs. 90-95 crores in FY 07-08. Moreover, with the expansion at its existing campus in Coimbatore getting completed by June 08, one can look forward to substantially higher revenues in the future.

(Rs. in Crores)

Particulars	*Quarter Ended (Dec. 06)*	*Quarter Ended (Dec. 05)*	*Quarter Ended (% Var)*	*YTD/ Latest Half (Dec. 06)*	*YTD/ Latest Half (Dec. 05)*	*YTD/ Latest Half (% Var)*	*Year Ended (Mar. 06) (12)*	*Year Ended (Mar. 05)(12)*	*Year Ended (% Var)*
Sales	18	13.31	35.2	48.5	37.7	28.6	51.18	40.55	26.2
Other Income	0.14	0.14	0	0.36	0.41	-12.2	0.58	0.56	3.6
PBIDT	4.4	2.97	48.1	11.15	8.15	36.8	9.9	5.96	66.1
Interest	0.21	0.23	-8.7	0.79	0.73	8.2	0.96	0.94	2.1
PBDT	4.19	2.74	52.9	10.36	7.42	39.6	8.94	5.02	78.1
Depreciation	0.85	0.78	9	2.57	2.33	10.3	3.07	2.69	14.1
PBT	3.34	1.96	70.4	7.79	5.09	53	5.87	2.33	151.9
Tax	1.11	0.26	326.9	2.53	0.51	396.1	1.16	0.19	510.5
Deferred Tax	0.35	0	-	0.3	0	0	0.83	0.98	-15.3
PAT	1.88	1.7	10.6	4.96	4.58	8.3	3.88	1.16	234.5

Source: Capitaline.

Dr. Vivek Saggar's Dental Care and Cure Centre, Ludhiana

The newest and fastest-growing area of medical tourism is a visit to the dentist, where costs are often not covered by basic insurance and by only some extended insurance policies. India, Thailand and Hungary attract patients who want to combine a filling, extraction or root canal with a vacation.

Dental Care and Cure Centre is, centrally located in Ludhiana, easily approachable from any part of Punjab by rail or road. It takes not more then two hours from any part of Punjab to reach this place. Theirs is a 6 chair operatory with an in house dental lab, the Dental Caps, Crowns and Beyond Dental Lab, which has been designed on the European standards. The office has been designed to provide an environment of comfort that combines exceptional skill levels, a respectful approach to treatment, Clinical and technical excellence with an individualized care approach by providing the most advanced, optimal dental care to the best of our ability. Theirs is a full service cosmetic and general dental office specializing in creating beautiful smiles. The in-house facility of Dental Caps, Crowns and Beyond. . . . Dental Lab gives them the unmatched time advantage plus international quality control. For NRI's and foreigners they provide special care in the form of appointments at a short notice and the work is completed within the span of 3-5 days keeping in mind your tight schedule.

Advanced technology

- Smile Designing.
- Crown and Bridge Work.
- Tooth Whitening.
- Dental Implants (single tooth or entire set of teeth).
- Oral and Maxillofacial Surgery (third molar extractions, apicoectomy surgeries, management of mandible fractures).
- Geriatric Patient (partial and complete dentures, implant supported dentures, complete extractions under local anesthesia).
- Diagnostic and Preventive (cancer screening, occlusal splints, tooth desensitization).
- Care of the Child Patient (fluoride treatment, milk teeth as well as permanent teeth restorations, preventive orthodontics, fixed orthodontics, habit breaking appliances, sedation dentistry.

How to Promote Medical Tourism in India?

The scope and concept of Medical Tourism (MT) has today transgressed and evolved from healing by mineral and hot spring in the Neolithic and Bronze Age to today's health advanced farms and Medi Cities with cutting edge technology and surgeries. India should provides the best of Eastern and Westerm healthcare systems. Ayurveda, Yoga and Siddha can be India's gift to the world. "Ayurveda is recognised as an official healthcare system in Hungary. Doctors in the West are increasingly prescribing Indian Systems of Medicine. More than 70 per cent of the American population prefer a natural approach to health," Dr. Bhaskar Shah, said. Americans are said to spend around USD 25 bn on non-traditional medical therapies and products. Addressing the conference organized by INDIAN EXPRESS, Anil Maini, said, "MT has gained prominence with the advent of cutting edge technologies in India in specialties like cardiology, oncology, neurology, molecular and receptor imaging, which have improved sensitivity and specificity, early diagnosis, accurate and precise staging in oncology, significant input in decision making, evaluation of treatment outcome and improved morbidity and mortality." The main deterrents to MT are poor airports and infrastructure, non-medical people getting into the business, unnecessary investigation and treatment, no replies to follow-ups and Indian doctors not providing sufficient information to patients. The threats to India are the practice of Indian hospitals raising their prices every now and then, while treatment in Eastern European countries like Poland and Hungary are good and cheap, with France being just around 25 per cent costlier.

"Selling points" of medical tourism

"Cost effectiveness, world class treatment" and its combination with the attractions of tourism are the key selling points. The latter also uses the ploy of selling the "exotica" of packaging of healthcare with traditional therapies and treatment methods. For example, open-heart surgery could cost up to $70,000 in Britain and up to $150,000 in the US; in India's best hospitals it could cost between $3,000 and $10,000. The outcome of such a surgery in Indian hospitals matches with the best in the world. MT has also received a boost with corporatisation of the hospitals sector and interest of international players with reference to investment and foreign direct investment. The growing international competition is another attribute with India facing a stiff competition with the East Europe having approximately half of US tariffs, Thailand having approximately 1/8th of US tariffs and India having 1/10th US tariffs.

National Health Policy

National Health Policy recognizes the treatment of international patients as an export, which allows private hospitals treating such patients to enjoy benefits such as lower import duties, increase in the rate of depreciation (from 25 per cent to 40 per cent) for life-saving medical equipment, and several other tax sops. Medical corporations in India serving medical tourists led by Apollo Hospital Enterprises are aggressively moving into medical outsourcing.

The following points merit attention:

- We need to club together 'pathies' because we have a very strong base of alternative healing therapies like yoga, naturopathy, ayurveda, etc.

- Creating awareness about India's facilities abroad is a must to establish credibility in foreign markets.
- Standardization of a price band for graded hospitals and a quality assurance model should be taken up immediately to take medical tourism ahead.
- India's relatively developing medical tourism segment has been anointed by healthcare and tourism industry pundits as the next 'best' thing for the country.
- There are plenty of challenges that need to be addressed for India to become the world's preferred healthcare destination.
- There is a need for a synergy between hospitals, state government and international tour operators.
- India will have to project itself as being a holistic medical destination to get an edge over other countries.
- The private healthcare industry is quietly facilitating a revolution to enable India to emerge as a health destination.
- STARK contrasts are no surprise in urban India, and in the healthcare sector, the difference between what is available (world-class techniques and service, at a price) and what the common denominator urgently needs is no less so.
- Private sector healthcare centres are gleaming "islands of excellence", as the industry calls them, all too often surrounded by seas of medical neglect.
- When the mix is just right (support from the government in the form of incentives and tax breaks, international healthcare accreditation standards in place, breakthroughs in insurance coverage for overseas patients, and savvy promotion of India as a tourism-plus-medical tech destination) the sector is certain the numbers will fall into place.

- The beneficiary of such growth will be the country's desperately overburdened public health system, say industry associations such as the Confederation of Indian Industry (CII) and the Federation of Indian Chambers of Commerce and Industry (FICCI).
- Look at the possibility of the public hospitals being technologically upgraded to world-class standards with this source of income.
- India's three-tier public health system—primary health centres (PHC) in villages, district hospitals, and tertiary care hospitals—is increasingly unable to attend to the medical needs of the population.
- Technology-centric approach to healthcare, such as that promoted by the private hospitals, will affect the cost of care to the common man.
- "If we can build our brand, there will be no stopping us," says Dr. Prathap Reddy, Chairman of the Apollo Group.
- Price-banding exercise by a CII-affiliated industry body, the Indian Healthcare Federation, completed late last year, indicates fair prices for standard treatments in a good hospital. This was preceded by complaints of wide variation in prices and indiscriminate fee-hikes.
- Imminent launch of campaign using brochures and advertorials by the tourism ministry to project Indian healthcare, will disseminate case-studies and the new pricing information. Targeting GP practices in western countries, especially those run by Indian doctors.
- Growing interest by foreign governments and public healthcare bodies in checking out Indian healthcare. Side-trip to hospitals being included in official itineraries, like the now-mandatory visit to Infosys.
- Satisfied customers and free publicity in the western media for top Indian hospitals for delivering on price and quality.
- A newly-created autonomous Indian accreditation

board to set standards in safety and patient care. Expects to accredit 50 hospitals this year. Simultaneously, a drive for American accreditation by leading hospitals.

What's not happening?

- Industry and government not working in a coordinated manner. Progress so far driven mainly by individual players and ministries. Inter-ministerial taskforce on medical tourism, with representatives from six ministries and the private sector, set-up two years ago, has little to show.
- The much-touted new 'medical visa' is a disaster, say facilitators, more expensive and cumbersome than a regular visa, and requiring an array of documents.
- Medical tourists still negotiate snake-like immigration queues at airports, despite promises of a fast-track for the last two years. Recently, a Pakistani child needing a liver transplant took an hour and a half to clear at Delhi airport.
- Government failing to deliver on quality of airports, roads and infrastructure which don't make India look like a destination for "world class" medical treatment.
- Much more needs to be done to enforce norms, standards and ethical practices in a notoriously unregulated healthcare sector.
- Big breakthroughs depend on insurance companies, corporations and public healthcare bodies like Britain's has picking up the tab for medical treatment in India. Such deals have so far proved elusive, but the industry maintains they will happen.
- Handful of top doctors' names crop up in testimonials by medical tourists. Hospitals will have to maintain quality as numbers increase. It takes thousands of testimonials to build a brand, but just a few brickbats can destroy one.

Noises from a global healthcare bazaar

"We have no health insurance. My wife suffers constantly with her back pain. We cannot even begin to think about treatment here in the US because of the extremely high cost. After seeing your operations on 60 Minutes, we both have new hope. Please contact us." Shortly after it was featured in the American TV programme 60 Minutes, e-mails began hitting the inbox of Delhi's Indraprastha Apollo Hospital, seconds apart from each other. From Illinois, Florida, Washington, Texas, New Mexico, California, Oregon, Oklahoma, Tennessee, Virginia, from British Columbia and Alberta, Canada. Curious, hopeful or frankly desperate, they were all looking for deals, asking prices, checking out packages: what will a new hip cost, by itself, and with bigger breasts thrown in? What about a package for two—a facelift for me, Lasik eye surgery for my companion? How much for a bridge, a root canal, IVF, angioplasty, gastric bypass surgery. . . . This is my budget, what can I get for it?

It might sound discordant, this price-tagging of body parts, but for Indian private hospitals, nothing is more musical than these noises from a global healthcare bazaar. They demonstrate that an idea that seemed absurd at the start of this decade has entered the realm of reality: that people from the West will travel thousands of miles, to so-called cholera country, for medical treatment—if the price is right, and the quality is right. It's an idea with big money attached to it: medical tourism is forecast to become a $2.3 billion business for India by 2012. Some analysts predict it could be the next major driver of the Indian economy after information technology—if the industry and the government play their cards right.

Western TV crews accompanied often elderly people to India, filmed them hobbling out of Third World airports, with bhangra on the soundtrack, and driving into First World tertiary hospitals with the best technology money could buy. They showed them being "swamped by staff" and "feeling like kings", as one delighted patient described it, and seen by western-qualified senior consultants within an hour of arrival—which could be 2 am.

The crews tracked the pilgrims' progress, finding their

way into an operating theatre where a surgeon obligingly delivered a tribute to the British system that trained him. But the main message came through loud and clear: white people getting knees replaced, hips resurfaced, and dental work done at bargain-basement prices by experienced doctors who knew their job. British tabloids went to town on teenager Elliot Knott who successfully underwent spine surgery here last August after being told to wait a year for an operation by the National Health Service U.K. Most private hospitals saw a marked upward trend in western arrivals last year, most of them from the UK, US and Canada.

The Apollo Group saw an overall five per cent increase in the number of western medical tourists, according to executive director (finance) Sunita Reddy, despite no special effort to market to them. But at Apollo's flagship Delhi hospital, which gets more medical tourists than its other hospitals, the arrivals from some countries seem to have doubled. For example, it got around 80 American patients from April to November 05, more than the entire number in the previous financial year. Any international marketing executive—and every upmarket private hospital now has one—can recite the numbers in her sleep: 8,50,000 waiting for a hospital bed in the UK, 47-million plus uninsured in the US. Medical value-travellers, as hospitals like to call them, are also people looking for body shapes that insurance companies won't pay for and dreams that even efficient public healthcare systems won't deliver, like those of the 5 feet 4 tall Frenchman who recently came to India for a leg-lengthening operation. Many are also in quest of treatments not available at home, like hip resurfacing, less radical than hip replacement, but yet to be approved by the US Food and Drug Administration.

Foreign medical tourists

Agonizing pain kept his wife in bed for 16 to 20 hours a day, and the wait for an appointment with the right kind of doctor was no less painful. Google took Smith to India. "Much of Marlene's pre-operative pain has gone. We're 100 per cent satisfied. We paid $19,000, including airfare. In the US, the metal alone would have cost $40,000."

Marlene and Paul Smith; Canadians

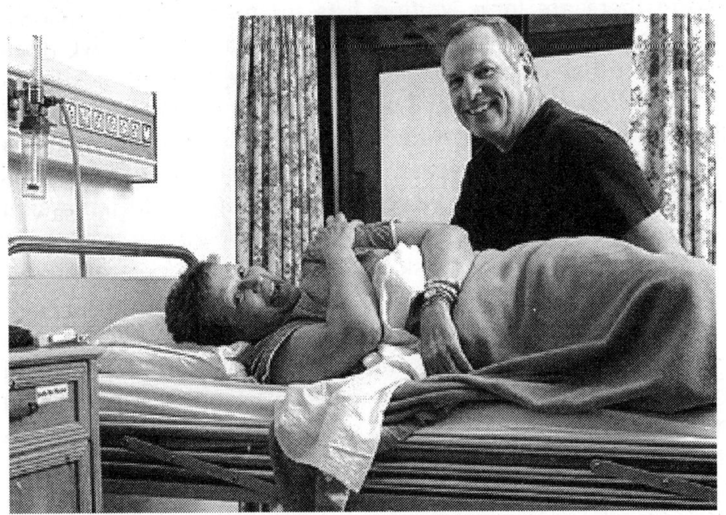

Treatment: Spinal fusion surgery

Contrary to the popular stereotype, not every medical tourist is dying to see the Taj. He could be someone for whom a hospital room is the only piece of India he can handle. In a month's stay at Apollo Hospital for complicated surgery to correct his wife Marlene's curved spine, Paul Smith, from Barrie, a small picture-postcard town in Ontario, left the hospital only once, on a trip to the airport to sort out ticketing. "With Marlene in bed, why would I want to sightsee?" he said.

In December, however, thanks to Elliot, and other high-profile visits arranged by their start-up, Taj Medical Group, they were able to send 27. They are going home in a few hours and they won't be returning. One giant leap into the unknown was probably enough. And yet, they couldn't be more grateful, raving about their doctor, dreaming about a better life for Marlene, determined to spread the word about India. Fortunately for the tourism ministry not all medical tourists confine themselves to hospital rooms.

Dr. Trehan says American citizens not covered by insurance—or those in countries such as the United Kingdom where there are long waiting lists for many National Health services—prefer to receive treatment in a country like India where top-tier institutions can provide high-quality healthcare at a fraction of the cost. Trehan recently operated on an 83-year old Canadian cardiac patient who needed a valve replacement with a bypass, but had been turned down by doctors back home. "No doctor was willing to do it for him. It's my specialization, patients with 10 or 20 per cent heart function. I told him the risk was less than five per cent," said Trehan.

Language is another big advantage in India, says Howard Staab, who spent more than three weeks in Escorts Hospital and at a resort, recuperating after surgery: "Doctors and nurses were all Indians, and many of the doctors were trained in the United States and Britain and most of them spoke very good English. I did not have any trouble understanding them." Howard Staab's partner Maggie Grace, who accompanied him on his medical trip to India, is writing a book about their experience. "We want to help people in the United States know they have choices," says Mr. Staab. "There will be our book coming out very soon. My partner Maggie Grace is writing it. The book title is "Patient Pilgrimage: A True Story of the First Americans Travel to India for Heart Surgery" and the website is www.howardsheart.com. Howard Staaab says one key to his trip's success was that it combined a high degree of medical excellence with a human touch.

Amitabh Kant, the bureaucrat who led 'Incredible India' and helped successfully reinvent Kerala as God's own Ayurvedic paradise, is leading the ministry's initiative to promote India as a "global healthcare destination". So, after incredible temples, incredible tigers and incredible yoga, it's now going to be incredible doctors backed by incredible technology. Glossy brochures, prepared with the help of ad agency Ogilvy and Mather, feature men and women in spotless white coats bending over patients against backdrops of sleek medical hardware. The patients in the brochure seem mostly white and middle-aged, for a reason: Kant is aiming way beyond the harried middle classes from SAARC countries, Afghanistan and poorer African countries who have been flocking to India for specialised medical care which their countries lack. They, too, are coming in rising numbers, especially from Afghanistan and Africa, and sure, hospitals want their custom.

But for reasons of both prestige and money, what really excites both government and industry is the fatter wallets in western countries with ageing populations and rising healthcare costs-and the Gulf, where seekers are finding it harder to access medical treatment in the West, post 9/11.

It's definitely not the titled rich that are showing up here. Cosmetic surgeon Mohan Thomas's upcoming patients include a pair of London cabbies, husband and wife, coming for facelifts. But even a school teacher from Bognor Regis can book a nice room when a hip replacement costs less than half of what it does back home. If they like the main course, western patients will also splurge on side dishes. Like Briton Barry Peters, who came to get a hip replaced, and got his teeth done as well, paying less for the whole treatment, including airfares, than just the dental would have cost him in London. Or Serena Taylor from California, who came to

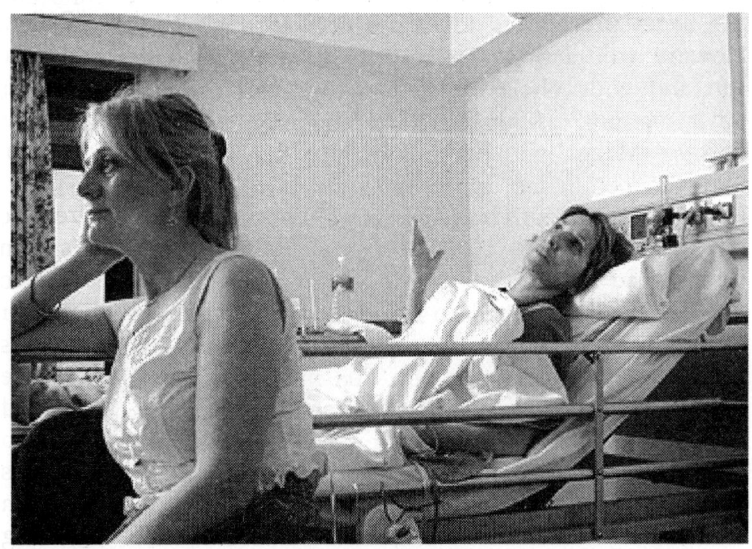

look after her friend seeking plastic surgery, and decided to buy an eyelift. It must be like eyeing a pricey handbag for several weeks and suddenly finding it at 80 per cent off. What else can you say but, "I'll have that"? "A hospital cannot replace a hotel. We should not keep these patients in hospital a minute more than required, we must send them to a place where they can recuperate," says Apollo group chairman Dr. Prathap Reddy. In Bangalore, patients can check out of leading private hospitals, and convalesce in places like Soukya, a sprawling health farm on the outskirts of the city. With an in-house team of ayurvedic physicians and allopathic doctors on call, when needed, its medical director, homeopath Dr. Isaac Mathai, claims to have the "lowest doctor-patient ratio in the world". It's the detox destination for Indian software and media tycoons, and its international guests.

> "I heard about medical treatment in India from the TV show 60 Minutes. Big American hospitals are full of Indian doctors, that's how I knew they'd be good."

Howard looked into state-of-the-art cardiac facilities in India, Argentina and Texas, where top US-trained doctors do the same procedures for a fraction of the cost. Of course, Howard would prefer to stay in the Triangle to be near his son and wide circle of friends. But who could resist these other options? After much deliberation Howard and his partner, Maggi, will fly to India for the surgery as soon as they can obtain the appropriate visas. Indian Hospitals Lure Foreigners with $6700 Heart Surgery.

Dhanyavaad

Staab was rolled into Escorts' operating room on Sept. 28. Grace, who'd picked up a smattering of Hindi, wrote "dhanyavaad," for "thank you," on his bare chest with purple marker. The surgeons first decided to repair Staab's mitral valve. A day later, the valve walls thickened and obstructed blood flow. Staab went in for a second operation on Sept. 30, and doctors replaced the valve. He was ready to leave on Oct. 8 when blurry vision from suspected blood clots kept him for another two days to thin his blood. Staab and Grace returned to the US on Oct. 24. Grace says finding out about India was the tough part. If not for Srivastava, she and Staab never would have figured out where to look, let alone gather the courage to make the trip. Back in North Carolina, Staab had an opportunity to compare healthcare in the US with his treatment in India. An early November checkup found that his blood was still too thick, and he entered Durham Regional Hospital.

Grace says she had to ask for sheets to make Staab's bed and get him water herself. The bathroom wasn't cleaned, and they had to ask twice for the intravenous bag containing blood-thinning heparin to be changed when it became empty, she says. Carol Clayton, senior public relations specialist at Durham Regional, says the hospital addresses patient concerns as soon as they are brought to the staff's attention.

In April, Ian Stuart Crombie, 64, couldn't finish his round of golf at the Bonny Island course in Rivers State, Nigeria, because of pain in his right hip. Doctors gave him two choices: live on painkillers or undergo surgery. Crombie opted for a route that more Europeans and Americans are

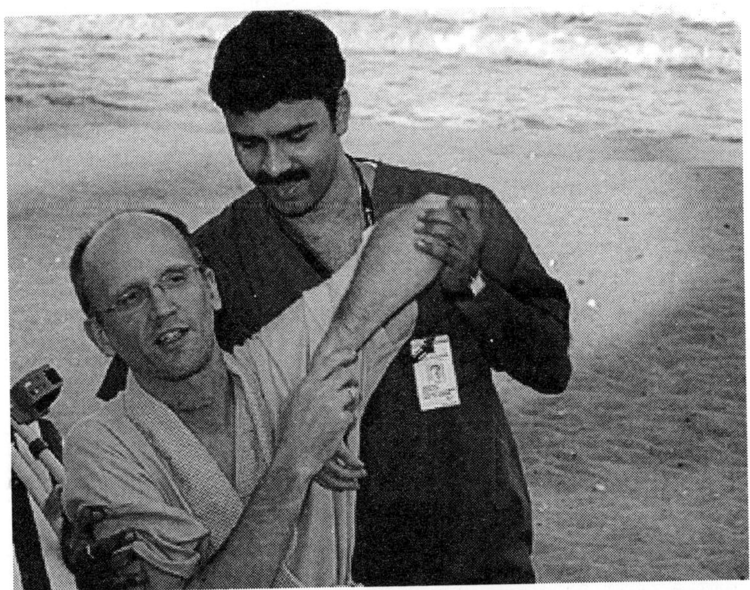

Scot Johnson; American Treatment: Cervical disc replacement.

taking. He looked beyond a decrepit airport and teeming streets and chose India for medical care. In September, the British citizen flew 5159 miles (8303 kilometers) from his home in Winchester to Apollo Hospital in Chennai. Doctors performed a hip resurfacing, which involved shaving his thighbone and fitting it with a metal head that was then anchored in his hip socket. With the operation, Crombie joined the international clientele flocking to India for cut-rate services that include telephone call centers, software design and financial analysis. Indian hospitals are a very cheap option where patients get the same quality they're used to back home," says Sanjay Dongre, who manages the equivalent of $237 million of shares at UTI Asset Management Co. in Mumbai, which owns Apollo stock.

For Crombie, who was working as a human resources manager in Africa, Apollo presented a low-cost option. He says his medical plan didn't cover the hip operation. He didn't bother with the U.K. National Health Service because of its waiting list and decided not to pursue treatment in Nigeria. A private hospital back home would charge 15,000 pounds ($27,965), he says. Instead, Crombie paid a total of 5000 pounds for his India trip, including the operation, airfare and a stay at the $130-a-night Park Hotel in Chennai. Crombie was familiar with India, where his job had taken him to recruit workers in Cochin, Mumbai and New Delhi. He found Bose on the Internet and checked his credentials with doctors Bose had worked with in the U.K. He decided on India after e-mail exchanges persuaded him that hip resurfacing rather than hip replacement would give him a better shot at playing golf again. "I can imagine someone who's not been to India before may find it intimidating," Crombie says.

On vacation in India in September, Brown experienced chest pain again and was rushed to Wockhardt Hospital in Bangalore. Wockhardt performed an angioplasty the next day, inserting a wire mesh tube called a stent to prop open an artery. "The hospital could have been in London," Brown recalls. "It was immaculately clean and had good standards." Back in England, Brown says, he got a letter from the National Health Service in November asking him to come in for his initial test—two months after he'd had the surgery in India.

Some Middle Eastern patients began choosing India after the Sept. 11, 2001, attacks on New York and Washington, says Suneeta Reddy, 45, director of finance at Apollo Hospitals and daughter of founder and Executive Chairman Prathap Reddy, 71. In November, Waleed Khalid Al-Zadjali, 40, a doctor in Oman, picked Apollo for his father's angioplasty and his mother's knee replacement. Oman hospitals often refer patients to India for complicated procedures because the country is familiar, closer than the US or Europe and cheap, he says. "After 9/11, people were scared to go to the US," he says.

Healthy competition in healthcare

Top private hospitals are also vying with each other in other ways to attract an international clientele. As in an accelerated race for the latest hardware—you can't miss the giant boards advertising the latest scanner—and for that prized certificate by the Joint Commission International (JCI) in the United States, a non-governmental body that accredits international hospitals meeting exacting American standards. The early birds who have it, such as Apollo in Delhi and Wockhardt in Mumbai, display it big, and other hospitals are in the queue. "The fact that we are JCI-accredited is a symbol of quality assurance for patients in the western world. The hospital room is changing too, with globalisation clearly the spur, though all CEOs maintain that demanding Indian patients are driving the changes, too. John Connell, a primary school teacher from Southampton in the UK, who came to Wockhardt in Mumbai earlier this month for a new minimally invasive procedure to treat a hole in his heart, had the following in his hospital room: a computer, internet, a DVD player with regional compatibility that could play British DVDs, a mini-bar, a coffee-maker, a cellphone. The hospital also offered him and wife Amanda "virtual family visits"—that is, a video of them shot in the room and uploaded for their families back home. A hospital car was made available for them to move around in the neighbourhood. John's room still managed to look like a hospital room, but at new hospitals like the Max Devki Devi Heart and Vascular Institute in Delhi, it's all blonde wood, expensive blinds, and leather sofas, the work of a British designer hired by the company to get the look right. And prices? Ashmeena Ghei, international marketing head, who is already facilitating visits by a stream of international patients, quotes them in dollars: $150 for a room, $300 for a suite.

The 2.3 billion dollar question

Judging by the talk on the hospital circuit, it won't be long before every upmarket private hospital offers ayurvedic massages, aromatherapy, mudbaths, pranic healing, yoga, the works. And full-fledged departments of alternative medicine, with homeopaths, naturopaths, and unani medicine specialists on board to deliver that authentic dose of India. The BPO sector, in comparison, earned $5.2 billion last year. (*Source*: CII-McKinsey report) The government hopes to encourage a budding trade in medical tourism, selling foreigners the idea of travelling to India for low-cost but world-class medical treatment. Naresh Trehan, former Executive Director of Escorts Heart Institute and Research Centre, a leading private healthcare provider, says India has established world-class expertise in practices such as cardiac care, cosmetic surgery, joint replacements and dentistry. Merging medical expertise and tourism became government policy when finance minister Jaswant Singh, in this year's budget, called for India to become a "global health destination". If foreigners respond, a new medical tourism industry could be generating revenues of Rs. 100bn ($2.1 bn, $1.9 bn, $1.3 bn) by 2012, according to a report by McKinsey Consultants and the Confederation of Indian Industry, a business group.

Take the rising popularity of "preventive health screening". At one private clinic in London a thorough men's health check-up that includes blood tests, electro-cardiogram tests, chest x-rays, lung tests and abdominal ultrasound costs $345 ($574, $500). By comparison, a comparable check-up at a clinic operated by Delhi-based healthcare company Max Healthcare costs $84.

Maharashtra Medical Tourism Council (MTC)

Initially the MTC plans to woo foreign patients who pay for private health-care in their own countries. But it also plans to work with state-run systems. For instance, Anupam Verma, the council's honorary secretary, believes Britain has a "huge potential" for medical tourism owing to its long waiting lists for surgery. He has already had exploratory conversations with some British National Health Service managers about the possibility of sending patients to India. For the MTC, its plans are the next chapter in globalization and the outsourcing of work to India. As Sanjay Agarwala, the Hinduja's chief neurosurgeon, says: "Wherever you can offer better services at a more competitive price, that is the place that is going to win in the end." Contrary to the claims of the council, Dr. Baru believes there will be no trickle down of money to the impoverished public health system, which currently receives just 0.9% of India's gross domestic product. The MTC's plans may well benefit the doctors and patients involved, but it is currently unclear how a country that still suffers from malaria and TB will reap the rewards of a new wave of medical tourists coming to India.

In recent years Indian Medical Tourism Sector has exhibited tremendous potential. Studies reveal that the Sector is growing at an exaggerated rate of 15% for last five years. It is expected that with the current growth rate the Industry will reach Rs. 270,000 crores by 2012. Statistics show that the medical tourism industry in India is worth $333 million at present (Rs. 1450 crore), while a study by CII McKinsey estimates that the country could earn Rs. 5,000-10,000 crore by 2012. Probably realizing the potential, major corporates such as the Tatas, Fortis, Max, Wockhardt, Piramal, and the Escorts group have made significant investments in setting up modern hospitals in major cities. Many have also designed special packages for patients, including airport pickups, visa assistance and board and lodging, healthcare industry officials said. Foreigners have already started trickling into India for medical treatment thus officials are hopeful that this will become a flood once the various initiatives being taken by the Government take-off. With world-class medical care, equipment and facilities now available in India, patients from the United States and other developed countries are going there for treatment. A number of private hospitals in India offer packages designed to attract foreign patients, with airport-to-hospital bed transfer service, Internet access, and other facilities. Some packages include add-ons, such as a yoga holiday or a trip to the world-famous Taj Mahal.

Religious tourism vs. Medical tourism in India

Synergy of religious tourism and medical tourism can work. It can improve healthcare for the countrymen and earn dollars from foreign medical tourists. It will not put any burden on the state exchequer or burden the country with debts. It will be self-financing as well as fulfilling to the community. This is in consonance with Indian tradition to help the people in pain and disability. If the donations from all over the country are channelised to healthcare, it will not only lead to healthcare for all in India, but also make it attractive for the medical tourists from abroad. Various religious sects and their heads have to come forward to further a common cause that is good for the humanity. See appendix on the list of religious places in India.

Agra moving forward

While the states of Karnatka, Maharashtra, Gujarat, Tamil Nadu, Andhra Pardesh are quite ahead in tourism promotion, other states are also making efforts to march ahead. Agra is definitely moving in the direction of a well developed medical tourism centre. With the new international airport coming up soon, and competent city doctors working abroad, this process will start soon enough. "Medical facilities in Agra have expanded immensely. Earlier we referred our patients to hospitals in Delhi, now with the latest gadgetry and facilities available locally, patients take advantage and save both money and time."

Apollo Hospitals has also entered into partnership with Pankaj Mahendru's medical outfit. The new venture is called Apollo Pankaj. Said Apollo Pankaj director Pankaj Mahendru: "Earlier during the British and Mughal empires also, Agra was the main centre of health services. Now embassies and corporate houses are referring patients to hospitals here which have a fairly competent base of manpower and facilities." An American company Mefcom Agro Ind has acquired stakes in Kamayani Patients Care India, a multi-specialty hospital, providing specialty cancer treatment. Metro, Heritage, Pushpanjali, Shanti Ved, Pareek's, Nawal Kishore's, GG Nursing Home and Sarkar's, the oldest nursing home in Agra, are some of the other hospitals that have broken new ground in Agra by modernizing their infrastructure and facilities. To support the fast growing medical tourism industry, at least a dozen training institutes for paramedic staff as well as research centres have come up. The Agra Mental Hospital is conducting several programmes to train personnel for this specialised sector. Even the 150-year-old S.N. Medical College now presents a new profile in a bid to attract patients from the rest of India and even abroad.

Rajasthan enterprise

For this, land would be provided at special prices to all new private medical institutions, including medical and dental colleges, diagnosis centres, blood banks, and nursing and paramedical training institutes. The policy will also boost other medical streams like ayurveda, homoeopathy and naturopathy. A "land bank" will be created to give land to medical institutions that are promoting and practicing alternative medical therapies.

To benefit from the policy, nursing and paramedical institutions will have to make an investment of at least Rs. 50 million. Similarly, nursing homes and 15-bed hospitals planning a facility within 50 km from regional headquarters or 20 km from district headquarters or in a village or town with a population of less than 50,000 will have to invest at least Rs. 5 million. Investors will also have to abide by environment protection rules for hospital waste disposal and follow the rules and regulations set by the committee of standards.

Obesity treatment looks attractive

In a development that could bring patients from US and Europe to the country, a private hospital today launched a world class bariatric surgery clinic in Gujarat to treat people suffering from severe obesity, a disease that is fast attaining epidemic proportions in India.

The star-studded launch of the clinic at Apollo Gleneagles Hospitals here saw at least 25 people queuing up for surgery to get rid of excessive body weight and in turn associated diseases like high blood pressure, diabetes and cardiac ailments. The new facility, first of its kind in India after sporadic attempts elsewhere in the country, is also eyeing patients from the west, where the cost of treatment is more and the waiting time enormous. "The facility, being backed by a support group for obese people, is a comprehensive unit, which will benefit not only domestic patients but also thousands of patients in the Americas and Europe, who are showing interest in flying down to get operated," says laparoscopic and bariatric surgeon, who heads the clinic. Quoting the WHO, he says 17 per cent of men and 15 per cent women in India were confirmed to be obese and the numbers were growing by leaps with changing lifestyles and eating habits. "Globally, over 1.7 billion people are affected by the disease. In the US, over 300,000 people die of obesity while in Europe around 250,000 people are killed by the scourge," he warned.

Tooth Tourism; Great Potential

Speaking on the subject of "Tooth Tourism—Destination India", Dr. Ajay Kakar and Dr. A. Kumarswamy said dental tourism has got a boost with dental treatment having comparable expertise, high technology and high value for treatment costs. Dental tourism in the country got a boost due to factors like Indians with foreign postings, NRI's and foreign nationals of Indian origin, foreign nationals working in India, casual tourists, dental tourists coming to India for treatment, said Dr. Kakar. "For a population of one billion, there are currently over 60,000 dentists with 15,000 dentists in metros and 5000 dental specialists, which include orthodontists, peridontists, endodontists, prosthodontists, dental surgeons and pedodontists, said Dr. Kumarswamy.

Common Surgical Interventions Sought by Foreign Patients

Globalisation has promoted a consumerist culture, thereby promoting goods and services that can feed the aspirations arising from this culture. This has had its effect in the health sector too, with the emergence of private hospitals that thrive by servicing a small percentage of the population that has the ability to "buy" medical care at "high end" rates. However, for foreign patients and profits to increase, India must remedy negative first impressions and persuade doubters that millions of the country's poor and ailing won't be left behind.

The following interventions are sought by foreign medical tourists.

Bone Marrow Transplant

Major hospitals in India have oncology units comprising surgical oncology, medical and radiation therapy as well as the crucial Bone Marrow Transplantation (BMT). The BMT unit with high-pressure Hipa filters has helped achieve a very high success rate in the various types of transplantation. Cord Blood Transplant and Allogeneic Stem Cell Transplant have been performed successfully, a feat that is remarkable and significant, considering the fact that the treatment costs one-tenth of what it does in the west. Special surgeons are available for individual organs. Plastic surgeons of repute provide treatment for head and neck cancer, breast cancer and other malignancies. Facilities offered include tele-therapy, which includes simulation work stations to ensure high precision and safety during treatment at the 18 MV linear accelerator or telecobalt machines, brachy therapy and 3-D planning systems. In orthopedics, the Ilizarov technique is practiced for the treatment of limb deformities, limb shortening and disfiguration.

Cardiac Care

Cardiac care has become a specialty in India with institutions like the Escorts Heart Institute and Research Centre, All India Institute of Medical Sciences and Apollo Hospital becoming names to reckon with. These centres have the distinction of providing comprehensive cardiac care spanning from basic facilities in preventive cardiology to the most sophisticated curative technology. The technology is contemporary and world class and the volumes handled match global benchmarks. They also specialise in offering surgery to high-risk patients with the introduction of innovative techniques like minimally invasive and robotic surgery.

Having accomplished what he had set out to do with Escorts, Trehan is planning a multispecialty hospital in Gurgaon, on the outskirts of New Delhi, that's patterned on the Cleveland Clinic in Ohio and the Mayo Clinic in Rochester, Minnesota.

There are several other hospitals, which offer world class cardiac care.

Interventional Cardiology

Interventional Cardiology is a specialty which uses imaging techniques and strategies for the diagnosis of the diseases of the heart and blood vessel. These novel, minimally invasive, non-surgical procedures make use of mechanical treatments for the diseases of the heart and blood vessels. These procedures are mostly performed under local anesthesia, have a considerably short hospitalization and recovery period with minimal post-operative pain and discomfort. Interventional Cardiology includes a number of procedures that can be performed to the heart by means of inserting a 'catheter' in one of your blood vessels of the groin, neck or forearm. Established in 2000, the Krishna Heart Institute and Specialty Clinic is known for its innovative diagnostics and treatment procedures, and its extensive work in areas such as cardiology and joint replacement. Located in Ahmedabad, Gujarat, this institute is one of Gujarat's leading hospitals. Initially specializing in cardiac care, the institute has grown into specialized areas such as hip and knee replacement surgeries, plastic and reconstructive surgeries, Onco-surgery, and other invasive and minimally invasive procedures.

The institute has an excellent record for providing quality medical care for its international visitors at affordable prices. An air conditioned lounge is on each floor and there is a cafeteria with an expert chef serving a selection of cuisines. The institute provides continuous central monitoring and International standard water filtration and distribution systems for pure water, hot and cold. This institute is only one of the several centres of excellence all over the country, in the field of interventional cardiology.

Percutaneous Transluminal Angioplasty (PTA)

PTA is a minimally invasive procedure which is used to open narrowed arteries of the legs (most commonly iliac arteries causing cramps when walking, known as claudication), those to the brain known as the carotid arteries (causing stroke) and the arteries to the kidneys (causing high blood pressure). These conditions belong to the group of Peripheral Vascular Disease. Another condition may be ballooning of the artery called aneurysm. Aneurysms commonly occur in abdominal aorta where it manifests itself with abdominal pain or tenderness and a throbbing mass in the abdomen. Peripheral Vascular Disease is diagnosed by a procedure called angiogram which is similar to Coronary Angiogram. Peripheral Angioplasty is very similar to Coronary Angioplasty where arteries of the heart are narrowed due to atherosclerosis (Coronary Artery Disease).

The blockage in the arteries is caused by deposition of fat in the form of plaques which accumulate along the arterial wall. Cost of procedure performed in the US: $18,171.

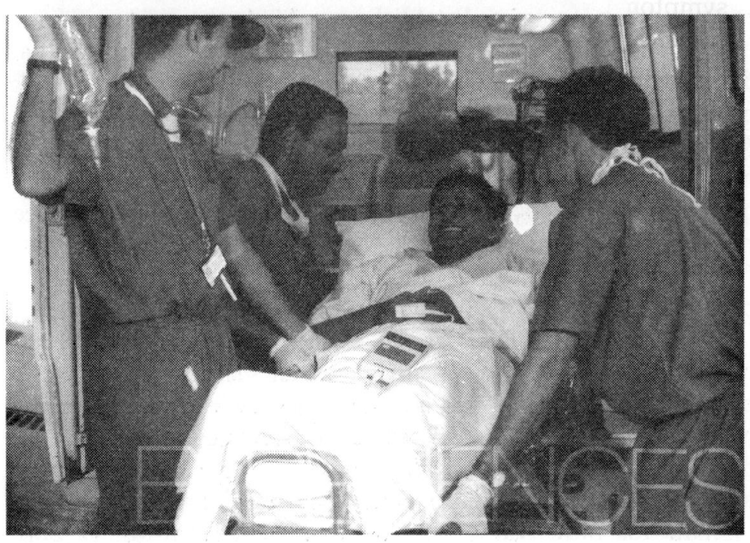

The procedure for PTA

The procedure comprises of three steps: Step one is also known as artherectomy involves removal of blockage (plaque) from peripheral artery either by laser or with specialized instruments to cut the plaque away and clear the arterial channel. The second step makes use of a balloon. An un-inflated balloon is inserted with the help of a guide wire to the site of blockage. The balloon is then inflated, which as a result enlarges the blood channel and increases blood flow. It can reduce a 70-90% blockage to about 20-30%. Step three of Peripheral Angioplasty consists of implanting a mesh stent which is tightly mounted on the Peripheral Angioplasty balloon into the walls of blocked artery.

If you have been diagnosed with intermittent claudication, i.e. aches, pain, cramps, or tightness in the calves, thighs, hips or buttocks when walking, which is relieved with a few moments rest, if you have leg ulcers or gangrene, if you have an aneurysm (abdominal aorta or cerebral artery), if you are a smoker who experiences numbness, tingling or coldness of legs and feet, if you suffer from high blood pressure, diabetes, high cholesterol, a family history of heart or vascular disease, and are overweight with symptoms of peripheral vascular disease, then you are an ideal candidate for PTA.

It has a success rate of almost 95% with the chances of re-stenosis occurring in 5% of the patients. This procedure is less painful and allows you to go back to your daily activities quickly. This means that you will not have the symptoms of Peripheral Vascular Disease any more. Insertion of Drug Eluting Stents have potentially improved the clinical outcome of the procedure of PTA. It has revolutionized the treatment of Peripheral Vascular Disease. Implantation of stents during angioplasty procedure reduces the chances of re-stenosis of the artery tremendously. The procedure of Peripheral Angioplasty is certainly not a treatment for Peripheral Vascular Disease however, accompanying lifestyle changes can definitely reduce your chances of further problems and complications. Cost of procedure performed in the US: $18,171.

What is Coronary Angiography?

Coronary Angiography is a procedure in which a non-ionic contrast dye is injected into the coronary arteries. This allows your cardiologist to visualize the coronary arteries on an X-ray and view the flow of blood through them. Cost of procedure performed in the US: $3,000 to $6,000. During the procedure you might experience some flushing and/or palpitation which will subside quickly. If you have chest pain which may or may not be increasing in intensity and duration, if you have unexplained pain in your jaw, neck or arm, if you have congenital heart disease or congestive heart failure, if you are planning to have heart valve surgery, if you have problems with your blood vessels like aortic aneurysm, if you have suffered a traumatic injury to your chest, then you are an ideal candidate for Coronary Angiography. Coronary Angiography is a relatively harmless procedure that can unfold tremendous amount of information and detail about the structure and function of your coronary arteries. Coronary Angiography is a diagnostic procedure that is used to confirm the diagnosis of the diseases affecting your heart and blood vessels.

Risks of Coronary Angiography

- Allergic reaction to the contrast dye
- Irregular heart beat (arrhythmias)
- Heart attack and death during the Coronary Angiography procedure
- Stroke
- Injury to the internal wall of the artery where the catheter was threaded in
- Perforation of coronary artery
- Kidney damage
- Excessive bleeding (hemorrhage)
- Infection
- Blood clots

Alternatives to Coronary Angiography

Magnetic Resonance Angiography (MRA)

In this procedure detailed images of your heart are captured using radio waves in a strong magnetic field without the use of catheters or X-rays

CT Angiography

This method does not require catheterization within the heart reducing some of the risks associated with Coronary Angiography.

Digital Subtraction Angiography (DSA)

This method combines the X-ray techniques of Coronary Angiography with a high-speed computer to improve the resolution of images obtained.

Cardiac Catheterization

This procedure is very similar to Coronary Angiography and consists of passage of a catheter in the coronary artery

Angioplasty?

Angioplasty or Balloon Angioplasty is a minimally invasive procedure in which the blocked or narrowed coronary arteries are opened (widened) to facilitate perfusion of the heart muscle. Coronary Angioplasty reduces the need for medication and to some extent eliminates chest pain due to Ischemic Heart Disease. Cost of procedure performed in the US: $35,000. The procedure for Coronary Angioplasty usually comprises of three steps: Step one of Coronary Angioplasty, also known as artherectomy involves removal of blockage (plaque) from your coronary artery either by laser or with specialized instruments to cut the plaque away and clear the arterial channel. The second step of Coronary Angioplasty makes use of a balloon (thus the alternative term Balloon Angioplasty). In this step, an un-inflated balloon is inserted with the help of a guide wire to the site of blockage. The balloon is then inflated, which enlarges the blood channel and increases blood flow through the artery. It is interesting to note that Coronary Angioplasty can reduce a 70-90% blockage to about 20-30%. Step three of Coronary Angioplasty consists of implanting a mesh stent which is tightly mounted on the Coronary Angioplasty balloon into the walls of blocked artery. The balloon is then deflated and removed leaving the stent in place permanently to hold the artery open. In this procedure of Coronary Angioplasty, the coronary arteries are accessed through a puncture made in the groin (femoral artery) or arm (brachial artery). Usually the femoral artery is used. Depending upon the extent of coronary artery narrowing, all three steps may or may not be carried out. The procedure of Coronary Angioplasty can take 30 minutes to several hours depending on the number of blockages being treated.

Benefits of Coronary Angioplasty

- Quicker and less painful recovery
- Short hospital stay, does not require general anesthesia
- Small incision
- Coronary Angioplasty can be done under local anesthesia

- The chest cage does not need to be opened
- Chances of major post-operative complications like stroke are minimized as heart-lung machine is not used during the procedure of Coronary Angioplasty

Risks of Coronary Angioplasty

- Allergic reaction to the dye
- Ruptured coronary artery
- Bleeding and infection at the site of insertion
- Arrhythmia
- Stroke
- Heart attack
- Kidney failure
- Rupture or dissection of the coronary artery
- Re-stenosis of the coronary artery requiring Heart Bypass Surgery

Coronary Stenting

Coronary Stenting is performed to hold your coronary artery open to facilitate flow of blood to the heart muscle and reduce your chest pain due to angina. The coronary stents physically hold your artery open and create a channel for your blood to flow through it easily. Coronary Stenting is usually performed as part of the Coronary Angioplasty procedure. So if you are an ideal candidate for Coronary Angioplasty, i.e. if one or more of your coronary arteries are blocked, if your chest pain due to angina is not well controlled with medications or if it is severe enough to disrupt your daily activities and also occurs at rest, then you are an ideal candidate for Coronary Stenting. Coronary Stenting has a success rate of almost 95% with the chances of re-stenosis occurring in 5% of the patients. This procedure is less painful and allows you to go back to your daily activities quickly. This means that you will not have chest pain any more and that your tolerance to exercise will increase. Drug Eluting Coronary Stents have potentially improved the clinical outcome of Coronary Stenting.

Benefits of Coronary Stenting

- Quicker and less painful recovery
- Short hospital stay, does not require general anesthesia
- Small incision
- Coronary Stenting can be done under local anesthesia
- The chest cage does not need to be opened
- Chances of major post-operative complications like stroke are minimized as heart-lung machine is not used during Coronary Stenting procedure
- Implantation of drug eluting coronary stents dramatically decreases the chances of re-stenosis and the need for a repeat procedure.

In the procedure for Drug Eluting Coronary Stenting, the implanted stent is coated with a medication that prevents re-stenosis. This type of stent consistently releases a chemical substance that prevents clot formation and narrowing of coronary artery. Drug Eluting Coronary Stenting has been 20-30% more successful than bare metal stenting. Cost of procedure performed in the US: $37,000.

Benefits of Drug Eluting Coronary Stenting

- Quicker and less painful recovery
- Short hospital stay, does not require general anesthesia
- Small incision (Minimally Invasive procedure)
- Drug Eluting Coronary Stenting can be done under local anesthesia
- The chest cage does not need to be opened
- Chances of major post-operative complications like stroke are minimized as heart-lung machine is not used during the procedure of Drug Eluting Coronary Stenting
- Implantation of Drug Eluting Coronary Stenting has dramatically decreased the chances of re-stenosis and the need for a repeat procedure.

Dialysis and Kidney Transplant

Common diseases like diabetes, hypertension and chronic glomerulonephritis can lead to permanent loss of renal functions—with dialysis and renal transplantation being the frequent outcome. The emergence of new therapeutic interventions has created opportunities in India to manage the progression of renal diseases. Major hospitals in India like Holy Family Hospital, Jaslok Hospital, Apollo Hospital, Sir Ganga Ram Hospital, Batra Hospital, Bombay Hospital and Hinduja Hospital have departments of Nephrology and Organ Transplant equipped with the latest computerised dialysis machines, reverse osmosis water plant to provide pure and trace element-free water supply, as well as state-of-the-art facilities in the operating rooms and Transplant Intensive Care Units.

For those who need renal replacement therapy, the following services are also available.

Patients can also avail of the bicarbonate dialysis facility at these centres. Round the clock service is available at these hospitals for the critically ill patients in the intensive care units who may need fluid, electrolyte management and renal supportive therapy.

The cost of getting a dialysis is around Rs. 1700 to Rs. 1800 per dialysis whereas the same costs about $ 300 in the U.S.A. Similarly a kidney transplant package in India is available for around Rs. 3 lakhs, which is comparatively much cheaper than what it would cost abroad.

Gynecology

Leading Indian hospitals with gynecology departments and women's hospitals have facilities for the prevention and early detection of gynecological disorders. Many hospitals have women check-up programmes designed to detect the earliest signs of disorders of the breast and the organs of reproduction as well as catering to the contraceptive needs of women. A mammogram, an ultrasound of the pelvis and a pap smear of the cervix are an integral part of any good medical check-up for women. Specialist medical as well as surgical care is available for all types of gynecological problems like menstrual abnormalities, prolapse, fibroids and other tumors of the uterus and ovaries, tubal re-canalization by microsurgery and care of the infertile couple. State-of-the-art gynecological surgery is available with world-class equipment and expertise using minimally invasive techniques.

Ectopic pregnancies, ovarian cysts and tumors, fibroids endometriosis, tubal blocks and even hysterectomies can be performed laparoscopically. Hospitals like Apollo have state-of-the-art IVF labs backed by highly experienced doctors who have been involved in the field of infertility and assisted Reproductive Technologies (ART).

Joint Replacement Surgery

Shoulder/hip replacement and bilateral knee replacement surgery using the most advanced keyhole or endoscopic surgery and arthroscopy is done at several hospitals in India including the Apollo Hospital, Sir Ganga Ram Hospital and Holy Family Hospital in Delhi, Bombay Hospital, Leelavati and Hinduja Hospital in Mumbai and the Madras Institute of Orthopaedics and Trauma Sciences. Some hospitals like Apollo in Delhi have Operation Theatres with Laminar Air Flow System, which compares with the best in the USA and the UK. A knee joint replacement costs only a quarter of what it costs in the UK. In the last 5 years arthroplasty has got established and has changed the face of osteoarthritis patients. More than 10 million people are supposed to suffer from this ailment in India alone. Dr. Dholakia was the first to introduce the technique in 1986. Ranawat performed surgery on the knees of the then prime minister of India in 2000. Now further advancement has occurred and new techniques have come in giving better results.

Osteoporosis

Several drug therapies now easily available in the market have been shown to be clinically effective in slowing down or reversing the bone-loss process. Leading hospitals in India are well equipped to detect and treat bone loss in its earliest states, so as to prevent the disease or lessen its impact. Doctors in leading hospitals have the expertise for the diagnosis and treatment of osteoporosis that involves an objective, quantifiable measurement of the patient's bone mass or bone density. Advanced technology called the DXA for bone densitometry is available. During a comprehensive bone valuation with DXA, the patient lies comfortably still on a padded table while the DXA unit scans one or more areas, usually the fractured spine or the hip. The entire process takes only minutes to scan depending on the number of sites scanned. It involved no injections or invasive procedures and the patient remains fully clothed.

Neurosurgery and Trauma Surgery

Other routine procedures performed with excellent results are replacement arthroplasty, diagnostic and operative arthroscopy, spinal surgeries including. Harrington Rod Instrumentation for scoliosis, corrective and reconstructive procedure for poliomyelitis and cerebral palsy, micro cascular surgical procedures and automated percutaneous lumbar distectomy. In addition, the advanced Luque technique is employed for the correction of complex scoliosis, and decompression and stabilisation of fractures of dorsal and lumbar spine with paraplegia, by neurosurgeons with excellent training and background. Many super-speciality hospitals in India like AIIMS, Ram Manohar Lohia Hospital, Vidya Sagar Institute of Mental Health and Neuro Sciences, Bombay Hospital, Jaslok Hospital, Nizam Institute of Mental Health and Neuro Sciences and Apollo Hospitals have advanced facilities devoted to the treatment of the entire range of brain and spinal disorders with highly experienced neurosurgeons, neurologists, Neuro-anaesthetists and Neuro-radiologists. Treatment of intra-and juxta-cranial, spinal tumours and vascular malformations, aneurysms and thrombolysis for brain attacks are done at these centres. Hospitals like Apollo employ state-of-the-art LINAC-based stereotactic radio surgery system outside the USA. The Clinic 6000 SR Linear Accelerator with XKNIFE system is a highly sophisticated computer-driven technology used for removal of appropriately selected brain tumours, arteriovenous malformations and other abnormalities.

Refractive Surgery

Refractive surgery is gaining popularity in India both among the public as well as among ophthalmologists. Till a few years ago only a few centres performed high volume radial keratotomy. Today, the highest international quality of eye care for cornea, cataract, squint and glaucoma is available in over 40 centres all over India. When it comes to reliability, India has the best ophthalmic surgeons with clinico-academic expertise honed to perfection in the best possible institutions. Apollo Hospital, Gurunanak Eye Centre, Dr. Rajindra Prasad Centre For Ophthalmic Sciences and Mohan Eye Centre in Delhi, Shankar Naytralaya in Chennai, L.V. Prasad hospital in Hyderabad are just some of the more popular eye care hospitals. The No Stitch Cataract Surgery with the most modern way of removing cataract through the use of Phacoemulsification procedure can be performed in India for as little as Rs. 20,000, for both the eyes, whereas the same surgery costs $ 45,000 in the USA. Facilities for PRK, myopia and astigmatism are now available in almost all parts of the country. Hyperopic and LASIK are available and even supra hard cataracts are treated using just 1 mm incision instead of the 3 mm incision size. Photo-refractive keratectomy or PRK treats the surface of the cornea with the Excimer laser while LASIK treats the inner tissue of the cornea. For this reason, with LASIK there is less area to heal, less risk of scarring, less risk of corneal haze, less post-operative pain and vision often returns very rapidly.

Urology

Several super specialty hospitals in India offer comprehensive Urologic services to diagnose and treat stone disease, Urologic cancer, incontinence, infertility, impotency and other urinary difficulties. Advanced methods such as lithotripsy for treating kidney and ureteric stones without surgery are available with complementary methods of treating stones endoscopically. Advanced machines like the Lithostar obvert the need for anaesthesia in the treatment of kidney and ureteric stones. High tech facilities for the treatment of prostate, bladder cancers, urethral strictures are also available. Investigation and treatment facilities for impotence and male/

female infertility exist with specialized facilities for pharmacotherapy, cavernosometry and cavernosography, in addition to doppler studies for the assessment of blood flow.

Other surgeries

Removal of the gall bladder, the spleen, the bowel and other organs like the adrenals, an operation for prolapse rectum and hiatus hernia repair have become fairly commonplace in almost all the major speciality hospitals in India. Experts are easily available and accessible and the workload at most of these hospitals ensures that the doctors have enormous experience. High intensive care treatment at much cheaper rates than in the west is available at most of these centers.

Preventive Healthcare

Preventive healthcare has been introduced for the first time in the country by Apollo Hospitals with hospitals in the metros of Hyderabad, Chennai and Delhi, within easy international air access. The professional chain also pioneered the concept of lifestyle clinics, established the first organ registry in the country and introduced non-invasive technique for treatment of lesions and tumours of the brain—Stereotactic Radio Surgery and Radiotherapy in the country. It recently installed a state of the art Cobalt Unit. Apollo Heart Hospital provides a complete network for cardiac patients. It has a total bed capacity of 500 beds distributed between Apollo Chennai, Hyderabad and Delhi. Apollo is linked to the Mayo Clinic and the Minneapolis Heart Institute, a premier heart institute led by the team of doctors who pioneered the Jarvik artificial heart.

Imaging with MRI, a hypertension research centre and facilities for hemodialysis and kidney transplantation are available at Akila Hospitals at Trichy. The hospital boasts a transplant team with 8 specialists, bone marrow transplant team along with five specialists on call to Sri Lanka, Sharjah, Kuwait and major Indian cities.

In Chennai, the Vijaya Heart Foundation's 79 beds have a state of the art cardiology and cardio-thoracic surgical unit manned by competent and experienced staff. The Vijaya

Health Centre with 270 beds offers diagnostic facilities in laboratory, X-ray, ultrasound, treadmill, Endoscopy. C.T. Scan, M.R.I. and nuclear medicine.

Fasting

Naturopath doctors at such centres mean a minimalist diet of 300 calories per day—veggie broths and juices-for two weeks to several months, accompanied by blood tests, purges and other treatments. They say many hard-to-treat conditions, from arthritis to allergies and various skin disorders, benefit from the metabolic switch that takes place when the body starts living off its own reserves. Of the thousands guests who come to fast each year (half from Southern Europe, America and the Middle East), about one third arrive with serious ailments—the rest come to lose weight or cut stress. Fasting has lately gotten a boost from medical research. Clinical studies in Scandinavia have shown that fasting is an effective treatment for rheumatism—especially if followed by a vegetarian diet. In one study, pain and swelling came down by a third in a week and stayed that way for a year. Other studies have shown success in lowering blood pressure and treating chronic pain like migraine or arthritis. They have shown that when patients fast, stress hormones levels go down and serotonin levels rise (which may explain the "fasting high" many patients report). "The more we look into it, fasting seems to work like a reset button for the body's own self-regulating mechanisms," say Naturopaths.

$800 vs. $18

Charging foreigners more than Indians is one way hospitals can make money to treat the poor, says Gautam Kumra, a McKinsey and Co. partner in New Delhi. An echocardiogram machine, used to picture the heart, costs about $200,000 anywhere in the world. Doctors can charge $800 per scan in the US; in India, they charge 800 rupees, or $18. One imbalance that works in India's favour is its lower salaries. A top cardiac surgeon in India makes about $330,000 a year compared with $5 million in the US, says Anupam Sibal, Director at Apollo Hospital, New Delhi.

Cosmetic and Plastic Surgery

This is a surgical specialty that corrects disfigurement caused by burns, tumor, congenital defects, developmental abnormalities, trauma, infection, disease or injuries, improves appearance and self-esteem and restores function. Cosmetic and Plastic Surgery is mainly concerned with correcting problems and enhancing appearance of exposed areas of the body and the face. Reconstructive Plastic Surgery is another term that is used in this context mainly referring to surgical procedures that correct severe functional impairments, fix physical abnormalities, and compensate for tissue lost to trauma or surgery.

Some disfigurations corrected include hair restoration (hair implants, hair flaps, and scalp reductions), rhinoplasty (reshaping or re-contouring of the nose), stalling of the aging process (face lift, cosmetic eyelid surgery, brow lift, sub-metal lipectomy for double chin), dermabrasions (sanding of the face), otoplasty for protruding ears, chin and cheek enlargement, lip reductions, various types of breast surgery and reconstruction and liposuction.

The problem of loose upper arm skin usually occurs after weight loss. This problem is more common in people who have lost a lot of weight. If you were over weight, the skin of your arm has to stretch to accommodate the increased volume of your upper arm. After weight loss, the skin usually fails to tighten and sags. Brachioplasty is performed to correct this problem of loose hanging skin of your arms. Brachioplasty is performed as an outpatient procedure in the plastic surgeon's office under local anesthesia with sedation. The entire procedure of Brachioplasty takes about an hour per arm. The surgeon makes zigzag, elliptical or triangular incisions along the inner surface of upper arm. The space contained between the incisions is exactly the area of skin that would be removed. Removal of loose skin tightens the surface of the arm however, it does not remove the fat. That is why it is usually recommended that Brachioplasty be accompanied with liposuction as well to remove extra fat from your arms. Make sure that you make arrangements for some one to accompany you as you will be allowed to go home after a couple of hours following Brachioplasty procedure.

Benefits of Brachioplasty

- Brachioplasty will help you get rid of the extra fat and skin after losing weight. Although this requires you to undergo a surgical procedure, the results are well worth it. To be able to get the lean and shapely arms that you have always longed for, Brachioplasty is the best option available.
- Brachioplasty is performed under local anesthesia, does not require hospitalization and you can return to work and resume your daily activities within 2 weeks.

What is Body Lift?

Body Lift or Total Body Lift is a Cosmetic and Plastic Surgery procedure performed to reshape your body to it's natural curves and contours. Body Lift is a surgical procedure where the loose and hanging skin of the entire body is tightened and implants are inserted, all in one procedure. Body Lift basically reshapes the breasts, chest, arms, thighs, hips, back, waist, abdomen and knees after losing weight (for example those people who lose lot of weight after undergoing weight loss surgeries like Gastric Bypass, Laparoscopic Gastric Bypass, Gastric Banding), aging and multiple pregnancies. Body Lift can be:

Central Body Lift

This procedure is also called Belt Lipectomy. In Central Body Lift, excess skin and fatty tissue is removed circumferentially from the belly, hips, back, buttocks, and outer thighs.

Lower Body Lift

Lower Body Lift is performed to shape buttocks and thighs by removing excess skin and fat from these areas.

Body Lift can be combined with other Cosmetic and Plastic Surgery procedures like Liposuction, Power Assisted Liposculpture (PAL), Tummy Tuck, Thigh Lift, Arm Lift, Breast Reduction, Breast Augmentation, and Breast Lift. Skin Grafting may also be performed in places of the body where needed. These procedures not only remove excess skin and fat, they also improve the unsightly stretch marks and create an uplifted, shapely, youthful and fuller appearance.

If you have lost large amounts of weight (50-300 lbs.) and have loose, hanging skin on your face, breasts, back, belly and thighs, or if you want to lose weight (especially if you suffer from central obesity) that is resistant to diet and exercise, if you have folds of loose, hanging skin due to aging or multiple pregnancies that might pose a danger of cellulitis or abscess, then you are an ideal candidate for Body Lift. This procedure can either be performed in isolation or in combination with other body contouring and weight loss procedures like Liposuction, Tummy Tuck, etc. If you are severely obese, are a smoker or an alcoholic or do not have a stable mental state to undergo a major surgical procedure and follow post-operative instructions to obtain optimum benefit or if you are allergic to the medication used for general anesthesia, then you are not an ideal candidate for Body Lift.

Body Lift is performed in a hospital setting under general anesthesia and can take about 5-7 or may be 10 hours depending on what other cosmetic surgery procedures are performed along with it. The Body Lift surgery is usually performed to remove excess skin from the belly first, i.e. from the area between the belly button and pubic hair and tightening of abdominal muscles is also performed. Excessive skin is removed, belly button is repositioned, remainder of the skin is approximated and the incision is sutured. The surgeon will then turn you on your side, make incisions in your buttock and back area, remove fat and excess skin to try and normalize the curves and contours of your sides and back. Body Lift also involves Liposuction of the buttocks, thighs and abdomen areas. Lastly your surgeon will work on the flabby arms (commonly called bat wings) and make them shapely. As mentioned above, Liposuction, Power Assisted Liposculpture (PAL), Tummy Tuck, Thigh Lift, Arm Lift, Breast Reduction, Breast Augmentation, Breast Lift and Skin Grafting can all be performed at the same time, whatever your need may be.

Body Lift is a comprehensive procedure that can take

care of flabby, bulges in different parts of your body. The best results are obtained when Body Lift is performed by skillful and experienced cosmetic surgeons. This procedure is as safe as multiple shorter cosmetic surgeries. The contours of your body will be better defined and if you commit yourself to exercising regularly and eating sensibly, chances are that the results of Body Lift will be good for the rest of your life. Body Lift is a revolutionary surgical procedure that quickly, safely and effectively re-shapes the normal contours of your body. Most people who undergo Body Lift are quite satisfied with the results. The procedure of Body Lift is unified approach to treat and skin laxity as a result of aging, pregnancy and dramatic weight loss. Body Lift is a remarkable procedure which can help you get started on the way to a new, more fulfilling life of normalcy and a level of self-esteem that you may have never imagined.

Alternatives to Body Lift

- Liposuction is commonly used in both men and women to remove localized excess fat deposits that are resistant to dieting and exercise.
- Power Assisted Liposculpture (PAL)—Power Assisted Liposculpture uses a powerized cannula which moves back and forth through the fat tissue in a rapid motion.
- Tummy tuck, also known as Abdominoplasty or Panniculectomy is a procedure where large amount of skin and fat are removed from the middle and lower part of the abdomen.
- Thigh Lift is a procedure which is performed to remove loose and excessive (hanging) skin around your thighs and buttocks, thus to tighten them and improve it's appearance and texture.
- Arm Lift—Brachioplasty or Arm Lift is a procedure where loose and excess skin are removed from your arm.
- Breast Reduction is a surgical procedure designed to remove excessive fat, glandular tissue, and skin from large and pendulous breasts, making them smaller, lighter, and firmer.

- Breast Augmentation or Breast Implant Surgery is a surgical procedure in which the size and shape of a woman's breast is enhanced by inserting an artificial breast implant behind each breast.
- Breast Lift or Mastopexy is a surgical procedure which is commonly performed in men and in women to reshape sagging or drooping breasts and to give them a firm, youthful contour.
- Skin grafting is a surgical procedure by which skin or a skin substitute is used to replace the damaged skin or provide a temporary wound covering.

Body Lift is fondly called the Face Lift of your body. The resulting body contour shows a remarkable and significant improvement in the areas of the belly, pubic region, hips, back, and buttocks and will bring you to the range of normal body contour.

What is a Breast Implant?

A breast implant is a soft shell or a rubber sac that is filled with silicone gel or saline (salt-water). The feel of the implant is very natural and close to the feel of the normal breast tissue. They are available in several different sizes to accommodate different patient's needs and surgeon's preference. The surface texture of the implant can be smooth or contoured. There are different approaches used for Breast Augmentation surgery:

(1) Infra-mammary Breast Augmentation

This is the most commonly used approach for Breast Augmentation operation. In this approach an incision is made in the crease just below the breast where the breast tissue meets the chest wall.

(2) Peri-areolar Breast Augmentation

In this approach a semi-circular incision is made around the lower part of the areola (areola is the dark area of skin surrounding the nipple).

(3) Trans-axillary or Axillary Breast Augmentation

In this approach an incision is made in the armpit to insert the breast implant.

(4) Trans-umblical or Umblical Breast Augmentation

In this approach, a breast implant is inserted through the umbilicus or belly button with the help of an endoscope.

Breast Augmentation surgery takes about 2-3 hours. Most commonly you can go home the same day or the following day. The sutures are covered with a gauze dressing to promote speedy healing. The outcome of Breast Augmentation is very satisfactory and successful. Your breasts will be enlarged for life. Clothes fit better and it certainly boosts your self confidence and self esteem. Some cases of leakage or breaking of the breast implant have been reported. In this case, a second Breast Augmentation surgery may be needed. The breast tissue is actually pushed to the surface as the breast implant is inserted behind the breast tissue. Following Breast Augmentation surgery it might become easier to perform breast self-examination to gain familiarity with your breast tissue. Of course the obvious benefit Breast Augmentation is improved look of your breasts and your overall body image remains undisputed without any doubt. Breast Lift is designed to regain you youthful look and vigor. This procedure of Cosmetic and Plastic Surgery is used world-wide by women as well as men to improve the appearance of drooping, sagging breasts. Breast Lift is performed in conjunction with Breast Augmentation to increase their size and give firmness. Breast Lift is a very popular surgery and the number of men and women undergoing Breast Lift has increased tremendously (214%) in the past five years. The beauty of Breast Lift is that it enhances your body image and maintains the normal shape of your breast as closely as possible. The operation for Breast Lift is an excellent option that reverses the changes that occur in your breast due to weight loss, pregnancy, breast feeding and aging. The goal of your plastic surgeon will be to restore the normal contour and firmness of your breasts as closely as possible. You will be extremely pleased with the results of Breast Lift surgery if you completely understand the procedure and make an informed decision but at the same time have realistic expectations.

Breast Reduction

Breast Reduction is a surgical procedure designed to remove excessive fat, glandular tissue, and skin from large and pendulous breasts, making them smaller, lighter, and firmer. During Breast Reduction, the size of the areola is also reduced in proportion to the breast size. Breast Reduction is also performed in men for the correction of Gynecomastia. Breast Reduction surgery is performed to alleviate both your physical and psychological problems due to large breasts. Physical problems include upper back and neck pain and discomfort, deep and sore indentations on the shoulder from bra straps, rashes on the under surface of the breast due to sweat and moisture and difficulty finding clothes or bra that fit you well. Psychological problems include feeling self-conscious due to large breasts. All the above reasons are definite indications for Breast Reduction surgery. Breast Reduction is also performed in men who have large breasts. Although certain health conditions and medications are known to cause male breast enlargements (Gynecomastia), there is no other known cause for this problem in men. If you are a woman who has large, pendulous breasts and are not planning on having any more children, if you have chronic headache, upper back or neck pain, then you are an ideal candidate for Breast Reduction surgery.

Benefits of breast reduction are:

- Reduction surgery not only alleviates your anxiety of being self-conscious about large, sagging breasts but it also relieves physical discomfort like chronic neck and back pain and skin rashes. Of course to say the least, Breast Reduction adds tremendously to your self-confidence and self-esteem as it enhances your body image and allows you to enjoy wearing clothes that you might have avoided to wear in the past. Breast Reduction also allows you freedom to enjoy sports and physical activities that might have been painful or uncomfortable due to bouncing of large and heavy breasts.

- You can feel the breast tissue better during Breast Self-Examination as the surrounding excessive fat surrounding the glands and ducts has been diminished.

Some other services

Tummy tuck

Tummy tuck or abdominoplasty surgery is a major surgical procedure that involves the abdominal area. The abdominal skin is trimmed and excess fat is removed. The stomach muscle is also tightened by stitching them together. The end result is a slimmer waistline. Being a major surgical operation, the recovery period can take anywhere from 6 to 12 months before you can enjoy the full benefits of a tummy tuck. A major surgery like a tummy tuck normally entails spending a few nights at the clinic or hospital so be prepared to fork out a bit more cash for a room. Once you have been discharged from the room or clinic, be prepared to budget for follow up visits to the tummy tuck specialist. The first few visits will be to remove the dressing and to check on the healing of the scar while monitoring your overall recovery progress. The doctor will also be prescribing you some medication to help you through the rest of your recovery.

Abnormal Uterine Bleeding

Heavy or irregular bleeding can disrupt your life. Having to be constantly on guard with pads can distract you at work, an evening out with friends and worse still you may feel worn out. You may wonder if this is normal and if so what is causing this. Normal menstrual cycle ranges from 24-35 days length, with an average bleeding for 2-8 days. The menstrual cycle is governed by a hormone "Estrogen" in the first half of the cycle which helps the lining of the uterus to grow. Mid-cycle hormonal surge causes the ovary to usually release an egg, which triggers the 2nd hormone called Progesterone to act on and nature the endometrium. At the end of the cycle, the hormone levels drop when there is no

Procedure	*U.S. Insurer's cost*	*U.S. Retail price*	*India*	*Thailand*	*Singapore*
Angioplasty	$25,704 to $37,128	$57,262 to $82,711	11000	13000	13000
Gastric bypass	$27,717 to $40,035	$47,988 to $69,316	11000	15000	15000
Heart bypass	$54,741 to $79,071	$122,424 to $176,835	10000	12000	20000
Heart-valve replacement (single)	$71,401 to $103,136	$159,326 to $230,138	9500	10500	13000
Hip replacement	$18,281 to $26,407	$43,780 to $63,238	9000	12000	12000
Hysterectomy	$9,591 to $13,854	$20,416 to $29,489	2900	4500	
Knee replacement	$17,627 to $25,462	$40,640 to $58,702	8500	10000	13000
Mastectomy	$9,774 to $14,118	$23,709 to $34,246	7500	9000	12400
Spinal fusion	$25,302 to $36,547	$62,778 to $90,679	5500	7000	9000

pregnancy and the lining is shed with blood, which is called Menstruation.

Executive Health Check-up

It's designed for busy professionals on the go (okay, so I'm faking it a bit) and involves several hours of all sorts of tests, and a follow-up session a few days later. It starts at 8:30 a.m., after 12 hours of fasting. The reception area looks like hotel lobby, in fact the entire place is spic n' span, with lots of natural light, potted plants, marble floors and views of the gardens.

I quickly check-in and am introduced to Mr. Singh, the hospital traffic co-ordinator. He leads me from appointment to appointment; readjusting my schedule depending on line-ups to make sure wait time is minimal.

The near-painless blood-taking is followed by a glass of glucose and the handing over of a cute and discrete little bag containing my sample containers. Then, it's off for a chest X-ray. The room looks like every other X-ray room on the planet, sterile and steely. The gowns aren't exactly award-show great, but they cover all the essential bits with more flair than usual. The radiologist cheerfully chats about Toronto doctors he's worked with as he takes snaps of my inner being.

From there, Mr. Singh takes me to my electrocardiogram test in the garden-view diagnostic centre. As she wires me up, the nurse tells me it's International Women's Day and that I should do something special with my friends. She is going to the movies later with her pals. She also administers my pulmonary function test, and cheerleads as I huff and puff, encouraging me to greater windy heights than I thought possible.

Next door is my ultrasound. Another nice gown and clean, professional room. Again the doctor has colleagues in Canada, and we commiserate about the weather as she pokes and prods.

Mr. Singh takes my lunch order and then, in quick succession, I have my bone density tested, a post-glucose blood test, a treadmill test and a meeting with a G.P. The G.P. answers all my questions with patience—so much so that

I start making up problems just to see if he'll kick me out, like my G.P. back home does. He doesn't, he just answers in a relaxed and friendly way, which is why I now know that to enails grow slower than fingernails (seems that circulation is poorer in the feet.) Time well spent, I think.

The same level of professional care holds through my next batch of appointments with the gynecologist, cardiologist, ophthalmologist and physiotherapist. Finally, a break for lunch, a nice light sandwich and juice that I eat in the garden.

Then, more appointments. The ear, nose and throat man discovers my deep (because it is several centimetres inside my head), dark (because, contrary to popular belief, there are no light bulbs in there) secret. Apparently I have slighted retracted eardrums. All the flying, probably. He prescribes some medicine, which I get for a few dollars at the hospital pharmacy. Then more tests. I barely spend any time in the waiting room, but what little I do, I end up next to a couple from Arizona who are on the same check-up circuit. They are more experienced, though.

Having been to India before, they also knew to stock up on cheap medicine, prescription glasses (she got two pairs, including prescription sunglasses, for $40 US) and to see a dentist (he is contemplating nine teeth implants for $2,000 US).

End result: seven hours of tests, half a dozen doctor appointments, a personalized diet plan, all my charts and scans to take back home, a nice lunch and a couple of slightly retracted eardrums. Total cost: $100 (US) Sitaram Bhartia, an excellent non-profit research institute, is a favourite of Indian politicians and bureaucrats, but is less well known to tourists.

Besides the above mentioned, there are several other procedures that are popular among the foreign medical tourists.

How much can you Save by your World-class Treatment in India?

The best part about treatment in India is that you enjoy world-class medical advantages at a fraction of the cost in comparison with destinations like US, Europe, Africa and the Middle East. The greatest cost savings is typically found in orthopedic/cardiac procedures (75-90% lower fees outside of the United States). If you have received quotes in the US for $10,000, you can expect the same procedure to cost between $2,500—$5,000 or less. One NRI patient, who came for consultation to the clinic of the author, said that he spent $24,000 for cataract surgery for one eye in USA. In India he paid $500 for the entire expense for similar surgery on the other eye.

If one is uninsured or under insured for medical treatment in U.S.A., the better option is to come to India. The significant cost reduction enables you purchase a round trip air ticket, recuperative holidays post-treatment in a exotic beach location in India and return home saving money. India aims to replicate the Thai model, which is still the first Asian destination for International Patients. Here are some examples of medical price savings.

Cost savings

The answer lies in the economics of healthcare in the United States and the amount of fraud and waste that is present in the US healthcare system. 80% of all healthcare dollars that go through their office cover nothing but paperwork.. As a medical tourist in another country, you

Nature of Treatment	*Approximate Cost in India ($)*	*Cost in other Major Healthcare Destination ($)*	*Approximate Waiting Periods in USA/UK (in months)*
Open heart surgery	4500	>18000	9-11
Cranio-facial surgery and skull base	4300	>13000	6-8
Neuro-surgery with hypothermia	6500	>21000	12-14
Complex spine surgery with implants	4300	>13000	9-11
Simple spine surgery	2100	>6500	9-11
Simple brain tumor:			
• Biopsy	1000	>4300	6-8
• Surgery	4300	>10000	6-8
Parkinsons			
• Lesion	2100	>6500	9-11
• DBS	17000	>26000	9-11
Hip replacement	4300	>13000	9-11

Treatment	*India (US $)*	*US (US $)*
Coronary Artery Bypass Grafting	6,600	60,000
Knee Replacement (single knee)	6,500	22,000
Rhinoplasty (nose job)	2,000	10,000
Bone Marrow Transplant	26,000	2,50,000
Root Canal Treatment	100	1000

Procedure	*United States (US $)*	*India (US $)*
Liver Transplant	3,00,000	69,000
Cataract Surgery	2,000	1,250

Dental procedure	Cost in US (US $)		Cost in India (US $)
	By General Dentist	By Top-End Dentist	By Top-End Dentist
Smile designing	--	8000	1000
Metal free bridge	--	5500	500
Dental implants	--	3500	800
Porcelain metal bridge	1800	3000	300
Procelain metal crown	600	1000	80
Tooth impactions	500	2000	100
Root canal treatment	600	1000	100
Tooth whitening	350	800	110
Tooth colored composite fillings	200	500	25
Tooth cleaning	100	300	75

eliminate these paperwork shufflers. And right there, you can save as much as 80% right off the bat. In the United States, your money is going to the insurance company and then the insurance company money is being used to pay paper shufflers. Doctors are not earning well, though they are paying huge amounts as the premia for medical indemnity insurance. The hospitals and insurance companies are earning the most. Many doctors have to close down shops due to this.

Some cost saving figures in dental treatment at a glance!

Case Study: An 87 year old US citizen who needed a mitral valve replacement turned to Madras Medical mission hospital Chennai, India as no hospital in US would touch him being a high risk patient. He had undergone a triple by-pass surgery years ago that costed him $40,000 in contrast the mitral valve surgery, a more complex and expensive surgery cost only $8,000 here in India. (The patient's damaged mitral valve was replaced with a bio-prosthetic valve whose life is said to be 15 years.) (The India Post Newspaper publication, USA; Feb. 2005)

Uninsured, Uninsurable or Underinsured: Americans

In the United States, healthcare is exorbitantly

expensive, and each year millions of Americans find themselves unable to pay for the healthcare they want or need because they are either uninsured, uninsurable or underinsured. Over 47 million Americans have no health insurance at all, and millions more are forced to forgo 'elective procedures' that do not qualify for coverage by insurers. An estimated 120 million Americans live without any form of dental insurance. A recent study describes fifty-percent of bankruptcies in 2001 as being related to medical crises*, and each year millions of Americans are forced to choose between incurring crushing debt or foregoing medical procedures.

Medical Tourism has emerged as a viable healthcare alternative for many Westerners for a variety of reasons. Furthermore, an increasing number of Western-trained physicians from the developing world have returned to their country of origin to practice. The result is that a "perfect storm" of positive factors have come together to offer real, high quality medical alternatives to Westerners faced with significant costs or waiting times at home. What may accelerate the trend is that some pioneering US corporations, swamped by rising health-care costs, are taking a serious look at medical outsourcing. Blue Ridge Paper Products of Canton, N.C., a manufacturing company, may soon offer employees outsourcing as a health-care option. The carrot? The patient would get to pocket some of the firm's substantial savings.

Americans looking to save money on medical procedures are increasingly traveling overseas for surgeries not covered by their insurance to avoid costly hospital stays in the United States. The trend is being driven by rising healthcare costs and frustrated ranks of uninsured American workers, said John Knox, a spokesman for MedSolution, a Vancouver, B.C.-based company that brokers transactions between American patients and foreign hospitals. Surgeries are cheaper in Third World countries where salaries and litigation expenses are lower.

Service providers

There are several service providers; some of them are mentioned elsewhere. One website, www.mediescapes.com

that aims to be an extensive resource for International patients needing affordable medical care in India at the same level one could expect from a "first-world" country service but with an third world prices tag!. The three main steps to complete successfully a treatment abroad are:

(a) Your medical insurance (private or governmental) or if any other, and be sure of having sufficient funds.
(b) Your medical travel itinerary.
(c) Your treatment procedure well explained itself.

Many major employers in the US are self-insured, which means they pick up the tab for much of their employees' medical care. That's why three major corporations that collectively cover 240,000 lives asked Dr. Arnold Milstein, national healthcare "thought leader" at the consultancy Mercer Health and Benefits, to assess the best places to outsource elective surgeries. Procedures in Thailand and Malaysia, he found, cost only 20% to 25% as much as comparable ones in the US; top-notch Indian hospitals sell such services at an even steeper discount. The bottom line: If more private payers sent patients abroad for uncomplicated elective surgeries, the savings could be enormous. "This has the potential of doing to the US health-care system what the Japanese auto-industry did to American carmakers," says Princeton University healthcare economist Uwe Reinhardt.

Employees who opt for India would get to take along a family member, says Darrell Douglas, vice-president of human resources, and the whole experience, including a recuperative stay at a hotel, would be covered. IndUShealth, a medical tourism start-up in Raleigh, N.C., will make all arrangements and coordinate care between US and Indian providers. The sweetener: the company will share with these intrepid employees up to 25% of savings garnered from the outsourcing.

Would people actually travel 10,000 miles for medical care just to make a few bucks? Polls commissioned by Milstein suggest that few consumers would opt for surgery abroad for incentives below $1,000. But raise the ante above $1,000, and the equation changes. Among people who have sick family members, about 45% of the underinsured or uninsured declare they would get on the plane; even 19% of those who have insurance say they're game. Above $5,000, the percentage of takers climbs to 61% and 40%, respectively.

Is the quality of care in Asian/Indian hospitals high enough? To cater to an international clientele, many private hospitals abroad are applying for accreditation (many of them successfully) from the Joint Commission International, the global arm of the institution that accredits most US hospitals.

A corresponding boom is taking place among Western agencies that funnel patients to Asia. Eight have popped up in Canada, where national healthcare can mean a yearlong wait for elective surgery. In the US several firms are aiming at the roughly 61 million people who are uninsured or underinsured. Planet Hospital's founder, "Rudy" Rupak Acharya, says his agency, which in the past seven months has sent some 200 patients abroad, got 11,000 inquiries in March alone. He has just retained Mercer to help him develop an insurance plan for the uninsured that will combine primary and emergency care in the US with surgery abroad.

Patrick Marsek, managing director of the agency MedRetreat, says his company sent 200 people abroad last year and is already processing 320 this year. He is demanding a deposit of $195 from customers because people posing as patients have been looking for information to start up their own agencies.

Why would someone travel to India and not to Thailand?

The cost difference between treatment in India and Thailand is favourable to India. Also India offers what you call a language advantage—a patient would surely prefer a country where English is widely spoken. Also, it is believed that the facilities in India are more suited for International patients.

How can you trust Indian Doctors?

Well, many highly qualified doctors have had some form of training from abroad, especially USA and UK. Indian surgeons and doctors are known for their skill and research throughout the world.

Why is India most suitable?

Indian corporate hospitals excel in cardiology and cardiothoracic surgery, joint replacement, orthopedic surgery, gastroenterology, ophthalmology, transplants and urology to name a few. The various specialties covered are Neurology, Neurosurgery, Oncology, Ophthalmology, Rheumatology, Endocrinology, ENT, Pediatrics, Pediatric Surgery, Pediatric Neurology, Urology, Nephrology, Dermatology, Dentistry, Plastic Surgery, Gynecology, Pulmonology, Psychiatry, General Medicine and General Surgery

The various facilities in India include full body pathology, comprehensive physical and gynecological examinations, dental checkup, eye checkup, diet consultation, audiometry, spirometry, stress and lifestyle management, pap smear, digital Chest X-ray, 12 lead ECG, 2D echo colour doppler, gold standard DXA bone densitometry, body fat analysis, coronary risk markers, cancer risk markers, carotid colour doppler, spiral CT scan and high strength MRI. Each test is carried out by professional M.D. physicians, and is comprehensive yet pain-free.

There is also a gamut of services ranging from General Radiography, Ultra Sonography, Mammography to high end services like Magnetic Resonance Imaging, Digital Subtraction Angiography along with intervention procedures, Nuclear Imaging. The diagnostic facilities offered in India are comprehensive to include Laboratory services, Imaging, Cardiology, Neurology and Pulmonology. The Laboratory services include biochemistry, hematology, microbiology, serology, histopathology, transfusion medicine and RIA.

All medical investigations are conducted on the latest, technologically advanced diagnostic equipment. Stringent quality assurance exercises ensure reliable and high quality test results.

Cutting-edge Vacations

In the US insurers negotiate discounts, but the uninsured pay retail rates for medical procedures. Here's how the prices of one surgical tourism agency compare. Its packages include airfare and hospital and hotel rooms, but costs can climb if there are complications.

Talks and views

Niraj Sharan: In Australia, medical tourism is a new concept. We are tying up with our hospital chains in India.

Stan Correy: And the Indians have done their research on what may attract Australians to medical tourism.

Niraj Sharan: Yes, especially the dental surgery—no doubt there's a lot of opportunities, especially as it's not covered under the insurance policy overseas, and in comparison to costs overseas it's very cheap in India.

Stan Correy: There's been a plethora of Australian media stories in recent weeks about long waiting lists in our public hospitals, higher fees in private hospitals and not enough dentists. So will the Indian corporate hospitals find a lucrative market? "In certain cases, it would make economic sense if you wanted to have a holiday and combine it, say, with having your teeth done." And with the money you save, you can pay for a little holiday afterwards. Dentistry is now a major cost for families, and most of the private insurance programs restrict you to a number of visits or a number of procedures per year.

Stan Correy: Poland and Hungary offer special cheap dental tours to other Europeans. India, Thailand, South Africa and the Caribbean also offer the joys of being an 'orthodontal tourist'.

Ian Crombie: So I got out there, met at the airport, VIP treatment, taken to a private hospital in Chennai, which is the modern name for Madras. I had a suite, which was a room with an en suite bath, choice of menu, daily newspapers, and it was like staying in a resort hotel. I got to meet Dr. Reddy; he is the founder of the Apollo Hospital Group, and he wanted to know how I'd been treated, whether I was satisfied and all that, and he took a great sort of interest. And there were other expats there at the same time, having hip replacements. There was a Kuwaiti having something done to his spine, etc. the anaesthetist was British trained, the cardiologist was British trained, and of course Dr. Vijay himself was British trained. So based on that, I thought, Why the hell not? I mean there is nothing the Apollo Group doesn't do. "The anaesthetist was British trained, the cardiologist was British trained, and of course Dr. Vijay himself was British trained. So based on that, I thought, Why the hell not?" In other words, I want competent people. It turned out

Stan Correy: Ian Crombie didn't feel lonely as he waited for surgery. There were several other non-Indian medical tourists.

Pauline Gately: Trade in services itself is not an area that's well understood, and part of the reason it's not well defined or understood, it's not like trade in other commodities. Part of the reason also that health services and health expenditure has risen is because of course of rising incomes, demographic changes, ageing populations, and the development and diffusion and uptake of new drugs and new technologies.

Stan Correy: Countries like Australia have been slower than other parts of the world to build themselves up for the potential business opportunities. As well, there's a general suspicion of Australians going to other countries for medical treatment.

Aadiyta Mattoo: If you were able to buy these services from other countries, it's not difficult to see that the ability to buy a service more cheaply outside your country than in your own country, can make you better-off.

Stan Correy: In the Gulf State of Dubai they've built a luxurious Healthcare City. Western healthcare corporations such as the Mayo Clinic, and Harvard Medical International are falling over themselves to get into this medical city.

Stan Correy: That health conference in Dubai took place last week. Dean of Surgery at the University of Sydney is Professor Andrew Coats. He's recently returned from the Middle East where he visited Dubai Healthcare City.

Andrew Coats: I think what we're seeing is very much part of the development of the Middle East; Dubai is a prime example, where we're seeing an area staking a place in the marketplace say for high quality area within the Middle East where people can get First World quality, hotels, resources, infrastructure, and health is a very major aspect of that. They have traditionally gone to the UK or the US, and the people in Dubai believe that if you set-up First World quality healthcare in Dubai, people will travel from the adjacent Middle East, and I think that's probably a fairly safe bet.

Stan Correy: So in a sense, it's not only what's happening in India or Asia, that kind of centre, or medical city, is also driving the competition in this medical area.

Andrew Coats: Yes. For some countries it will be good quality healthcare at low cost, in other countries it will be the highest quality healthcare at a higher cost, and others will offer a geographical advantage, and that's where Dubai might fit in where they can say, we can offer you a US, UK, Australian quality healthcare, but you don't have to fly eight to twelve hours to get there.

Derek Morgan: This is probably what we're now seeing as the development of a second wave in terms of medical tourism.

Stan Correy: The second global wave of medical tourism is creating new players, new companies, that are not health specialists, but facilitators, brokers between the international patient and the hospital networks.

Derek Morgan: There are two forces I think, that are external to the healthcare market, which are really contributing to this. The first I mentioned earlier on, is the relative decline of the cost of air travel across the world. And the second is the rise of the internet. "The internet enables increasingly knowledge-rich patients to seek out service providers, to make comparisons for themselves, or for specialist firms to grow up in order to broker patients and specialist services."

Stan Correy: Medical insurance and medical broking are not the same thing. A medical broker is someone who operates as a middleman who, for a fee, will act as a go-between to find the best deal for your personal needs. Medical insurance is self-explanatory, but there are very few medical insurers who will let you take your insurance cover to another country.

Leslie Smith: We then found individuals calling us, asking us for help, saying that they were on an NHS, National Health Service waiting list, couldn't get surgery and were suffering considerable pain levels.

Stan Correy: India is becoming a popular destination for Americans, and there are 47-million poor Americans who have no medical insurance at all, and who might simply die because they can't pay for treatment.

Bob Couch: And you know, you've got to remember we're retired. I mean I'm 81 you know. We're not broke, but these are big sums of money to take out of the bank, because we haven't got the income, we're just living on our savings all the time.

Stan Correy: Before his operation he had to fill in a questionnaire regarding his medical history and the normal documents that patients sign before surgery.

Leslie Smith: I'm particularly concerned always with hundreds and hundreds of patients, you're going to get things go wrong because they're under the surgical knife and anesthesia. So things will go wrong, and I just want to make sure the patients are fairly treated, they can sue properly in the appropriate country, they can be reimbursed, they can be brought home.

Stan Correy: How do you come under as a financial company?

Leslie Smith: No, we're still under the insurance regulator here for our insurance advice. But so far, the industry of facilitating patients to other hospitals around the world, without giving medical advice, there's no regulator for that as far as I'm aware in Europe at this time. I think there will be in the future.

Stan Correy: Acting as a broker for international patients is in its early days, and Leslie Smith admits that there are large regulatory issues involved. Many countries don't have the protective legal systems westerners are used to.

Derek Morgan: You've identified a difficult issue within this whole sort of boutique market that's now developing. What is the legal status? we don't really know. We're not entirely sure. Complications do arise in any potential operation that is undertaken. You can't guarantee that healthcare and the sequelae to operations are always going to run smoothly, there will always be issues about problems that arise. And how one deals with those on a patient who, let's say, has made a contract with a company or a broker in London to travel to Johannesburg for surgery, to travel on to another country for recuperative holiday and such like, and something goes wrong in the operation itself, trying to resolve these legal issues really is going to become a quite fundamental issue over the next 10 or 15 years. And of course it's going to differ from jurisdiction to jurisdiction. It may even differ from where the patient comes from.

Stan Correy: You can have a hip replacement in India, or heart surgery in Dubai, or dental work in Malaysia, but you may find it hard to get insurance, or a legal comeback if you're badly treated.

Leslie Smith: The interesting thing about Singapore and Thailand, is the involvement of state government, where they're investing millions of dollars in state-of-the-art hospitals, recognizing that the kind of health tourism from Australasia or Japan is hard currency, which is dollars. "They have all the skills there, they have huge numbers of nurses and they can do this just as good as the westerners, if not better."

Stan Correy: So let's hitch a ride on one of those big white aeroplanes, full of medical tourists from UK, Canada and the US, refugees from overstretched and expensive healthcare systems. Waiting with open arms and beds are a whole chain of new Indian healthcare corporations. The Fortis Healthcare, Max Healthcare, Wockhardt, and the largest, the Apollo Group, which is the most aggressive in promoting its business abroad. They're also lobbying the Indian government to make India more attractive for medical tourism.

Sangita Reddy: I think in any other sector some things can wait, it's not as critical. But healthcare is life. And also we come from a culture of people expecting the government to provide healthcare, as we transition from a country where the private sector is playing such an important role. It's important for the private sector and the public to work together and try and give more efficient solutions, reach people quicker, extend our reach, and there are many examples of win-win solutions when we work together.

Stan Correy: Indian corporate hospitals say business is good and they offer world class treatment. But there are critics who see medical tourism as a sick concept. In India, NGOs say the reason we're hearing so much about medical tourism is that too much money is being spent on building expensive hospitals, and that the vast majority of ordinary Indians can't afford them.

Ravi Duggall: Without regulated healthcare market insurance will find it very difficult to operate because the younger people are not insuring themselves. So you have a very small, about 2% of the population which seeks this kind of voluntary insurance, and the private sector has stayed away, the study that they did, the private insurance companies said they've gone into life insurance or other general insurance, but they have stayed away from health because they realise that the people who are insuring themselves are high risk people. So that would have been a good base for many of these elite hospitals to fill up their vacant occupancies. But that has somehow not worked. So the other option is now looking to developed countries to cater to their over-supply of patients which they can't handle.

Stan Correy: Apollo and other Indian hospital corporations have recently asked the Indian government to relax foreign investment guidelines to allow international health insurance companies to set-up in India. But insurance companies demand better government regulation of healthcare. In India, the only accreditation these relatively new groups have isn't by any health authority. Apollo, for example, is accredited by Crisil, an Indian financial and credit rating company which isn't really the same thing.

Ashok Ananthram: If you look at the Apollo Group, we are touching 60,000 cardiac surgeries to date. At a success rate of well past 95%, 98%. Now JCI *et cetera* is a tangible proof of the fact that the systems, your processes, your entire hygiene, perhaps the quality of blood, *et cetera* is at international levels. I think we need to get international accreditation to be counted amongst the world's best.

Stan Correy: And after you had the operation, what was the experience like then?

Ian Crombie: I spent a couple of weeks in Chennai. In the Taj Hotel, where I came across Warnie and Gilchrist and all the other lot about to play the second Test Match down there, and we had a great time. And during that time that I was in the hotel, every day they sent over a nurse to make sure the dressing, the stitches were OK. They also sent a physio across every day to make sure I was doing my exercises. I mean, you couldn't have asked for better care.

Stan Correy: In the Bloomberg's article, it says you paid a total of 5,000 pounds for the trip.

Ian Crombie: By the time I would have paid for my air fare, plus my hotel stay, yes, it would have come out at about 5,000 pounds.

Stan Correy: Outsourcing of IT has already given the Indian economy a huge boost, and it's no secret that India has turned around from being one of the poor countries of the world to an emerging economic power. There's talk of Indian medical care being worth billions of dollars.

Guy Ellena: I don't believe that they've established management of hospitals in such a strong way, that they can guarantee consistent quality of healthcare, a consistent quality of services around healthcare. They have fantastic doctors, no doubt, I mean OK a lot of them being trained either in India, but also trained in the US, in the UK, in Australia, and different countries. If something was to happen, or people started to be dissatisfied, because if big numbers were really to flock into India I think the system would be very much stressed.

Stan Correy: He's concerned that the Indian healthcare corporations may be over-hyping the market for medical tourists.

Guy Ellena: The private sector is not going to address the needs of the entire population, because they have private hospitals, they need to generate profits, if not OK they would close the doors. Clearly they need to sell their services to a population that can pay.

Stan Correy: Ellena's more critical perspective on the profits to be made from medical tourism comes from first-hand experience.

Guy Ellena: I'm traveling all around the world. We are financing hospitals in Latin America, in Central Europe, in Russia, in East Asia, Africa, all over the world. They all believe that they have a comparative advantage. There have been, up to 9/11, it's true, a trend where wealthy patients from the Middle East felt reluctant, or a difficulty, to be treated in the US because of getting a visa, or they didn't feel comfortable to go, and they have moved back to other places where is easier. Europe, and/or to some extent the subcontinent or Thailand. But still these are very, very small numbers.

Stan Correy: Once a trend and hype bubble gets rolling in the global economy, it's hard to stop. Everyone wants to be a healthcare hub. The surgery itself, it seems, is first class in the best places. And it's much cheaper than what you pay in the UK, the USA and Australia. But it's not only all about providing better healthcare. It's about business and commerce and trade.

Debra Lipson: Our members, along with thousands of unrepresented workers, are now being confronted with proposals to literally export themselves to have certain "expensive" medical procedures provided in India. When you're there, you give up your legal rights that you have here. You can't sue if there's malpractice. Who would send their 7-year-old child or their 80-year-old grandmother to a foreign country for surgery and you couldn't do anything if something goes wrong? Exacerbating this crisis by attempting to outsource healthcare is not only shameless; it does nothing to solve the nation's skyrocketing healthcare costs.

So America is also aware of its shortcomings and wants to improve its healthcare. If it does it may have impact on the medical tourism plans of countries across the globe.

Foreign Medical Tourists

Some Illustrative Examples

Patients pay in India a fraction of what it might cost in USA. Post-operative care may be provided at what you might think are 4 star resorts or luxury hotels. What may cost a fortune—say the standard $ 100,000 may be available for a more affordable $ 10,000 here. It all can work out even with airfare overseas and accommodation overseas to only 10-15% of the standard US healthcare costs. Such is the world of globalization.

Until recently, medical tourists were usually a very select few who chose to travel for elective surgeries such as tummy tucks and face-lifts, combining surgery with a holiday in a far away locale that ensured both privacy and a pleasant stay. Today there is a swelling rank of medical tourists comprised of ordinary citizens who seek a wide variety of healthcare services and medical care outside their home country, and every year that number grows. For some, medical tourism or international medical travel can literally be a lifesaver, enabling patients to access quality medical services that they might not otherwise be able to afford. By using the services of Medical Tourism companies, Americans would experience a seamless and carefree world-class experience in health-care in a foreign country.

In Punjab alone, more than five lakh NRIs make annual visits home. This single largest group of visitors is a big source of revenue, especially for the dental treatment and cosmetic surgery market. The cost of a tummy tuck in the UK is about £ 7000-10,000, while in India it costs approximately £ 1500. Add £ 300 (Rs. 24,000) for the round trip airfare on a Sahara flight and you have a deal!

Trickle of British patients

Four years ago the first trickle of British patients, frustrated by long NHS waiting lists and the high cost of private surgery, began to organise operations abroad. James Campbell, from Aberdeenshire, flew to Ahmedabad in 2003 for a double knee replacement at less than half the cost of private treatment in the UK, after organizing the trip and treatment himself. Now an agency such as the Taj Medical Group receives 200 inquiries a day from around the world and arranges packages for 20-40 Britons a month to have operations in India. Taj also offers follow-up appointments with a consultant in the UK. "Generally people don't see any difference in the care they receive in India from private care in the UK," says Dipa Jethwa, of the Taj group. With more Indian hospitals admitting foreign patients, it is easier for tourists to arrange their own surgery there but packages offered by agencies make organization simpler.

One foreigner laments I took my children aged 5 and 13 to a reputed hospital in Bangkok for hepatitis A vaccine. The doctor looked at my younger son and said he cannot have the vaccine because he has running nose. He gave medicines for the boy and charged me some 550 baht. Surprise of surprises, he charged 330 baht for "treating" my elder son. Just being in the cabin, the doctor charged a fee. This was ridiculous. Compare this to a bridge which I got it implanted. It cost me just a pittance at Leroy's dental clinic in Hubli, Karnataka (South India).

Howard Staab; trend setter indeed

A 53-year-old carpenter-contractor from North Carolina, was diagnosed last year with a serious heart condition. Mr. Stabb's doctor recommended surgery as soon as possible. But he had no health insurance. The cost for the surgeon, the cardiologist, the anesthesiologist, the radiologist, and the pathologist, along with the cost of a heart valve and prescription drugs, had brought the total up to a staggering $200,000—assuming no complications. Howard Staab decided to go to Dr. Trehan of Escorts Hospital in New Delhi, where the estimated cost was under $10,000, including airfare, surgery, and rehabilitation! Howard Staab said, "I was apprehensive in the beginning because I had no experience with India or about the quality of care, and the situation there. But my experience was superb. From the time we arrived at the airport, Escorts (Hospital) people escorted us to the hospital, gave us excellent care. The surgeons and all the staff were extremely professional, kind and caring. Everything went very well and I was so satisfied and impressed with the care."

Howard Staab's partner Maggie Grace, who accompanied him on his medical trip to India, is writing a book about their experience. "We want to help people in the United States know they have choices," says Mr. Staab. There will be our book coming out very soon. My partner Maggie Grace is writing it. The book title is "Patient Pilgrimage: A True Story of the First Americans Travel to India for Heart Surgery" and the website is www.howardsheart.com. Howard Staaab says one key to his trip's success was that it combined a high degree of medical excellence with a human touch.

Dr. Naresh Trehan said, "Now we do over 4,000 heart operations a year, and the mortality, which is an index of how well things are, is 0.8% which is even better than most places in the world. The other thing that we measure is infection rate. Ours is 0.3% as compared to the world average of 1%."

- 65 years okd C. Shaw from U.K. had cancer of the liver, who came to India for surgical intervention. Within 3 weeks he was operated successfully.
- Sohail, 35 years male came to India to watch cricket match, but developed kidney stone pain on the way. Indian surgeons removed his kidney stone through endoscopy and he went back hale

and hearty. 'The kind of care I received here, made me forget my pain and that I was in a foreign country'. Laproscopic/endoscopy surgery is applied routinely in India in various specialities, viz. General surgery, Paediatric surgery, Urology, Colorectal surgery.

- 64 years Robert Beeney from San Francisco came to India for joint resurfacing—not covered by his insurance. He paid $6600 in all, instead of $25000 he would have paid at home, for the surgery. After getting his surgery in a Hyderabad hospital, he was walking around Taj Mahal after 2 weeks.
- Julie lost her smile 3 year back and in trying to get it back she spent $88,888 in U.K. Finally, she came to India, spent just $3333 and within 12 days treatment from a dentist she got her smile back. That shows Indian dentistry has come of age.
- Salma chose an Indian hospital for her spinal surgery, instead of her hometown, Dubai. With surgical treatment, yoga, acupuncture and regular saunas and massages. She was on her feet again before 3 months.
- A British citizen, Cyril Parry (59), came all the way to Chennai to get himself a new hip. Ironically, the procedure that was performed on him is called Birmingham Hip Resurfacing procedure.
- Yet another British national, 47-year-old Elaine Ackrill was treated in Chennai for cancer of the cervix.
- A Canadian national, 50-year-old Arunadevi Thurairajan, who was suffering from degeneration of the cervical spine, found relief only after treatment in Chennai.
- Gregory Bates, the former power lifting champ from the UK, had chest pain while holidaying in Goa last year. He agreed to be operated at a Mumbai Hospital, rather than go back home and wait in a long queue. After undergoing coronary by-pass surgery, Bates spoke of his experience in

India, "there are hospitals here which give medical care similar to what the best hospitals in the world offer." After returning, Bates spread the message of quality healthcare and three more patients came to India for treatment from the UK.

- Azim Premji, a Tanzanian politician of Asian origin, had the option to go to UK but came to India for his coronary by-pass surgery because his friends advised him, "India is the best for heart surgery. The cost of treatment was an equally important issue. "Europe would have been at least three to four times more expensive", he says. Premji came to a Mumbai Hospital with his wife and two daughters and they were in the city for three weeks. The total cost of the family's visit, including Premji's hospital bill, was much less than what Premji would have paid for his surgery in the UK.
- Henry Mclnnes, a software engineer based in Seattle, not only had his root canal treatment done in Bangalore last year, but also enjoyed a vacation for just $4,000—the amount that he would have otherwise spent in US for his treatment.
- When Charles Keiser, a professor in New Mexico, US, decided to look for medical help for his lower back pain and stiff neck, he knew he would have to look for it abroad. The earliest he would get to even consult a specialist in the US would be at least 6 months and the waiting period for surgery another 4-5 months.
- On an NRJ doctor's recommendation Keiser flew to India in January and underwent surgery for cervical spondylosis of the neck and lumbar spondylosis of the back. Besides the sensitive expertise required for neurosurgical procedures, the total cost of the package here, including stay and travel, comes out to be less than what the surgery alone would cost in the USA and UK. After his experience in India, Kaiser says "I never believed India had expertise in neurosciences!"

Apart from the fact that the three were treated in Chennai, they are among the large number of foreign nationals who come to India, in search of medicare. Speaking to the press along with Mr. Parry, Ms. Ackrill and Ms. Thurairajan, the chairman of the Apollo Hospitals, Prathap C. Reddy, said over 95,000 international patients had undergone treatment in the chain of hospitals all over the country. "This is truly a testimony of faith in the Indian healthcare system and the country's medical talent", Dr. Reddy said.

Fairfield woman becomes a "medical tourist" in India

A fall down a hill in Palo Duro Canyon on the last day of her vacation began a journey for a Fairfield woman that would take her and her husband through almost a year of doctor visits and Internet research, and would end in a hospital in India where they became part of a trend called "medical tourism."

They climbed high atop a mountain, stopped for Sherber to take a picture of his wife, and as they began to climb back down, Mrs. Sherber slipped and fell. It wasn't a long fall, but it was enough to do quite a bit of damage to Mrs. Sherber's leg and knee.

The next morning, Mrs. Sherber had surgery at a Waco hospitalin Texas. After the surgery, where they inserted a number of pins in her knee, the doctor warned the Sherbers that the patient would need a total knee replacement "sooner, rather later." Mrs. Sherber says "the Texas Hospital estimated the surgery, with one night's stay in the hospital, at $40,000 to $50,000." This was unaffordable.

Mrs. Sherber's surgery—which didn't require total knee replacement—was done in May of this year at Wockhardt Hospital in Mumbai, India, previously known as Bombay. Estimated to cost some $40,000 at a hospital in Waco, Texas the entire trip to India, including a 24-night stay at the hospital for Mrs. Sherber and her husband, meals, laundry, sightseeing and even airline tickets, cost the couple less than $10,000 total.

And, Mrs. Sherber says, "It was the experience of all experiences." From the start, Sherber says, he investigated credentials, and found that the doctor who would be treating his wife had been educated in England. "They were all very well qualified." Before they left the US, the Sherbers had received phone calls from several of the medical professionals who answered all of their questions. "Sam and I prayed about it and a lot of others prayed for us as well, and we decided to make the trip", Mrs. Sherber says. At the airport in India, the Sherbers were met by a hospital representative who stayed with them until they were registered and comfortable in their room. The nurses, called "sisters". All spoke good English and treated Mrs. Sherber "like a queen," she says. Her physician, Dr. Malhan, examined Mrs. Sherber and ordered an "executive exam," a complete physical, to get the full picture of her health status. The surgery was a success. While she was recovering, when she could get out, someone from the hospital took the couple sightseeing, at no extra charge, and they saw the Gateway to India, the Prince of Wales Museum and one of the many temples. They also visited some of the area's markets and shopped at a mall, where Sherber bought his wife two Saris, which are the brightly colored silk wrappers Indian women fashion into a dress.

Traffic in India was wild, the Sherbers say, but they enjoyed their rides in a rickshaw, a 3 wheel contraption that weaves in and out of traffic. "It was like a bumper car," Mrs. Sherber points out. A highlight of their trip was a birthday celebration held for Mrs. Sherber by the hospital, complete with cake.

While his wife recovered, Sherber also "enjoyed" some healthcare: Three root canals, four fillings, five caps and a partial bridge, all costing some $1400. After that, the dentist and her husband took the Sherbers out to dinner. Mrs. Sherber says she shares her experience with people who now contact her on the Internet looking for information about medical tourism.

"I am telling you it was such a delightful experience, I would go again in a heart-beat," she says. "And I hope this is an eye-opener for those who need medical care but cannot afford it." Mrs. Sherber says this is a great alternative for people who have little or no medical insurance. "I think it's a shame that we are one of the richest countries in the world, but our residents have to fly for 23 hours to get affordable healthcare," she notes.

Now, Mrs. Sherber is feeling much better. She gets around well, and still hears from her doctor in India. "I feel blessed that we were given the opportunity to do this," she says. "And I recommend it to anyone."

"I completely agree with Mrs. Sherber as I have experienced this first hand myself. I was a global tourist in 2006 when I went to India to get LASIK, a laser eye surgery done (http://healthbase.wordpress.com/2007/01/14/lasik/). However, unlike Mrs. Sherber, I needed to visit only one website to do my research, get quotes, talk to surgeons as well as book my travel itinerary online. It is one of the leading providers of global medical tourism which works with only JCI certified hospitals in South and Southeast Asia", said another satisfied patient.

Eliot suffered spinal injury

One of the notable arrivals at Apollo Hospitals, New Delhi, was 14-year-old Elliot Knott. In December 2004, the boy had a fall while ice-skating and was bed-ridden due to a major spinal injury. The doctor gave him an appointment in June 2005 and then told him that his surgery could only be possible in December that year or early 2006. The family decided to come to India and within two weeks of his arrival, Elliot was walking. He rejoined school as soon as he went back to the UK.

After living with pain for nearly 15 years, Russell Cole, 62, travelled from California to Mumbai November 5 to have three joints operated—knees and right hip—at the L.H. Hiranandani Hospital. Cole, who suffered from severe arthritis, paid Rs. 6 lakh for the surgeries that would have cost him over Rs. 25 lakh in the US. Three weeks later, he was back on his feet and on the way home. "I would definitely recommend India to my friends who have been putting off orthopaedic surgeries for years because they can't afford it," Cole said. George Marshal, a retired policeman, underwent an angiography in the UK. But when he was put on an eight-month waiting list for surgery, Marshal decided to get his operation done at Wockhardt Hospital, Bangalore. The operation was conducted last year and he is doing well.

Healthcare system

Raudaschl, an Austrian who lives in Canada and earns his living as a mountain guide. Suffering from osteoarthritis in his hip, Raudaschl last year decided to undergo "hip resurfacing," a relatively new procedure that involves scraping away damaged bone and replacing it with chrome alloy. He learned he would have to wait as long as three years if he wanted to have the operation under Canada's national health plan, a delay that would have cost him his job, Raudaschl said. In the United States, the procedure would have cost $21,000, he said. So, Raudaschl flew from Calgary to Chennai, on India's east coast, where a surgeon at Apollo Hospital performed the operation for $5,000, including all hospital costs. "They picked me up at the airport, did all the hotel bookings, and the food is great, too," said Raudaschl, whose private room was equipped with Internet service, a microwave and a refrigerator. Most important, Raudaschl said the surgeon told him he would be "skiing again in a month." "Nobody ever questions the capability of an Indian doctor, because there isn't a big hospital in the United States where there isn't an Indian doctor working," he said.

Toni Wildish's world collapsed around her when a breast augmentation in Prague went wrong. With a bleeding, infected implant, doctors back home in the UK told her she could have died of septicaemia. After one implant was taken out, she arrived in India with skewed breasts. Her search for health and beauty brought her to India. The surgery and hospital stay cost her £ 1500, while in the UK it would have between £ 3500 and £ 8500. Her compatriot, Anne Marie, a mother of five, came over for a tummy tuck and liposuction of thighs and flanks. After the surgery, she plans to come back for a vacation and breast reduction.

Reproductive tourism picks up

In what is called "reproductive tourism" in India, the couples—many of them of Asian origin—find arranging for surrogate mothers in India far cheaper than the thousands of pounds they spend on fertility treatment in Britain. British patients waiting in long queues for normal operations traveling to India for speedier treatment is no longer news. But reports say that the Indian medical infrastructure is now being increasingly used by British nationals for reproductive purpose. The Guardian recently reported the case of a couple from Leicester, Ajay and Saroj Shah, who used the services of Daksha, a 31-year-old surrogate mother in Gujarat. She is loaning her womb for Rs. 150,000 ($3300).

The Shahs reportedly spent £ 60,000 on fertility treatment in Britain, with little success. The newspaper report said: "The British couple appear to be part of a flourishing trade in reproductive tourism in India, which has a more relaxed attitude towards paying women for pregnancy, a practice prohibited in many other countries. "Indian clinics report that the incidence of surrogacy has more than doubled in the past three years, with the demand driven by fertility requests from abroad and the decision by some professional women to delay trying for a family until their late 30s". The report claimed that such treatment had become big business in India and was now worth Rs. 20 billion ($450 million). "The increase in requests from abroad is partly fuelled by the relatively cheap costs. At about £ 3,000 in Britain, an IVF cycle costs five times what you might pay in India," the report said.

Neuro surgeon's delight

Dr. A.K. Singh, Director, Neurosciences, Fortis Hospital, Noida, recently operated on 62-year-old Charles Keiser, a sociology professor from New Mexico, USA, for lumbar and cervical spondylitis. An ecstatic Suzane, the professor's wife, recalls how they were made to feel special and comfortable. Six months back, when Charles found he was unable to walk after suffering from neck constriction for five years, doctors in the US suggested surgery in India. After two neuro-surgeries, which cost one-tenth in India, he and his wife were off to the vibrant Rajasthan as part of his medical package. His wife can't get over the hospital's nine-dish fare and three nurses in attendance all at the same time. The professor, who landed up practically immobile in India, wants to trek in the Himalayas on his next visit.

Kevin Miller, 45, suffered in a car accident on July 5. The second was sticker shock. The self-employed and uninsured chiropractor from Eunice, La., learned that it would cost $90,000 to get the herniated disk in his neck repaired. So, over the objections of his doctors, he turned to the Internet and made an appointment with Bumrungrad Hospital in Bangkok, the marble-floored mecca of the medical trade that—with its liveried bellhops, fountains and restaurants—resembles a grand hotel more than a clinic. There a US-trained surgeon fixed Miller's injured disk for less than $10,000. "I wouldn't hesitate to come back for another procedure," says Miller, who was recovering last week at the Westin Grande in Bangkok.

Wayne Steinard, 59, a general contractor from Winter Haven, Fla., is one of those US patients "who fall through the cracks" of the health-care system, as he says. Steinard landed at Max Healthcare's Devki Devi Heart and Vascular Institute in New Delhi with his daughter Beth Keigans to get a clogged artery cleared and a stent installed. Steinard, too rich for Medicaid and too poor for insurance, certainly didn't have the $60,000 he would have had to pay back home.

Howard Aschwald, 52, of Belvedere, said, he saved nearly $4,000 on a laser eye procedure to correct myopia that was not covered by his insurance and nearly $2,000 on a heart screening he had done in Mumbai, India. Aschwald and his wife also scored a long-awaited vacation to India, but at a cost: They paid nearly $3,000 for their combined airfare and stayed in a $185-a-night hotel.

Freelance writer Jeannine Walston, 32, of San Rafael, is planning a trip this month to Cologne, Germany, for a series of cancer treatments that have not been approved in the United States. She estimates the treatments will cost her up to $40,000.

Fernanda Wagland from Britain was traveling in India with her husband when he was hit by a stomach infection. She brought him to Apollo Hospital and describes the experience as "pleasant." She may even consider seeking treatment here in the future. "In England, we would be in the kind of multiple (bed) ward, a bit more hectic, so we are getting more exclusive treatment here. If you really wanted something special done with more care and one-to-one treatment, perhaps one could consider coming here," she said.

Insurance muddle

Insurance companies in USA and the NHS in UK do not underwrite health-care expenses incurred overseas—unless an already-insured person needs emergency-care while traveling abroad. But then Medical Tourism Companies like Panacea Overseas began to come up when finally, in 2006, Insurance and Finance Company called Union Group Programs in Boca Raton, Florida, USA, convinced 40 of their Corporate Clients to opt to send their employees overseas for surgical procedures (Newsweek International, 30th Oct. 2006). They broke the taboo! The fundamental reason to do so: save up to 80-90% of what it would cost in USA. Demand exists because:

1. In USA, Rising Health-Care Costs and commensurately rising Health-Insurance Premiums are critical today.
   - 16% of America's GDP is spent on Health-Care, in 5 years it might be 20%.
   - Millions of workers in the 18-33 years age-group do not enroll for Health-Insurance.
   - 47 million Americans have no Health-Insurance at all.
   - Another 30-to-40-million Americans have Inadequate-Health-Insurance.
   - Industry and Businesses are suffering the burden of Employees' Health-Insurance.
- 50% of Domestic bankruptcies and major Corporate Failures like Airlines and Steel industry are grim evidence of the severity and magnitude of the problem.
2. In UK and Canada, though the government delivers free-health-care, the Waiting Lists for important surgical procedures are so long that people are compelled to suffer. Immediate surgery in Private hospitals being exorbitantly expensive, they have no choice but to seek treatment overseas.

3. In Africa, medical technology has not yet reached and infrastructure not yet developed—so even money cant buy it there—and so they flock to other countries.
4. India offers the cheapest rates for all surgical procedures be they Cardiac, Spinal, Cosmetic, Orthopedic, Dental or Transplant Surgery as compared to Thailand, Malaysia and Singapore.
5. The latest technological equipment is available in India—be it a Flat-Panel Detector Cardiac CathLab system, combined Gamma Camera/CT systems, a Brain-Suite with Intra-Operative MRI, a 3-Tesla MRI-scanner or even a 64-slice CT-scanner.
6. Delhi has Apollo Hospital, Escorts Hospital (International fame; 15,000 open-heart surgeries annually with 0.8% mortality) and Max Hospital—which are already receiving patients from developed Western Countries. Artemis Hospital and MediCity in Gurgaon (near IGI Airport) will be State-of-the-Art Hospitals, planned to be ready by 2008-2009.
7. Most of the Surgeons in these hospitals are qualified and trained in the USA or UK and gained experience there too.
8. Delhi has excellent airlines connectivity with direct International Flights from New York, Newark, Chicago, Toronto, London and Manchester available almost daily.
9. Overseas patients from UK and Canada can Avoid Waiting Lists altogether. They can undergo any major surgical procedure the very next day after arrival in Delhi as long as the Pre-Anesthetic tests are acceptable.
10. JCI is the International arm of Joint Council on Accreditation of Healthcare Organizations (JCAHO), the same organization that certifies quality of health-care services in every medical establishment in the USA. JCI Accreditation is the gold-standard for Quality in health-care. Until now, Five hospitals in India have acquired JCI

Accreditation:

- Apollo Hospital, Delhi
- Apollo Hospital, Hyderabad
- Apollo Hospital, Chennai
- Wockhardt Hospital, Mumbai
- Shroff Eye Hospital, Mumbai

Now several other Indian hospitals have been given JCI accreditation including Forrtis, Mohali and Grewal Eye Institute at Chandigarh.

11. Escorts Heart Institute and Max Hospital in Delhi are not JCI Accredited but have ISO 9001-2000 ratings. Escorts Heart Institute conducts 15,000 open-heart surgery annually and has a global reputation due to amazing post-operative mortality rates of 0.8%. Max Devki Devi Heart and Vascular Institute has just started 3 years ago, but in Cardaic surgery they are getting so many international patients. Max Institute of NueroSciences has the 3rd Brain-Suite in the world, which is the ultimate in technological advancement for Brain-surgery.
12. All these hospitals look like 5-Star deluxe hotels and have services and facilities to match.

Three factors hinder the growth and usefulness of the Medical Tourism industry:

1. There is no reliable database of all those who need major surgical treatment urgently amongst the 47-million Americans who have No-Health-Insurance at all or even the 30-to-40 million Americans who have Inadequate-Health-Insurance. It is very difficult to identify and locate them and yet they would benefit the most from Medical Tourism. It is a problem for Medical Tourism companies to specifically identify the unfortunate patients in UK or Canada whose sufferings are compounded by long unbearable Waiting-Lists.
2. Health-Insurance companies in USA are reluctant to embrace the very concept of Medical Tourism.

A probable reason might be that they fear that in case something goes wrong, it would be very difficult to bring malpractice suits against the Surgeons and Hospitals in foreign lands, but it stands to reason that an individual, who can't even afford health-insurance, would rather seek life-saving and life-improving health-care first and worry about litigation later.

3. Acquiring JCI Accreditation is an expensive venture considering it is valid for limited time. A JCI accreditation would cost a hospital approximately US$ 60,000—US$ 100,000, for about 2 years. However, the industry continues to grow due to sheer necessity.

Kerala the God's own Paradise

Kerala is probably the greenest place you will ever see. The coconut palms, the red tilted houses, the innumerable lakes and beaches will remain long lasting impressions to any visitor. The colourful festivals like ONAM and VISHU, various dances like Kathakali, Kaikottikali, Mohiniyattom and Koodiyattam, martial arts like Kalaripayattu and wildlife sanctuaries are the other attractions.

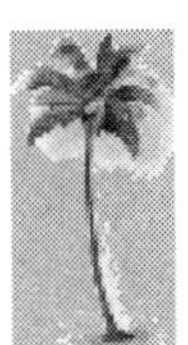

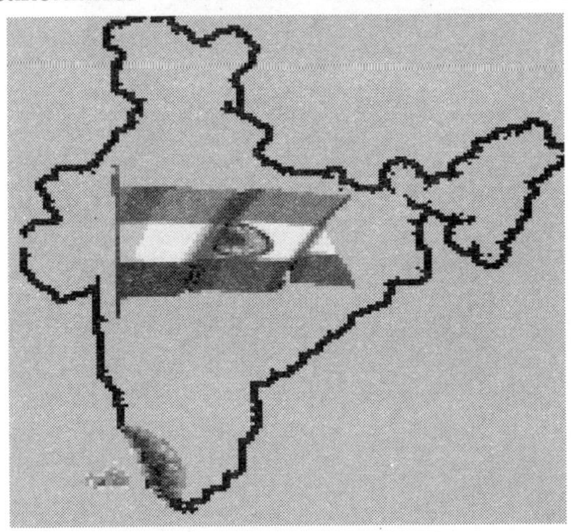

Kerala is a very attractive tourist place in India. Kerala is a narrow strip of land located on the south western edge of the Indian Subcontinent as it looks on the map. It is sandwiched between the Western Ghats mountain range on the East and the Arabian Sea on the West.

The Pioneer State

Kerala, 'God's Own Country', has pioneered health and wellness tourism in India. Kerala and Ayurveda have virtually become synonymous with each other. However, wide array of treatments and medication are also available in the other forms of medicine as well as in modern medical treatment. Ayurveda the 3000 year old system of medicine (recognized by World Health Organization as a system of alternative medicine), is becoming very popular all over the world. Estimates have shown that by 2010, Kerala could

witness a growth of more than one lakh medical tourists. The Government is aiming to make the state a global hub for medical tourism. Two million Keralites who work abroad, has huge allocation to India, which is estimated to be around Rs. 200 billion a year. The government of Kerala has come up with a new health tourism policy that promises investment opportunities for Non-Resident Keralites, which ensures steady returns in the long-run. (See Appendix 2 for more on the wellness centres in Kerala and other places in India).

Traditional form of Indian medicine

Many people from the developed world come to India for the rejuvenation promised by yoga and ayurvedic massage. Ayurveda the traditional form of Indian medicine was developed by ancient sages whose astute observations led to the development of constitutional medicine. Traditional Chinese Medicine too has similar origins. Over the past 5000 years the Ayurvedic and Chinese traditions have developed sophisticated systems of medicines.

Benefits of Ayurveda

When alternative lifestyles and stressful schedules are talking points in the cosmopolitan circuits, Ayurveda, the art of ancient Indian healing cannot be far behind. The inability of modern medicine to allay all sicknesses and diseases has made an increasing number of people turn to Ayurveda, which has a cornucopia of ancient secret cures for stubborn diseases. Along with yoga, Ayurveda is the new balm for fevered souls. It uses natural herbs and their oils to treat ailments and ensure a healthy life. Most of the centres for Ayurveda, called Ayurveda Shalas, are in Kerala on the South Coast. This is beach country as well, so bring along your sunscreens and hats. In fact many westerners have made Ayurvedic spas their annual treat, combining a relaxing holiday with cleansing for their bodies.

The Massage; Oils and herbs

Say "massage" in the context of an Asian country, and the first thoughts that come flooding in are those of the exotic massage parlours of Pattaya. But with Ayurvedic massage, be

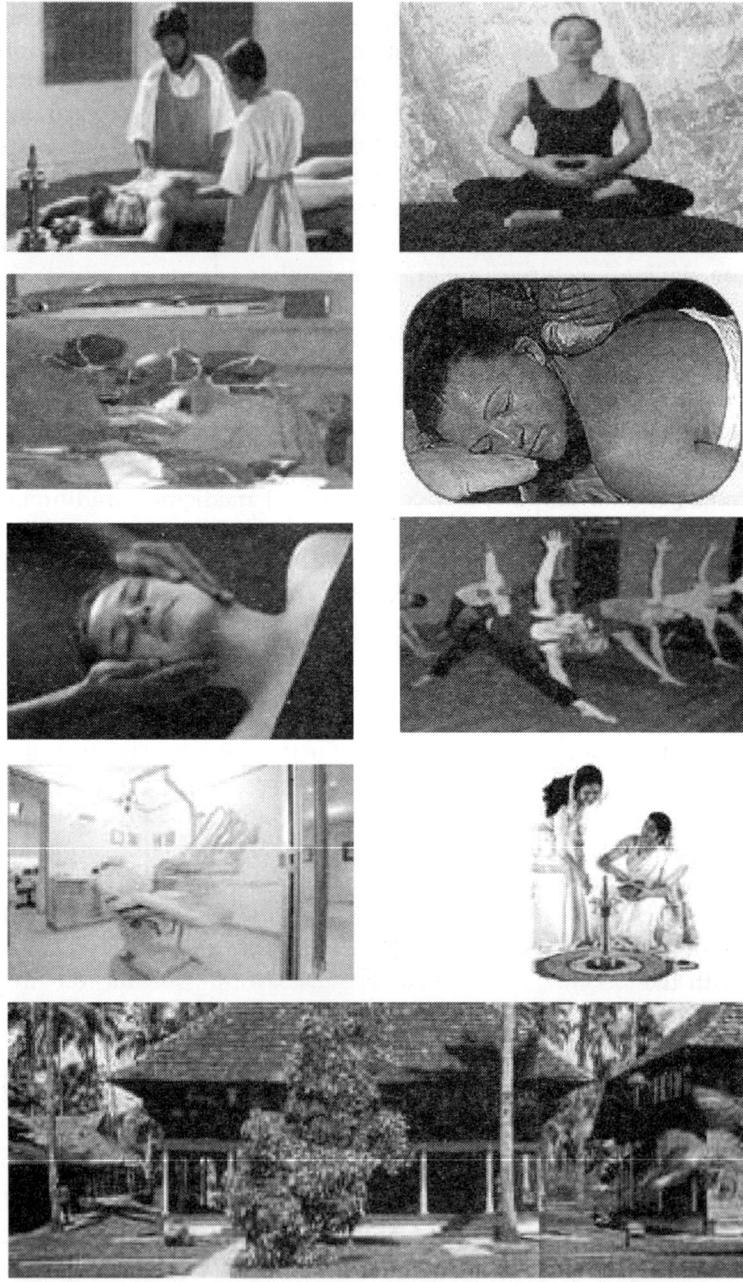

prepared to get some energetic flesh pounding from experts. While you soak in the herbs you can watch the beaches of Vizhinjam packed with boats out to sail in the sunset. From the beach you can see their lights strung out like pearls in a necklace from the coast. Look forward to being draped with pieces of linen, dipped in lukewarm herbal oils, all over the body by two to four trained therapists in a special rhythmic way. This goes on continuously for about 60 to 90 minutes per day for a period of 7 to 21 days, and is said to be an effective remedy for rheumatic diseases. It's supposed to be good for your nerves too and should pep up your overall energy levels as well. Ayurveda believes that the imbalance of fire, air and phlegm causes disease in the human body and tries to correct it majorly through cleaning and massage. Once the balance of humours is restored, the body copes better with external factors like pollution, strain and infections. The type of oil used for massage differs according to the ailment being treated. It is one of these: camphor, neem, mustard and castor. To these are added various powdered herbs, nuts and the bark of trees. The Ayurvedic practitioner may conduct the massage using the palm of the hand, poultices, and cloth.

YOGA

This ancient health and fitness practice provides both physical and mental therapy. It considers ageing as largely an artificial condition, caused mainly by autointoxication or self-poisoning. By keeping the body parts clean and well lubricated, cell deterioration can be greatly reduced. To get the maximum benefits of yoga one has to follow three main guidelines, i.e. practice of asanas, pranayama and yoga nidra. With the regular practice of asanas, we control our cholesterol level, reduce weight, normalise blood pressure and improve cardiac performance. Asanas harmonize our mental energy flow by clearing any blockages in the subtle body, leading to mental equilibrium and calmness.

Pranayama

The practice of pranayama, the correct breathing technique, helps to manipulate our energies. Most of us breathe incorrectly. Pranayama is a technique where in it re-educates our breathing process, helps to release tensions and develop a relaxed state of mind. It balances our nervous system, reduces the need for sleep and encourages creative thinking. Increasing oxygen to our brain, improves mental clarity, alertness and physical well-being. Yoga nidra performed while lying on the back in the shavasana pose, it relaxes the physiological and psychological systems. This technique completely rejuvenates the body and mind, giving a sense of wellbeing. YOGA continues to be practiced in the traditional way in India and its gentle stretching and mental concentration exercises have been proven to have a beneficial effect on the body and mind. Each posture or asana exercises some of the muscles of the body and combinations of these asanas can provide you with a complete physical and mental workout routine. Asanas such "Suryanamaskara," an invocation to the Sun god can be the ideal way to start your day. Savasana while involves meditation while lying flat on ones back, can provide relief from stress and restore a sense of calm.

The doctors are prescribing meditation as a way to lower blood pressure, improve exercise performance in people with angina, help asthmatics breathe easier, relieve insomnia and generally ease the everyday stresses of life. Meditation is a safe and simple way to balance a person's physical, emotional and mental states. The concept of meditation works on the principle that when the mind is calm and focused on the present. Neither is it reacting to memories from the past nor being preoccupied with plans for the future: two major sources of chronic stress known to impact health. There are several techniques of meditation but they all have one thing in common—focus on quietening the busy mind. The concept is not to remove stimulation but rather to direct concentration to one healing element: one sound, one word, one image, or one's breath. The simplest form of meditation is to sit quietly and focus attention on the breath. Yoga and meditation practitioners believe that there is a direct correlation between one's breath one's state of the mind. For example, when a person is anxious, frightened, agitated or distracted, the breath will tend to be shallow, rapid and uneven. On the other hand, when the mind is calm focused and composed the breath will tend to be slow, deep and regular. As one focuses one's awareness on the breath, the mind becomes absorbed in the rhythm of inhalation and exhalation. As a result, breathing will become slower and deeper, and the mind will become more tranquil and aware. This helps to gain a more calm, clear and non-reactive state of mind. Studies show that after meditation, reactions are faster, creativity greater and comprehension broader. In addition, by silencing the mind, meditation can also put one in touch with the self, allowing the body's own inner wisdom to be heard.

Abhyanga

A synchronized full body massage performed by two therapists using specific herbal oils prescribed according to the body type. Improves eyesight, promotes sleep and gives a glow to the skin.

Shirodhara

Treatment for chronic headaches, insomnia, mental tension and cases of hysteria, hallucination and insanity. Lukewarm herbal oil is poured in a continuous stream on the forehead, while a gentle massage is simultaneously given, also on the forehead, for rejuvenating and revitalizing the body and mind. It relieves stress and strain related problems, slows the aging process, improves memory, and is known to have a curative effect on paralysis and other neurological malfunctions. Herbal oils, medicated milk or buttermilk and decoctions are poured on the forehead/whole body in a special manner.

Dhara (good for diseases of the eyes, ears and skin)

Choornaswedan

A vigorous massage, with a cloth bundle containing herbal powders. Induces profuse perspiration leading to relief of neurological disorders, rheumatism, arthritis and sports injuries.

Takra Dhara

Medicated buttermilk (takra) is poured in a stream (dhara) on the forehead to calm and give relief from conditions like insomnia, depression and other stress related problems. (For those suffering from memory loss, severe headache or insanity)

Sarvanga Dhara (for both head and body)

Snehapanam

Treatment to alleviate Osteo-arthritis, leukaemia, etc.

Kashaya Vasti

This therapy is usually taken after a course of Sneha Vasti. A cleansing enema of honey, oil and herbs leads to nourishment and rebuilding of the Dhatus (body tissues), strengthens their respective functioning, restores and fortifies the body's immune system. Medicated ghee is given internally in a gradually increased quantity for specific periods.

Sirovasti

Treatment for dryness of nostrils, mouth and throat, severe headaches, facial paralysis and burning sensation in the head.

Lukewarm herbal oils are poured into a leather cap fitted on the head for specific durations as per physician's recommendation

Kaval

Holding in the mouth and gargling with medicated oil/ decoction. Is highly beneficial for ear, nose, throat disorders; improves the voice and brings a glow to the face.

Pizhichil

Treatment for spondiliosis, rheumatic diseases like arthritis, paralysis, hemiplegia, nervous weaknesses and nervous disorders. A combination of two classical Ayurvedic treatments: Snehana (oliation) and Swedana (sudation). Pizhichil is considered to be the most natural way to purify different body systems, to protect from illnesses and build up immunity for a healthy life. Lukewarm herbal oil is applied with fresh linen all over the body by trained masseurs in a rhythmic manner for a period of 1 to 11/2 hours daily for 7 to 21 days.

Udvarthanam

Treatment for diseases like hemiplegia, paralysis, obesity and certain rheumatic ailments. A deep, dry massage using herbal powders to stimulate hair follicles and tissue in order to break down the subcutaneous, stored fat. Slimming of the body is the significant effect. Therapeutic massage with herbal powders.

Marma Chikitsa

Treatment for musculo-skeletal ailments due to trauma or accidents. Treatment that works on the extremely sensitive vital points of the body (the 107 marmas).

Gandusa

Retention of medicated oil/decoration in the mouth for several minutes. Lends a radiance to the face, improves lines and wrinkles, tones the skin and assists with any kind of mouth, voice or teeth disorders while cleansing the ear, nose and throat pathways.

Nasyam

Treatment for nasal ailments. The face, shoulders and chest are massaged with specific herbal oils, inducing perspiration. The medicine is measured out in the exact doze and poured into the nostrils while inhaling. A highly effective treatment for headaches, sinusitis and migraine. Inhalation of medicated herbal preparations, decoction oils, ghee, etc. to eliminate the morbid factors from the head and neck area.

Karnapooranam

Treatment for ear ailments. Medicated oils are applied to the ear for 5 to 10 minutes daily to clean as well as treat specific ailments. Tharpanam—Preventing cataract and strengthening vision. Medicated ghee made with black gram powder, is smeared on the eyes. This has a cooling effect on irritated and stressed eyes. A treatment for the eyes effective in preventing cataract and strengthening the optic nerve.

Njavarakizhi

Treatment for wasting of muscles, rheumatism, sports injuries, pain in the joints, emaciation of the body or parts of the body and certain kinds of skin diseases. Massage with small linen bags filled with cooked Njavara rice. This procedure is highly rejuvenating, nourishing and prepares the body for the stress and strain of a busy lifestyle. The whole body is made to perspire by the external application of medicated rice packs in the form of boluses tied in muslin bags.

The ayurvedic physician will decide on a separate programme for every individual after evaluation. Short dutation treatments for minor ailments like back pain, muscular pain,, etc. with herbal steam bath, spinal bath and therapeutic massages will be provided only on the advice of the physician. Often women have female technicians for body massage and other health programmes. Some of the programmes are not suitable for the very aged, very young (under 7) infirm, heart patients and pregnant women.

Naturopathy

The nature cure movement was started in Germany by a farmer named by Vincent Priessnitz (1799-1851) but it gained momentum in India under the aegis of Mahatma Gandhi. He established a Bapu nature cure Hospital in Uruli Kanchan in Pune. Naturopathy believes that nature is the greatest healer and the body has the capacity to prevent itself from the diseases regain health. The treatment can include consultations on lifestyle and diet, recommendations of mantras medication, moxibustion (burning of herb mugwort), use of supplements and massage with specially formulated herbal oil, and occasionally, acupuncture. The practice of nature cure is based on the three principles: 1. Accumulation of morbid matter; 2. Abnormal composition of blood and lymph; and 3. Lowered vitality

The system of nature cure states that the basic cause of disease is not bacteria. Bacteria develop after the accumulation of morbid matter when a favourable atmosphere for their growth develops in the body. All diseases arise due to this morbid matter in the body, and if latitude is given for its removal, the body provides a cure. Nature cure takes into account the totality of factors responsible for diseases such as habits in living, working, sleeping, relaxing, sexual indulgence and considers the environmental factors involved, which on the whole disturbs the normal functioning of the body and leads it to a morbid, weak and toxic state. The five main modalities of treatment are air, water, heat, mud and space. The recent development of nature cure advocates the practice of drugless therapies like massage, electrotherapy, physiotherapy, acupuncture, acupressure and magneto therapy.

Other forms of complimentary and alternative medicine (CAM) are given below:

Acupuncture and Acupressure

Acupuncture is based on an ancient Chinese theory. This theory states that life force flows through human body via fourteen invisible channels regulating the mental and physical processes. The 'puncture' in the word acupuncture, refers to the insertion of tiny needles in specific points on the surface of body. The use of this therapy has been widely successful in easing withdrawal from the addiction to drugs and alcohol, and is used in many detoxification clinics in the United States. Although it has been practised for many years as a method of traditional healing. Indians have only recently started to embrace this method Acupressure deals with the human body and the flow of natural energy within the body. It is practiced with the use of only one tool, the human thumb. Pressure is applied on different pressure points on the body stimulates the corresponding glands of the body.

Gem therapy

Crystals, gems and minerals are solidified reflection of properties that are already within the human body. Gems and precious metals are used to balance planetary influences and to act directly on life forces. Having the capacity to both attract and dispel positive or negative energies, their healing properties are applied by wearing them in or having them in some way close to the body. The healing effect of gems can be experienced even by placing them in water overnight and drinking the water the next day, drinking water from vessels made of specific metals such as gold, silver or copper. Precious stones and metals are also oxidized and purified in medicines in India. Called 'bhasma', these substances go deep into the body and can help in the healing of deep-seated illness or in rejuvenation. If gems are to be used for healing they should be purified. Immersing gems in salt water for two days purifies them. There power can also be enhanced by chanting sacred mantras over them. Gems are most effective when they weigh more than two carats and are worn in contact with skin. Some of the commonly worn stones include the—

- Topaz, which is said to help overcome fear.
- A yellow Sapphire is worn to enhance energy and vitality and is generally considered good for health.
- Opal is considered to have a positive influence on the wearer, promoting friendship, compassion, creativity and understanding.
- Precious stones like Diamond Sapphires Rubies and semi-precious stones like Lapis Lazuli, Coral, Beryl and Moonstone, have their own attributes and are recommended to correct various imbalances in the body.

Aromatherapy

Aromatherapy has been around for over 6000 years. In India and other ancient civilizations of the East, plant essences were used for their fragrance to purify the air. Agarbattis and dhoop (incense sticks) are still in use as they were in ancient times in India. The modern era of aromatherapy in 1930 when the French chemist Rene Maurice Gattefosse coined the term 'aromatherapy' for the therapeutic use of essential oils.

Our sense of smell works at a subconscious level. Olfactory nerves conduct smell sensations to a part of the brain, which also regulates and controls our moods, emotions, memory and learning. Studies with 'Briar wave frequency' have shown that smelling lavender increases alpha waves, which are associated with relaxation in the back of the head. Fragrance of jasmine increases beta waves, which are associated with a more alert state in the front of the head. Aromatherapy is particularly effective for stress, anxiety, and psychosomatic induced problems, muscular and rheumatic pains, digestive disorders and gynecological problems, such as PMS, menopausal complaints and postnatal depression.

Magnet therapy

The earliest mention of the magnet being used as a healing agent is in the Atharva Veda, the ancient Indian treatise on medicine and a part of one of the four Vedas. The ancient Egyptians were also familiar with the properties of magnetic forces, as they utilized it to preserve mummies. Their legendry queen, Cleopatra was said to have worn a tiny magnet on her forehead in order to preserve her charm. Dr. Samuel Hahneman, the father of homoeopathy, was convinced of the magnet's healing powers and recommended its use. Magnetic therapy is very effective in drawing out pain and reliving stiffness.

The magnets influence the iron in the blood, thereby removing calcium, cholesterol and other deposits. It cleanses, purifies and ionizes the blood. The ionized blood flows easily, resulting in case in the activity of the heart and normalization of blood pressure. The secretion of hormones is also regulated and this improves the luster of the skin. Magnet of various shapes, sizes and strengths are used to regulate and strengthen the natural system and preserve the balance of magnetic field in the body. Two types of artificial magnets are used electromagnets and permanent magnets. For most treatments, disc-shaped magnets of medium to high potency are generally used.

Chakra therapy

Energy healing is one of the most profound and fundamental alternative therapies in the field of alternative medicine and holistic health. It employs spiritual healing methods which expand the awareness of the energy healer and uses energy, colour and light healing techniques to catalyze healing in the patient's energy field (aura and chakra system)—helping the patient break free from afflictions and limitations of body, mind and spirit. It may provide enhanced quality of life for the patient, and facilitate spiritual growth. Energy healing is often a powerful spiritual path for the practitioner, as well.

The stress of everyday life takes a toll on your physical body, but also on your energy system. Some chakras are affected more than others, creating an imbalance in your aura, or energy field. Chakra meditation is a useful way to restore balance.

Those ancient Singing Bowls, found to be spiritually attuned to each chakra, are allowed to dominate in this music, so affording the maximum stimulation to the chakra in question, i.e. it is possible to focus one's listening attention upon the bowl(s) in question in each piece whilst allowing them to convey teaching or whatever other form of spiritual communication to your Being.

REIKI

Allowing energy to flow through peoples and directing the excess energy either to our selves or to others is the essence of REIKI. 'Re' means universal and 'Ki' means vital like force. Disease according to Reiki is caused by an energy imbalance, the depletion or congestion of energy. The treatment in this system of medicine consists of correcting imbalance. Reiki is similar to pranic healing; as it also uses Prana or energy to affect a cure but the technique of Reiki vary from pranic healing. Here the healer draws the prana or energy through his or her crown (chakra), and allows the energy to flow through the hands or the chakra. The healer or therapist is the energy channel

Homoeopathy

Dr. Samnal Hahnemana sought to create a system of gentler healing. He began creating a new system using plants, minerals and animal substances, combining them into energetic compounds. The word 'Homoeopathy' is derived from two Greek words, 'homeo' meaning similar 'pathos', meaning suffering. Homoeopathy simply means treating diseases with remedies, prescribed in minute quantity, which produce symptoms similar to the disease when taken by healthy people. It is based on the natural law of healing—'Similia Similibus Curarantur' which means "like is cured by like". For example, the effects of peeling an onion are very similar to acute cold. The remedy prepared from the red onion Allium cepa is used to treat that type cold.

Homoeopathy is concerned with the treatment of the whole person as an individual. Rather than the disease alone a Homoeopathy does not concentrate his therapy on, say arthritis or bronchitis or cancer. Rather he treats the mental, emotional and physical aspects of the patients. The physician's interest is not only to alleviate the patient's present symptoms but also his long-term well-being. Homoeopathic medicines contain extremely small quantities of substance called potencies. These high dilutions not only enhance their curative properties, but also avoid undesirable side effects. Homoeopathy has been serving humanity for over two centuries and has emerged as a time-tested therapy.

Rejuvenating Programmes: Rasayana Chikitsa—Rejuvenation Therapy

Tones up the skin and rejuvenates and strengthens all the tissues so as to achieve ideal health and longevity. Increases 'Ojas' (primary vitality) and improves 'Sattva' (mental clarity) and thereby increases the resistance of the body. Includes head and face massage with medicated oils and creams, body massage with herbal oil or powder by hand and foot, internal rejuvenating medicines and medicated steam bath. Herbal baths are also used.

Kayakalpa Chikitsa—Body Immunisation and Longevity Treatment

This therapy is a prime treatment for retarding the ageing process, arresting the degeneration of body cells and immunisation of the system. Includes intake of Rasayana (special Ayurvedic medicines and diet) and comprehensive body care programmes. Most effective if undertaken before the age of 50.

Sweda Karma—Body Sudation

Medicated steam baths eliminate impurities from the body, improve the tone and complexion of the skin, reduce fat and are recommended for certain rheumatic diseases, particularly for pain. Precious herbs and herbal leaves are boiled and the steam is passed over the entire body for 10 to 20 minutes daily. Hand massage with herbal oils or herbal powder improves blood circulation and tones up the muscles.

Beauty Care

Herbal face pack, herbal oil massage, intake of herbal tea, etc. improves complexion and beautifies the body.

Mental And Physical Well Being (Meditation and Yoga) Mental and Physical exercises meant to isolate the ego from the body and mind—designed to hone your concentration, improve health and help attain peace of mind through eight stages of training: Disciplined behaviour (yama), Self-purification (niyama), Bodily postures such as the lotus position (asana), Control of breathing (pranayama), Control of the senses (pratyahara), Fixing of the mind on a chosen object (dharana), Meditation (dhyana) and Samadhi—a state of being where you experience absolute tranquillity and well-being.

Panchkarma

Panch Karma is the cornerstone of Ayurvedic treatment. While diet, lifestyle, and herbal supplements play roles in creating and maintaining health Panch Karma is the process, which gets to the root cause of the problem. There are several eliminative procedures in Panch Karma: This purification therapy aims at correcting the imbalance of the body's Doshas or bio energies (Vata, Pitta and Kapha) in order to maintain their inherent equilibrium and Ama, which forms as a result. Panchakarma therapy has three main stages: Poorvakarma, Pradhanakarma and Paschatkarma. Poorvakarma, the first stage, comprises essential preliminary procedures for preparing the body to unload stored toxins. The treatments help to loosen Ama (toxins) and move it out to the deep structures into the gastro-intestinal tract, where Panchakarma's cleaning therapies can then eliminate it.

Pradhanakarma is the second stage and includes the main cleansing therapies.

Paschatkarma is the final stage and describes the measures employed after the main treatment, such as diet, medicines and daily routine.

Vamana—therapeutic Vomiting—promotes elimination from the stomach and thoracic cavity—Administering herbal decoction to induce therapeutic vomiting. Very beneficial for Kapha imbalances such as asthma, cough, psoriasis and other skin disorders.

Virechana—puragation—promotes elimination from the small intestine—Administration of Virechak Aushdhi, a purgative, in milk or warm water. Alleviates excess Pitta in the body and helps treat dermatitis, chronic fever, heartburn and jaundice.

Vasti—therapeutic enema—works on the colon—An oil enema. The main seat of the Vata Doshi is Pakwashaya (large intestine), therefore Vasti is the main therapy for all Vata disorders such as constipation, neurological ailments, paralysis, flatulence, lower backache, gout and rheumatism

Unani

This ancient medical tradition, with its origin in the Mediterranean world was developed in the Middle East. The Unani system of medicine was founded on the principles propounded by Galen, a Greek practitioner. Unani system of medicine revolves around the fact that food is transformed by the natural warmth in the stomach into different substances. A part of these substances that are useful to the body are transported by the blood to different organs, while the waste is excreted. The main products of this process according to the Unani system were the four cardinal humours:

- Blood
- Mucus
- Yellow bile
- Black bile

These humours were combined with the four primary qualities:

- Warmth (or heat)
- Cold
- Moisture (or damp)
- Dryness

This system of medicine states that if the four humours and the four primary qualities are all in a state of mutual equilibrium, man is healthy. It is the influence of external factors such as climate, age, profession and the customs that causes a dominance of one of the four humours observed in every human body. Both rules and noblemen from the beginning of the Muslim rule, built hospitals that followed the Unani system. During the reign of Akbar, there was a mass exodus of learned men from regions where Arabian medicine was taught.

Later when the English took over, these medicine practices lay neglected and forgotten. Towards the last quarter of the nineteenth century that a national reawakening aroused the interest of a few educate Indians to this system of medicine. Today various charitable organizations colleges throughout the country promote this form of medicine.

Siddha

This system of medical practice is associated with the Tamil speaking parts of India. The term Siddha is dehived from Siddha, which means attainment of perfection. The origin of this system of medicine is associated with the desire of saints who relentlessly took efforts to attain salvation. These saints realised that a good physical body free from disease was required to attain eternal bliss. They evolved a system of medicine primarily for the healthy living and also for the elimination of disease. This traditional Tamil system was refined by Saivite saints called siddhars. It's also known as Agastya after it's famous exponent, sage Agastya.

Like all the traditional India medicines, siddha is based on body humours and other characteristics similar to those in Ayurveda. According to siddha system, the universe consists of 5 elements—earth, water, fire, air and ether that correspond to the five senses of the human body. A suitable proportion of these 5 elements in combination with each other produce a healthy person.

Mercury and sulphur play a major role in the therapeutics of this medical science and often, they are used in combination. Siddha medicine has an interesting way of categorizing drugs. On the basis of mutual interaction the drugs are called enemies or friends based on the compatibility with each other. The Siddha practitioner considers these aspects while administering the drugs. The diagnosis in Siddha is based on findings from eight aspects: pulse, eyes, voice, touch, colour, tongue, faeces, and urine.

Tibetan

Two thousand years ago the indigenous people of Tibet had a traditional medical system, which was closely connected to their native spiritual system. They use an ancient form of medicine known as Gso-wa Rig-pa or the "knowledge of Healing" whose origins are believed to be based on the teachings of the Buddha. Tibetan medicine has existed in its present form for over one thousand years. Over the several centuries, medical knowledge was incorporated from the Indian Ayurveda, the Chinese system and the Greek medical systems. In addition it also incorporated the buddhist thought. In Buddhist thought, all suffering and hence all illness, is caused by attachment, anger and ignorance, known as the "three interior poisons". The physical manifestation of the three poisons assume the form of three humours which are rlung (pronounced long), mkhris-pa and Bad-kan. In English these are generally translated as wind, bile, phlegm. When they are in harmony, they maintain well being, but when they are disturbed or out of harmony, they are the cause of illness.

- Desire corresponds to disharmony of rlung (wind). Some symptoms of that are frothy urine, a rough and dry tongue or a 'jumpy' pulse.
- Hatred corresponds to disharmony of bile. Some symptoms are presence of thick or yellowish red urine, thick yellowish fur on the tongue or a 'full' pulse.
- Ignorance causes phlegm disorders. The urine in odourless, thin whitish and the pulse is "sluggish or heavy".

Furthermore Tibetans believe that karma (the law of cause and effect) from one's previous incarnations can also be responsible for our illnesses in our present experience.

Ignorance generates other negative states of the mind such as desire, hatred, jealousy and pride, which also contribute to our suffering. Understanding one's emotions is an essential part of the Buddhist journey to full awakening and freedom from unwanted conditions or all sorts. However, since most of us have very little ability to work with our emotional energies, medicines and other remedies are required. Treatment can include consultations on lifestyle and diet, recommendations of mantras and meditation, moxibustion (burning of the herb mugwort), the use of supplements and massage with specially formulated herbal oils and occasionally, acupuncture.

Spiritual healing

India has no equal for those in search of spiritual healing wellbeing. The traditions date back millennia, the choice of location is endless; when it comes to connecting the body, mind and soul, all roads lead east. India's spiritual heritage is vast and intact. yoga is not just the physical exercise. Yoga is much more than a way of keeping physically fit and mentally calm, it's the first step on the journey to inner peace and contentment. Designed to tone, cleanse and purify the body and relax the mind, yoga is unlike any other exercise every part of the body, stretching and toning muscles and joints, and massaging internal organs. The twin technique of meditation, another crucial ingredient for health and well-being, has it's roots here, too. Across India, courses for the novice and expert alike are held in temples, meditation centres, spas, hotels and ashrams. In contrast to the Western approach to medicine, Ayurveda works to remove cause of illness, not just treat the disease, by suggesting lifestyle and nutritional guidelines to reduce the excessive dosha. Programmes are always individual, tailored to treat the person, not a physical symptom. Though Ayurveda is found across the country, its heart lies deep in the south, in Kerala, where there's plenty of choice, whatever your needs. So close your eyes, relax and cast your mind east. The spirit of India lives on.

The Art of Living

The Art of Living Foundation is the largest non-governmental volunteer based organization in the world. The Foundation's service projects, programs on yoga, meditation and stress elimination have benefited over 20 million people from all walks of life. As a Non-Governmental Organization, Art of Living Foundation works in special consultative status with the Economic and Social Council of the United Nations, participating in a variety of committees and activities relating to health, education, sustainable development and conflict resolution. Millions of people around the world have experienced physical and emotional healing from these the Art of Living programs, which help eliminate stress and create a sense of belonging. Sri Sri Ravi Shankar is the founder of the Art of Living Foundation

The Art of Living Course

Developed by H.H. Sri Sri Ravi Shankar, these courses offer simple and effective techniques for eliminating stress, resolving conflict thus improving health and living life with new joy and enthusiasm—A combination of the very best of ancient wisdom and modern science.

The Art of Living courses offer simple but effective techniques, which eliminate toxins, and stresses that accumulate in our systems over time. They are a unique way to harmonize and energize the Body, Breath, Mind, Emotions and Spirit.

The course is done in two parts.

The first part is simple exercises aimed at relaxation, rejuvenation and improved circulation. The Course incorporates practical wisdom, ancient spiritual knowledge and health practices to increase the physical, mental, and emotional well-being of an individual. The Sudarshan Kriya is a powerful technique that purifies and rejuvenates both the mind and body. It is known to have beneficial effects on the physiology, nervous system, endocrine system and the immune system.

Part two of the course is about true relaxation. It's more about practice than learning. It includes a combination of

- "Silence" takes you deeper into yourself
- "Sadhana" (Meditation), builds Energy
- "Satsang" (Group Prayer), Supports and maintains it
- "Seva" (Service), Energy is channelised into service for others

Sudarshan Kriya

The Sudarshan Kriya uses specific rhythms of breath to re-establish balance in life as it simultaneously floods the cells of the body with oxygen and energy. The Kriya links the breath to the mind-body system in a specific way, that rids the system of accumulated stress and toxins, releasing negative emotions and rejuvenating the body.

- Reduce levels of stress
- Reduce cholesterol
- Relieve anxiety and depression (mild, moderate and severe)
- Increase anti-oxidant protection
- Enhanced brain function (increased mental focus and recovery from stressful stimuli)
- Enhance health and well-being.

These simple, yet powerful breathing practices have a unique advantage over many other forms of treatment: they are free from unwanted side-effects, cut healthcare costs, and are easy to learn and practice in daily life.

Vipassana Meditation

The technique of Vipassana Meditation is taught at ten-day residential courses during which participants learn the basics of the method, and practice sufficiently to experience its beneficial results. There are no charges for the courses—not even to cover the cost of food and accommodation. All expenses are met by donations from people who, having completed a course and experienced the benefits of Vipassana, wish to give others the opportunity to also benefit.

11

Medical Tourism and Healthcare Services

Health is vital for ethical, artistic, material and spiritual development of man. Unfortunately our healthcare institutions are deficient in several ways. Poor financial allocation is one of the maladies. The sight of the country's overcrowded public hospitals, open sewers and garbage-littered streets would unsettle most foreign visitors' confidence about public sanitation standards in India. The government has to improve public health services to adequately cover the healthcare of Indian people first, following Thai Model. This entails (i) massive investment in healthcare, (ii) public-private partnership, and (iii) chain of Medicare Cities all over the country.

Private healthcare providers argue that foreigners can be sheltered from such nastiness, and that the quality of India's corporate hospitals is world-class. "In a corporate hospital, once the door is closed you could be in a hospital in America," says P.V.R.K. Prasad, Director-General of the Dr. Marri Channa Reddy Human Resource Development Institute. Vishal Bali, president of Wockhardt Hospitals, points out as proof of quality that the US private health insurers Blue Cross and Blue Shield insure so that patient's are treated at his group's hospitals in India.

In sharp contrast to the generally impoverished economical background and poor infrastructure in public hospitals, there are private healthcare centers that offer sophisticated medical services, comparable to and at times even better than those offered by developed countries. A recent market study forecasts a growth from US$ 18.7 billion to around US$ 45 billion—equivalent to 8.5 per cent of GDP by 2012.

India's healthcare industry

India's healthcare industry along with its IT and tourism sectors will helped it move into the economic renaissance. It is poised to become a major driver of economic growth as first-world patients, driven out of their own systems by high costs and crowded conditions, look for cheaper places for medical care. The Government of India provides Tourist Visa of short duration and a special Medical Tourism Visa (M) of longer duration (up to 1 year) for patients. Patient is also provided Visa (MX) for his accompanying spouse coming to India for Medical Treatment. Private healthcare units are constantly improvising their health infrastructure and attracting a regular stream of international patients by appending alluring benefits to their package.

Stark contrasts are no surprise in urban India, and in the healthcare sector, the difference between what is available (world-class techniques and service, at a price) and what the public urgently needs is no less so. In Mumbai, as in New Delhi, Chennai and Hyderabad, private sector healthcare centers are gleaming "islands of excellence", as the industry calls them, all too often surrounded by seas of medical neglect. These "islands" are quietly facilitating a revolution. When the mix is just right (support from the government in the form of incentives and tax breaks, international healthcare accreditation standards in place, breakthroughs in insurance coverage for overseas patients, and savvy promotion of India as a tourism-plus-medical tech destination) the sector is certain the numbers will fall into place. What's more, the beneficiary of such growth will be the country's desperately overburdened public health system, say industry associations such as the Confederation of Indian Industry (CII) and the Federation of Indian Chambers of Commerce and Industry (FICCI), which see medical tourism a mirror of the early years of India's info-tech growth.

Medical tourism will finance public healthcare

India's three-tier public health system—primary health centres (PHC) in villages, secondary level in district hospitals, and tertiary care hospitals in bigger cities—is increasingly unable to attend to the medical needs of the population. Government expenditure on public health infrastructure is shrinking. At present, India spends 0.9% of its gross domestic product (GDP) on healthcare, lower than the average of 2.8 per cent of GDP spent by some less developed countries. Many optimistic planners says, "Look at the possibility of the public hospitals being technologically upgraded to world-class standards with this source of income. Also, with exposure to the paid medical service market, the spirit of competition will

A WIDENING GAP: Can public healthcare catch up?

germinate in public hospitals to enhance their efficiency and service delivery levels." Such optimism apart, According to a World Bank study released in January 2004, nearly 82 per cent of all health spending in India is private.

The study also pointed to health inequities such as the poorest quintile getting only 10 per cent of subsidies, while the richest 20 quintile captures 33 per cent. Jean Dreze of the Delhi School of Economics calls it a "paradox". Bed capacities in five-star private hospitals remain under-utilised, he has observed, forcing the industry and government to promote health tourism.

Medical tourism can destabilize the public healthcare?

Many believe that a technology-centric approach to healthcare, such as that promoted by the major private hospitals, will inevitably affect the cost of care to the common man. Given the fiscal imperatives (healthcare is also an industry, after all) how does the private sector in India propose to make services accessible and affordable to the average Indian, and how does the private sector define its responsibility to public healthcare? "The role and responsibilities of the government are clearly in the areas of primary healthcare, epidemics, public health and sanitation," says S.K. Venkataraman, chief financial officer of the Apollo Hospitals Group, "whereas the private sector can cater to secondary, tertiary and quaternary care and the increasing burden of diseases due to lifestyle factors, like cancer, cardiac ailments and diabetes." Dr. Naresh Trehan, former executive director of the Escorts Heart Institute and Research Centre, says the private sector can "contribute in small but significant ways given its resource constraints". Escorts runs a rural healthcare programme under which it deputes specialists to conduct cardiology camps that examine patients free of cost, he says. Villages are "adopted" to "improve their basic levels of sanitation and health and awareness, which goes a long way towards improving the health index", Trehan adds. The dream of a million medical tourists, establishing India's status as a health hub and boosting an industry to growth rates rivalling that of info-tech, is seen as within reach by the private sector.

Confidence-inspiring performance

In the last two years, international news coverage of India's major private hospitals—Apollo, Asian Heart Institute, Escorts, Fortis, Hinduja, Max Healthcare, Wockhardt and Woodlands among them—has been upbeat and confidence-inspiring. At home, however, the question increasingly being asked by public health practitioners is: how will this affect the country's health indices? Thailand is currently the Asian leader both in number of foreign patients and revenue. Malaysia and Singapore too have set in motion aggressive plans, with ambitious targets, for the years 2010-12, which is also seen as a defining period by CII and the Indian Healthcare Federation (IHCF), an association of about 60 hospitals. Now, private healthcare groups are lobbying for the adoption of measures they say will encourage growth—some of these are tax allowances for rural doctors, relaxations in the norms for setting up medical colleges, and relaxation in indirect taxes on purchase of equipment, medicines, medical consumables and devices. S.K. Venkataraman emphasises that the industry urgently needs infrastructure status "with attendant benefits like a tax holiday, concessional utilities and preferential land allotments, in order to create an enabling environment for the healthy growth of this sector". These demands are questioned by health policy analysts. Ravi Duggal, health researcher with Mumbai's Centre for Enquiry into Health and Allied Themes, points out that private hospitals have obligations for their not-for-profit status under the Public Trust Act to provide healthcare free to the extent

of 20 per cent of their resources. "Where is the accountability of this provision?" he asks.

Dr. K.C. Ojha, financial director of the Bombay Hospital for 27 years says bluntly: "Medical tourism will not affect Indian healthcare. It will mean greater profits for the private hospital sector and creation of more jobs. Hospitals that provide for medical tourism will not create subsidized treatment for Indians." With charges for specialty services steadily rising, healthcare moves out of the reach of the common man, she adds, often propelling them into either indebtedness or to quacks. Nevertheless, Dr. Nilima Kshirsagar, dean of the King Edward Memorial Hospital in Mumbai, sees the possibility of leveraging the expertise and experience teaching hospitals have in clinical medicine and surgical skill. "With augmented infrastructure we can provide services to foreign patients and revenues earned can subsidize poor Indian patients," she says, which is a view close to that of the CII and IHCF. In any case setting up of new hospitals and increasing bed capacity is a dire necessity, respective of Medical Tourism Promotion.

International patients look for World-class care

Chennai's Frontier Lifeline Hospital (Dr. K.M. Cherian Heart Foundation) began healing the hearts of international patients on March 1, 2004. "They were treated free of cost," says Dr. Cherian. Chennai is truly the health hub of Asia. Over the course of a year, Frontier Lifeline has seen more than 200 patients from Fiji, Iraq, Kenya, Malaysia, Mauritius, Palestine, Tanzania and Uganda. In the first year of operations, Dr. Cherian says Frontier Lifeline generated $2,00,000 (or approximately Rs. 86,00,000). "If a small hospital like this can earn so much foreign exchange, imagine if we built dedicated health hubs and medical cities with all the facilities."

The St. Gregorios Cardiovascular Centre in Parumala in Alleppey district, Kerala, feels that his institution could become a holistic centre with the right kind of support. He describes it as a rural area with all the facilities of an urban hospital and just one hour from Kochi. "It's a 30-bed hospital, in one year, we have performed more than 500 angioplasties and 400 open-heart surgeries. It's set in the middle of a village by paddy fields and a river. . . . it's the kind of place that is ideal for surgery, recovery and relaxation," he says. This is accessible and affordable for the Indian people as well.

Vacation and surgery clubbed by private entrepreneurs

Eager to cash in on the trend, posh private hospitals are beginning to offer services tailored for foreign patients, such as airport pickups, Internet-equipped private rooms and package deals that combine, for example, tummy-tuck surgery with several nights in a Maharajah's palace. Some hospitals are pushing treatment regimens that augment standard medicine with yoga and other forms of traditional Indian healing. The phenomenon is another example of how India is profiting from globalization—the growing integration of world economies—just as it has already done in such other service industries as insurance and banking, which are outsourcing an ever-widening assortment of office tasks to the country. A recent study by the McKinsey estimated that India's medical tourist industry could yield as much as $2.2 billion in annual revenue by 2012. "If we do this right, we can heal the world," said Prathap C. Reddy, a physician who founded Apollo Hospitals, a 6,400-bed chain that is headquartered in the coastal city of Chennai and is one of the biggest private healthcare providers in Asia. Patients from the United States and Europe still are relatively rare—not only because of the distance they must travel but also, hospital executives acknowledge, because India continues to suffer from an image of poverty and poor hygiene that discourages many patients.

India may have problems

Medical tourism is going to result in a number of demands and changes in the areas of financing and regulations. There will be a greater push for encouraging private insurance tied to systems of accreditation of private hospitals. There is a huge concern in the developed countries about the quality of care and clinical expertise in developing countries and this will push for both insurance and regulatory regimes. The potential for earning revenues through medical tourism will become an important argument for private hospitals demanding more subsidies from the government in the long-run. In countries like India, the corporate private sector has already received considerable subsidies in the form of land, reduced import duties for medical equipment, etc. Medical tourism will only further legitimise their demands and put pressure on the government to subsidise them even more. This is worrying because the scarce resources available for public health will go into subsidising the corporate sector. It thus has serious consequences for equity and cost of services and raises a very fundamental question: why should developing countries be subsidising the healthcare of developed countries?

It is a myth that the revenues earned by these corporates will partly revert back to finance the public health sector. There is ample evidence to show that these hospitals have not honoured the conditionality for receiving government subsidies—in terms of treatment of a certain proportion of inpatients and outpatients free of cost. If anything, increased demand on private hospitals due to medical tourism may result in their expansion. If they expand then they will need more professionals, which means that they will try to woo doctors from the public sector. Even today the top specialists in corporate hospitals are senior doctors drawn from the public sector. Medical tourism is likely to further devalue and divert personnel from the public sector rather than strengthen them.

Medical tourism promotes an "internal brain drain" with more health professionals being drawn to large urban centres, and within them, to large corporate run specialty institutions.

However, the segment of patients, who take treatment in corporate hospitals needed to be attended too. If this capacity was not created, they would have further crowded the public health system and further skewing the balance of 'Demand and Supply' against the ordinary Indian patient.

12

Medical Tourism as a Distortion of Priorities

As medical tourism grows, it is attracting critics. They slam medical tourism as a gross distortion of priorities for a country failing miserably to meet the healthcare needs of its own people. About 40 per cent of Indian patients admitted to hospital have to borrow money or sell their assets to pay for medical care that public hospitals fail to provide adequately. They do not agree with the healthcare industry's argument that medical tourism will benefit Indian patients by raising standards in private hospitals. Many say they are not against people coming to India for treatment they can't get in their own countries, like complicated paediatric heart surgery or a liver transplant. "What I am against is encouraging patients from western countries looking for cheap treatment. Healthcare is different from buying and selling goods. It should not be treated as a commodity. Medical tourism of this kind will distort prices in the private sector and make doctors even greedier than they are. Market forces will be in favour of selling to western patients, and the priorities will be: first western patients, then rich Indians and finally poor patients." Where will the poor go?

"Eighty per cent of Indian patients are dependent on

private doctors and hospitals. Medical tourism will result in Indians competing for treatment with people whose incomes are 30 times higher. We must substantially and visibly improve access to state health services before we go in for medical tourism. Thailand first created its medical infrastructure and then went for medical tourism. "If you go to a public hospital in Thailand, the quality of care is the same as in private hospitals, minus the frills. The poorest of the poor can avail of it. . . . medical tourism is a form of export. Will you export wheat when there is a severe shortage of wheat in India?"

Can the cost of treatment come down for poor patients?

Hospitals say there is little reason to fear medical tourism. "Costs will come down," Anupam Verma, a Director of the Hinduja Hospitals, Mumbai, told Asia Times Online. "A ballpark figure of 500 to 700 medical tourists daily use facilities in Mumbai. But since most big hospitals here are run by non-profit charitable trusts, medical tourism will feed infrastructure." Domestic patients will not run out of hospital beds, assures Verma. "Currently, 30% capacity of private hospitals is not utilized, and this can be offered to medical tourists." Wockhardt's, Dr. Nazareth belives, a large inflow of foreign tourists will not affect local patients. "Our primary concern now is working out a strong accreditation system for hospitals to ensure uniform, quality standards of service with a transparent fee structure," he says.

A lack of accreditation is a major roadblock in drawing patients from abroad, however, most corporate hospitals are already in the process of upgradation and accreditation. Rating agencies like Crisil and other Indian Credit Rating Agency have graded a few hospitals for setting standards, but certification also needs to come from international agencies like the Joint Commission on Accreditation of International Standards. While accreditation from an international body such as the Joint Commission International facilitates better response from Europe and the US, recognition from the National Health Services ensures international standards in terms of patient care, quality improvement and patient safety.

In south India, the Tamil Nadu Tourism Development Corporation (TTDC) and Apollo Hospitals cut a deal giving TTDC tourists a 15% discount for healthcare check-ups in any Apollo center in India.

Problems with medical tourism

- Government, insurance company, and sometimes—extended medical insurance, often do not offer cashless facility or do not pay for the medical procedure at all, meaning the patient has to pay cash.
- There is little follow-up care. The patient usually is in hospital for only a few days, and then goes on the vacation portion of the trip or returns home. Complications, side effects and post-operative care are then the responsibility of the medical care system in the patients' home country.
- Most of the countries that offer medical tourism have weak malpractice laws, so the patient has little recourse to local courts or medical boards if something goes wrong.
- There are growing accusations that profitable, private-sector medical tourism is drawing medical resources and personnel away from the local population.

Unethical practices

"Transplant tourism" is on the rise because organ donations are not keeping up with growing demand, especially for kidneys, the World Health Organization (WHO) said on Friday. The United Nations agency said it was concerned about a rise in cases where people in countries such as India, Pakistan, Egypt and the Philippines were persuaded to sell their body parts to outsiders, mostly through a broker. The practice has increased over the past decade. Transplantation is increasingly regarded as the best solution to end-stage organ failure. Medical advances in transplantation surgery have resulted in surging demand from those needing new kidneys, livers, hearts, corneas and bone marrow. Long waiting lists for organs from cadavers have caused frustrated patients to look overseas for new sources. "The wealthy, in search of their own survival, will sometimes seek organs from the poor". WHO has recommended stricter organ donation and transplantation rules to confront the practice. Many of those who sell their organs and tissues do not receive adequate follow-up medical care, increasing their health risks.

Farhat Moazam of the Sindh Institute of Urology and Transplantation in Karachi, Pakistan, said increasing numbers were travelling to her country to buy kidneys. "There are villages that are in the poorer parts of Pakistan whereas many as 40 to 50 percent of the population of the village we know only has one kidney," Moazam told the briefing. She said donors are often promised as much as 150,000 rupees ($2,500) for an organ but may only get a fraction of that after brokers' fees and associated medical costs are paid. It is possible for healthy individuals to donate organs and tissues which they can live without, such as one kidney, part of the liver, blood or bone marrow. Situation in India is no better than Pakistan.

Opportunities in Healthcare

The striking feature about the Indian Healthcare sector is that it has the potential to grow at a much faster rate in the foreseeable future and shall present new 'sectors of opportunity' within healthcare, which shall emerge as growth drivers. The key areas of opportunity within the Indian Healthcare are:

- Medical Infrastructure
- Telemedicine
- Medical Equipment
- Medical Textiles
- Health Insurance
- Clinical Trials
- Health Services Outsourcing
- Medical Value Travel
- Training and Education

Hospital beds

Medical infrastructure forms the largest portion of the healthcare pie. As per our analysis the current (2006) bed per thousand population ratio for India stands at 1.03 as against an average 4.3 of comparable countries like China, Korea and Thailand (2002 data). Our analysis points out that in spite of the phenomenal growth in the healthcare infrastructure, we are likely to reach a bed to thousand-population ratio of 1.85 and in a best-case scenario, a ratio of 2 by 2012. Beds in excess of 1 million need to be added to reach a ratio of 1.85 per thousand. Out of the total about 896,500 beds will be added by the private sector with a total investment of 69.7 Billion US$ (Rs. 222,000 crores) over the next six years. However, the gains are commensurate in this capital-intensive industry, since the revenues generated by private hospitals in the year 2012 will be to the tune of US$ 35.9 Billion (Rs. 161,440 crores) growing at a CAGR of 15%. Despite this investment, the bed to thousand population ratio would be far from comparison with other similar developing countries. (*Source*: Ernst and Young Analysis: Cumulative Investments)

Telemedicine is another exciting opportunity, which allows even the interiors to access quality healthcare and at the same time, according to the model proposed by us, significantly improves the productivity of medical personnel. In a country of over 1.1 Billion people, the Healthcare system will have to innovate to double the utilization of its existing resources just to reach a stage at which comparable developing countries were in 2002. Telemedicine in our opinion is one such innovative technology, if used effectively it can double utilization of scarce human resources. We believe that it is difficult to make standalone telemedicine models feasible but if telemedicine models are integrated in a Healthcare model, such models can become viable. One important reason is that Telemedicine shall increase the patient base, which in turn will increase occupancy rates of hospitals in the integrated telemedicine model.

Acute shortage of trained personnel

The biggest challenge for the healthcare industry today is an acute shortage of trained personnel, ranging from doctors, nurses, technicians and even healthcare administrators. We foresee a shortfall of over 450,000 doctors in the year 2012. Such challenges present an opportunity for both domestic and foreign players in the form of 'training and education'. Our analysis shows the foreign players can enter the market to take a two-fold advantage. One, they also get a piece of the booming education sector and two, they can source some of the talent for their own countries as human resources shortage in healthcare will be a global phenomenon. Not only the numbers, the paucity of highly trained manpower and the medical teachers/trainers is even greater.

Medical equipment

Medical equipment forms another promising opportunity within healthcare. The analysis peg the medical equipment industry at US$ 2.17 billion (Rs. 9,790 crore) in 2006 growing at 15% per year and will reach US$ 4.97 billion (Rs. 22,396 crore) by 2012. Currently over 65% of the medical equipments are imported and thus is a key area for forging partnerships across borders. Engineering excellence, cost-effective labour, increasing emphasis on intellectual property rights and most importantly a fast growing domestic market makes India an ideal manufacturing base.

Another such important industry is medical textiles, which shall almost double to a US$ 753 Million (Rs. 3,388 crore) industry by 2012 from the current US$ 405 Million (Rs. 1822 crore). Medical value travel has finally come of age and is poised to grow at 22% annually. With hospitals moving in for quality accreditations like JCI, NABH and ISO and tie-ups between insurance players and hospitals, this sector has the potential to be a latent growth driver. A percentage of high end beds will provide treatment to medical tourists and the estimated value of the industry will reach US$ 1.48 billion (Rs. 6,678 crore) by 2012 from its current size of US$ 450 Million (Rs. 2025 crore).

Health insurance has the potential to show fantastic top line growth. Premiums grew 133% for private players and for the overall industry premiums grew at 47% in Q1 of 2006. The Health insurance sector will grow to US$ 3.8 billion (Rs. 17,100 crore) in collected premiums by 2012 as compared to US$ 711 Million (Rs. 3,199 crore) in 2006.

Clinical trials has the potential of becoming a US$ 1 billion (Rs. 4,500 crore) industry by 2010, even though the advantages of trials in India is well known, the industry needs a boost in terms of effective government policies and active interest by the government including effective utilization of established government infrastructure.

The Health services outsourcing sector has real potential as most of the key components needed for success are present in India. Plus India has demonstrated potential in outsourcing. As per our analysis the total size of the industry is set to grow to US$ 7.4 Billion (Rs. 33,300 crore) by 2012 growing at 11% per year.

The analysis points towards the need for stronger partnerships in healthcare, between the government and private sector. Even a realistic targets of 1.85 beds per thousand population by 2012 needs an investment of US$ 77.9 Billion, the government and private players need to focus on their core competencies/responsibilities and work together to reduce inefficiencies and complement each others effort.

Reservations

The main concern is that it might distort our priorities.

Just look at our flight attendants and the way they smile and kowtow to foreign flyers. Bring that kind of discrimination into our entire healthcare system and you can imagine what could happen.

If quality is not maintained, our medical tourism program could be shot down even before it takes-off. All you need is a few well-publicized complaints of botched medical procedures from the visitors and we're finished.

A foreign patient may be totally pleased with the medical services, but if he or she is mugged while out on a shopping trip or overcharged at some tourist trap, then they're likely to discourage friends from coming here. But if we get our priorities right, medical tourism could help somewhat to serve the needs of natives, with revenues derived from it going back into improving equipment and services and, in a sense, subsidizing costs for Indian patients.

Appendix I

LIST OF SELECTED HOSPITALS

(Compiled by Ministry of Tourism, Government of India for its Brochure on Health Tourism)

Cardiology and Cardiac Surgery

Apollo Hospitals Enterprise Ltd.
Ali Towers, Ground Floor
No. 55, Greams Road
Chennai-600 006
Tel: 044-28291696/28294265
Fax: 044-28291407/28295706
www.apollohospital.com

ASIAN Heart Institute
G/N Block, Opp. ICICI Towers
Bandra-Kurla Complex
Bandra (East)
Mumbai-400 051 (India)
Tel: 022-56986666/26542088/56986585
Fax: 022-56986639/56986506
www.ahirc.com

B.M. Birla Heart Research Centre
1/1, National Library Avenue
Kolkata-700 027 (India)
Tel: 033-24567777/24567890
Fax: 033-24567000
www.birlaheart.com

Batra Hospital and Medical Research Centre (Also for Ortho)
1, Tughlakabad Institutional Area
Mehrauli Badarpur Road
New Delhi-110 062 (India)
Tel: 011-26057284
Fax: 011-26057284/29957661
www.batrahospitaldelhi.org

Breach Candy Hospital Trust (Also for Ortho)
60-A, Bhulabhai Desai Road
Mumbai-400 026 (India)
Tel: 022-23671888/23672888/23667555
Fax: 022-23680750/23672666
www.breachcandyhospital.org

Care Hospital
Road No.1, Banjara Hills
Hyderabad-500034 (India)
Tel: 040-55668888/23372424
Fax: 040-23327025/55625003
www.carehospitals.com

Escorts Heart Institute and Research Centre
Okhla Road
New Friends Colony
New Delhi-110 025 (India)
Tel: 011-26825000/26825001
Fax: 26825012/26825013
www.ehirc.com

Fortis Healthcare Ltd
Sector-62, Phase VIII

Mohali (Chandigarh)-160062 (Punjab) (India)
Tel: 0172-5096222
Fax: 0172-5096221
www.fortishealthcare.com

GNRC Heart Institute (Also for Ortho)
Institute of Critical Care Dispur
Guwahati-781006 (India)
Tel: 0361-2227700-04
Fax: 0361-2227711/2227715

G. Kuppuswamy Naidu Memorial Hospital (Also for Ortho)
Post Box No. 6327
Pappanaickenpalayam
Coimbatore-641 037 (India)
Tel: 0422-2213501-07/2211000
Fax: 0422-2213509
www.gknmhospital.org

Jaslok Hospital and Research Centre (Also for Ortho)
15, Dr. G. Deshmukh Marg
Mumbai-400 026 (India)
Tel: 022-56573333/56573313/56573321
Fax: 022-24950508/23520508
www.jaslokhospital.net

Kerala Institute of Medical Sciences (KIMS) (Also for Ortho)
Anamukham, Post Box No. 1, Anayara P.O.
Kumarapuram Poonthi Road
Thiruvananthapuram-695 029 (Kerala)
Tel: 0471-2447575/2447676/: 98470-67687/98470-64166
Fax: 0471-2557169/2446535
www.kimskerala.com

K.G. Hospital and Post-Graduate Medical Institute (Also for Ortho)
No.5, Government Arts College Road
Coimbatore-641 018
Tel: 0422-2212121-29/2218001-09 Fax: 0422-2211212
www.kghospital.org

Kovai Medical Center and Hospital Limited
P.B. No. 3209, Avanashi Road
Coimbatore-641 014 (Tamil Nadu) (India)
Tel: 0422-2627781/2627784-90
Fax: 0422-2627782
www.kmchonline.com
Lilavati Hospital and Research Centre (Also for Ortho)
A-791, Bandra Reclamation
Bandra (West)
Mumbai-400 050 (India)
Tel: 022-26438281/26455891/26421111/26552222
Fax: 022-26451809/26407655
www.lilavatihospital.com

Max Devki Devi Heart and Vascular Institute
2 Press Enclave Road, Saket
New Delhi-110017 (India)
Tel: 011-26515858
Fax: 011-26565060
www.maxhealthcare.com

Manipal Hospital (Also for Ortho)
98, Rustam Baugh
Airport Road
Bangalore-560 017 (India)
Tel: 080-25266646/25268901/25202269/25202271
www.manipalhospital.org

Mallya Hospital (Also for Ortho)
No. 2, Vittal Mallya Road,
Bangalore-560001 (India)
Tel: 080-22277979
Fax: 080-22242326
www.mallyahospital.net

Narayana Hrudayalaya Institute of Cardiac Sciences and Health City
No. 258/A, Bommasandra Industrial Area
Anekal Taluk
Bangalore-560 099 (India)

Tel: 080-7835000-18
Fax: 080-7832648
www.hrudayalaya.com

P.D. Hinduja National Hospital and Medical Research Centre (Also for Ortho)
Veer Savarkar Marg
Mahim
Mumbai-400 016 (India)
Tel: 022-24451515/24452222/24449199/24447718-19
Fax: 022-24449151
www.hindujahospital.com

Rabindranath Tagore International Institute of Cardiac Sciences
124, Mukundpur, E P Bypass
Near Santoshpur Connector
Kolkata-700099 (India)
Tel: 033-24363000/24363401-05
Fax: 033-24264204

Ruby General Hospital Limited (Also for Ortho)
Kasba Golpark
E M Bypass
Kolkata-700 107
Tel: 033-24420291/24426091/24420857/24420887
Fax: 033-24426577
www.rubyhospital.com

Ruby Hall Clinic (Also for Ortho)
40, Sassoon Road
Post Box No. 70
Pune-411 001 (India)
Tel: 020-26123391-92/56065368
Fax: 020-26124529
www.rubyhall.com

Sir Ganga Ram Hospital (Also for Ortho)
Sir Ganga Ram Hospital Marg
Rajinder Nagar

New Delhi-110 060 (India)
Tel: 25861463/25730501/25721800
Fax: 25864754/26257816
www.sgrh.com

Sri Ramachandra Medical College and Research Institute (Also for Ortho)
No.1, Ramachandra Nagar
Porur
Chennai-600 116 (India)
Tel: 044-24768403/24765997/24761549-50/24768027-29
Fax: 044-24767008/24765995
www.srmc.edu

The Bombay Hospital Trust (Also for Ortho)
1402/03, Raheja Centre
Nariman Point
Mumbai-400 021 (India)
Tel: 022-22820240
Fax: 022-22875380/22079485
www.bombayhospital.com

Wockhardt Hospitals Limited
14, Cunningham Road
Bangalore-560 052 (India)

Wockhardt Multispeciality Hospital
Bangaghatta Road
Bangalore
Tel: 080-51994444/22281146
Fax: 080-22281149
www.wockhardthospitals.com

Woodlands Medical Centre Limited (Also for Ortho)
8/5, Alipore Road
Kolkata-700 027 (India)
Tel: 033-24567075-89
Fax: 033-24567090
www.woodlands-hosp.com

Westbank Hospital (Also for Ortho)
Andul Road
Howrah-711 109
Tel: 033-26448673/26448888/26445516
Fax: 033-26448673
www.westbankhealth.org

Orthopedics—Joint Replacement

Apollo Hospitals Group
Indraprastha Apollo Hospitals
Sarita Vihar
Delhi-Mathura Road
New Delhi-110 044
Tel: 011-26925911/26825602
Fax: 011-26823629
www.apollohospitals.com

Escorts Hospital and Research Centre Limited
Neelambata Road
Faridabad-121001 (Haryana) (India)
Tel: 0129-2416096/2416097/2426590/5009999
Fax: 0129-2416260/2426586/5009973
www.ehirc.com

Fortis Healthcare Limited
B-22, Noida-201301 (Uttar Pradesh) (India)
Tel: 0120-2400222/3945603-5
Fax: 0120-2402031
www.fortishealthcare.com

Indian Spinal Injuries Centre
Sector-C, Opp. Police Station
Vasant Kunj
New Delhi-110070 (India)
Tel: 011-26898446/26898448
Fax: 011-26898810
www.isiconline.org

Kovai Medical Center and Hospital Limited
P.B. No. 3209, Avanashi Road
Coimbatore-641 014 (Tamil Nadu) (India)
Tel: 0422-2627781/2627784-90
Fax: 0422-2627782
www.kmchonline.com

Lilavati Hospital and Research Centre
A-791, Bandra Reclamation
Bandra (West)
Mumbai-400 050 (India)
Tel: 022-26438281/26455891/26421111/26552222
Fax: 022-26451809/26407655
www.lilavatihospital.com

Rockland Hospital
B-33-34, Qutab Institutional Area
New Delhi-110 016 (India)
Tel: 011-51688752-64/51222222
Fax: 51688765
www.rocklandhospital.com

VIMHANS
No.1. Institutional Area, Nehru Nagar
New Delhi-110065 (India)
Tel: 011-26310510/26310520
Fax: 011-26919916
www.vimhans.org

Wockhardt Hospital Limited
Muland Goregaon Link Road
Mumbai-400021
Tel: 022-55994444/5594400
Fax: 022-55994242
www.wockhardthospital.com

Minimally Invasive Surgery and Therapeutic Endoscopy

Apollo Hospitals Group
58, Canal Circular Road
Kolkata-700 054 (India)
Tel: +91-33-23585211-15
Fax: +91-33-23585218/23585198
www.apollohospitals.com

Breach Candy Hospital Trust
60-A, Bhulabhai Desai Road
Mumbai-400 026 (India)
Tel: +91-22-23671888/23672888/23667555
Fax: +91-22-23680750/23672666
www.breachcandyhospital.org

Fortis Healthcare Limited
B-22, Sector-62, Noida-201 301 (Uttar Pradesh) (India)
Tel: +91-120-2400222/3945603-5
Fax: +91-120-2402031
www.fortishealthcare.com

Manipal Hospital
98, Rustam Baugh
Airport Road, Bangalore-560 017 (India)
Tel: +91-80-25266646/25268901/25202269/25202271
www.manipalhospital.org

Max Devki Devi Heart and Vascular Institute
2, Press Enclave Road
Saket, New Delhi-110 017 (India)
Tel: +91-11-26515858
Fax: +91-11-26565060

P.D. Hinduja National Hospital and Medical Research Centre
Veer Savarkar Marg
Mahim, Mumbai-400 016 (India)
Tel: +91-22-24451515/24452222/24449199/24447718-19
Fax: +91-22-24449151
www.hindujahospital.com

Sri Ramachandra Medical College and Research Institute
No. 1, Ramachandra Nagar
Porur
Chennai-600 116 (India)
Tel: +91-44-24768403/24765997/24761549-50/24768027-29
Fax: +91-44-24767008/24765995
www.srmc.edu

Tata Memorial Hospital
Dr. E. Borges Road, Parel,
Mumbai-400012 (India)
Tel: 022-24177000/24146750
Fax: 022-241469937
www.tatamemorialcentre.com

Wockhardt Hospitals
Mulund-Goregaon Link Road
Mumbai-400 078 (India)
Tel: +91-22-55994444/55994400
Fax: +91-22-55994242
www.wockhardthospitals.com

Westbank Hospital
Andul Road
Howrah-711 109 (India)
Tel: +91-33-26448673/26448888/26445516
Fax: +91-33-26448673

Oncology

Apollo Hospitals Group
Jubilee Hills
Hyderabad-500 033 (India)
Tel: +91-40-23608850/23607777
Fax: +91-40-23608050
www.apollohospitals.com

Fortis Healthcare Limited
Plot No. 7, Block 22
W.E.A. Karol Bagh

New Delhi-110 005 (India)
Tel: +91-11-25815145-7/25716781
Fax: +91-11-25745267/25815148
www.fortishealthcare.com

K.G. Hospital
No.5, Government Arts College Road
Coimbatore-641 018 (India)
Tel: +91-422-2212121-29/2218001-09
Fax: +91-422-2211212
www.kghospital.com

P.D. Hinduja National Hospital and Medical Research Centre
Veer Savarkar Marg
Mahim
Mumbai-400 016 (India)
Tel: +91-22-24451515/24452222/24449199/24447718-19
Fax: +91-22-24449151
www.hindujahospital.com

Rajiv Gandhi Cancer Institute and Research Centre
Sector-V
Rohini
New Delhi-110 085 (India)
Tel: +91-11-27051011-32
Fax: +91-11-27051037
www.rgci.org

Sir Ganga Ram Hospital
Sir Ganga Ram Hospital Marg
Rajinder Nagar
New Delhi-110 060 (India)
Tel: +91-11-25861463/25730501/25721800
Fax: +91-11-25864754/26257816
www.sgrh.com

The Bombay Hospital Trust
1402/03, Raheja Centre

Nariman Point
Mumbai-400 021 (India)
Tel: +91-22-22820240
Fax: +91-22-22875380/22079485
www.bombayhospital.com

Wockhardt Hospitals
Mulund Goregaon Link Road
Mumbai-400 078 (India)
Tel: +91-22-55994444/55994400
Fax: +91-22-55994242
www.wockhardthospitals.com

Cosmetology

The Cosmetic Surgery Institute
169, St. Andrew's Road
Opp. Macronells Roof Garden
Bandra (W)
Mumbai-400 050
Tel: 022-26405578/26456045
Fax: 022-26557990
Email: cosmodoc1@yahoo.co.in
www.csisite.com

Holistic Healthcare

Soukya International Holistic Health Centre
Soukya Road
Samethanahalli
Whitefield Road
Bangalore-560 067
Tel: 080-7945001/04
Fax: 080-7945010
www.soukya.com

Arya Vaidya Sala
Vaidyaratnam PS Varier's
Arya Vaidyasala, Kottakal
Kerala-676503 (India)

Tel: 0483-2742216-19/2742561-64
Fax: 0483-2742210/2742572
www.aryavaidyasala.com

Sir Ganga Ram Hospital
Sir Ganga Ram Hospital Marg
Rajinder Nagar
New Delhi-110 060 (India)
Tel: +91-11-25861463/25730501/25721800
Fax: +91-11-25864754/26257816
www.sgrh.com

The Bombay Hospital Trust
1402/03, Raheja Centre
Nariman Point
Mumbai-400 021 (India)
Tel: +91-22-22820240
Fax: +91-22-22875380/22079485

Sri Ramachandra Medical College and Research Institute
No.1, Ramachandra Nagar
Porur
Chennai-600 116 (India)
Tel: +91-44-24768403/24765997/24761549-50/24768027-29
Fax: +91-44-24767008/24765995
www.srmc.edu

Woodlands Medical Centre Limited
8/5, Alipore Road
Kolkata-700 027 (India)
Tel: +91-33-24567075-89
Fax: +91-33-24567090
www.woodland-hosp.com

Westbank Hospital
Andul Road
Howrah-711 109 (India)
Tel: +91-33-26448673/26448888/26445516
Fax: +91-33-26448673
www.westbankhealth.org

A LIST OF SOME OTHER HOSPITALS AND INTERNET SITES FOR MEDICAL TOURISTS

All India Institute of Medical Science—Delhi

AIIMS' contribution in the fields of medical education, research and specialized treatment is widely acknowledged.

Apollo Heart Hospital—Delhi

Have eight state-of-the-art cath labs. Plain balloon angioplasty, directional coronary arthectomy, rotablatory coronary artery stenting.

B.M. Birla Heart Research Centre

A specialized hospital dedicated exclusively to the diagnosis, treatment and research related to cardiovascular diseases. It has established itself as India's most advanced heart center.

Christian Medical College—Vellore

Occupies a prominent place among medical institutions in India and in the world as a 1,700-bed multicampus complex that is a vital, diverse, interdenominational community.

Tata Memorial Hospital

Located at Dr. Ernest Borges Marg, Parel, in the Central District of Mumbai, a short taxi ride from the local stations, the hospital has private and deluxe rooms.

Apollo Cancer Hospital Chennai

The first hospital in the country to be awarded the ISO 9002 certificate.

Indraprastha Medical Corporation

India's first corporate hospital and the third largest corporate hospital outside the USA.

Institute of Cardiovascular Diseases

Has gained a reputation for being one of the most advanced centers in the world.

Sahaj Dental Clinic

A Complete Dental Care. Offering a great oppurtunity to experience Mystic India with World Class Dental Treatment. Where you Save and Enjoy both.

Medical Tourism India

The India Health Tourism Directory.

Medical Tourism India

Healing Opportunities in India. . . . Don't forget that Medical Treatment in USA equals to A tour to India + Medical Treatment + Savings.

Inspiration Kerala

One of the leading professional Kerala tour operator and travel agent in Kerala, South India, offering Kerala tour packages, honeymoon packages, ayurveda packages, backwater cruises and also wide range of travel and tourism-related services.

Advent Medical Services

A leading medical service provider based in India with accomplished and distinguished physicians and surgeons with vast experience in medical field.

GaramChai

Medical Tourism in India.

MediTours

Medical Tourism at your service. Kerala has been described by National Geographic as one of the must see places in the world. Meditours has tied up with some of the major hospitals. . . .

Indian MediCare

Prerana Healthcare Services. A managed care service organization providing affordable and innovative services towards healthcare requirements.

Hinduja Hospital

Indian National Hospital and Medical esearch Centre.

MediEscapes India

Indian Medical Tourism operator which offers world class medical and health treatments combined with leisure holiday packages in India

Care and Cure Medi-Tours

Offers comprehensive services to facilitate ailing patients in neighbouring countries to utilize the specialized treatment being provided in the speciality hospitals in Chennai (India) for a reasonable fee.

Howard's Heart

The story of Howard Staab, 53 years old, who has to treat a flailing mitral valve in urgence and required a surgery as soon as possible to replace the mitral valve with no medical insurance. . . .

Incredible India

General Tourism Information in India.

Doctors at Distance

Quality Healthcare at Affordable Cost.

Medorama

Healthcare and Leisure in India, the Medorama way.

Randhawa Hospital

The oldest non-invasive cardiac center in North India. Hundreds of patients have avoided Heart Byepass Surgery in the last 10 years and are leading active, healthy lives!

Longfield Management

World Class Economical Healthcare.

Express Healthcare Management

India's First Newspaper for the Healthcare Business.

Dr. Agarwal Vasans Eye Hospital

One of the leading eye hospitals in Tamilnadu with state of art facilities for comprehensive eye care. Lead by world renowned Ophthalmic surgeons Dr. Amar Agarwal.

India Full Circles Tours

Health Holiday Tours.

Swagatam Tours

Medical Tours in India.

KG Hospital

Medical tourism in India.

Appendix 2

A typical Ayurvedic Center in Kerala offers following facilities to visitors planning to visit India for Medical Tourism:

1. Review of your old Medical Records and past/present medication by Doctors (preferably prior to your arrival in India) to determine the true state of your health. Modern methods are used to evaluate your Blood Reports based on Internationally accepted Standards of Optimum Values corresponding to perfect health. Consultation Cost is US $70.00 per person.
2. Root cause investigation and Root Cause diagnosis of all your chronic medical problems based on your Medical History and present symptoms.
3. Complete Detoxification and Rejuvenation of Colon, Kidneys, Liver, Lungs, Blood (preferably 4 to 8 weeks prior to your arrival in India) by means of a user friendly Do It Yourself Kits which comprises of Safe Natural Herbal/Dietary Supplements. Each Program lasts approximately 4 weeks. Cost US $ 99.00 each for Detoxification and Rejuvenation Kit respectively.
4. On your arrival in India the following is carried out:
   (a) Evaluation of your Cardiac function and Ragland Postural Measurements to determine the state of your Cardiac Health/Adrenal Function. Check up for missed Heart Beats.
   (b) Complete Body Scanning on a special Microprocessor Controlled Electronic Machine to determine—Weight, Fat Mass, Bone Mass, Hydration Level/Water Retention, Average Calorie intake and Metabolic Age of the Body.

(c) Measurement of Body pH to determine the level of acidity in your Blood.
(d) Evaluation of your present diet pattern and recommendations for any changes if required. Cost of above Consultation lasting approximately 1 hour is US $100.00 per person.

5. Next day a complete evaluation of your Health by a Comprehensive Health Check Up Program. Time required: approximately 1 day. The following Tests are conducted:
   (a) Laboratory Tests—Complete Blood Count, ESR, Urine/Stool Examination.
   (b) Tests for Diabetes—Fasting and Post Breakfast Blood Sugar.
   (c) Tests for Kidney Function—BUN, Uric Acid, Creatinine, Serum Sodium, Potassium, Chlorides and Phosphorous.
   (d) Tests for Cholesterol/Lipids—Cholesterol, HDL, Triglycerides, Ratios, LDL Cholesterol, VLDL Cholesterol, Cholesterol/HDL Cholesterol Ratio.
   (e) Tests for Liver Function—Bilirubin, SGPT (ALT), SGOT (AST), Gamma GT (GGTP), Alkaline Phosphatase, Total Proteins (Albumin and Globulin).
   (f) Special Tests—Serum Calcium, Acid Phosphatase, HBsAg.
   (g) Tests for Heart Disease—Risk Factor Review, ECG, Stress Test (Tread Mill).
   (h) Sonography—Abdominal Organs, Prostate Scan for Males, Ovaries/Uterus Scan for Females.
   (i) X-Ray Chest.
   (j) Eye Check-Up—Fundoscopy, Tonometry, Refraction Error By Opthalmologist.
   (k) Women's Check-up—Gynaecological Exam, PAP Smear Test.
   (l) Spirometry—Lung Function Test.
   (m) Dental Check-Up—Dental And Oral Cancer Check-up.

Complete Reports are available within 2 to 3 days. Cost US $ 200.00 per person.

Optional Tests which can be done simultaneously on the same day:

(a) EEG
(b) 2D Echo (Digital)
(c) Color Doppler (Digital)
(d) CT Scan
(e) Wide Open MRI
(f) PFT, Audiometry
(g) Mamography for Females
(h) PSA for Males
(i) Thyroid Free T3, Free T4, Ultrasensitive TSH
(j) HIV Test ELISA
(k) 2D Echo Color Doppler for Heart
(l) Glycosylated Hemoglobin for Diabetes

Optional Tests are at an additional cost not mentioned above.

6. Additional Blood Tests to evaluate Hormonal and Nutritional Imbalance and Heavy Metal Toxins. Time required: 1 day. Cost can vary from US $100 to US $500.00 maximum depending on the number of Blood Tests relevant and chosen as per each person's requirements and desire during Consultation. Blood sample is collected from your Hotel Room and Reports are normally available within 3 to 5 days. Heavy Metal Toxin Reports normally require 10 days.
7. Additional Blood Tests for:
   (a) Cardiac Risk Profile—US $120.00
   (Homocysteine, Lp(a), D-dimer, hsCRP, LDL, direct Apolipoproteins, A1(b)
   (b) Cardiac Injury Profile—US $140.00
   (Includes CK-MB, FABP, Glycogen Phosphorylase, Myoglobin, Troponin-l)
   (c) Diabetes Risk Profile—US $100.00
   CBC, FBS, PPBS, Cholesterol, Triglycerides, Creatinine, Electrolytes, Urine routine, Insulin antibody, Microalbumin, Insulin, C-peptide, HbA1c)

(d) Infertility Profile (Male)—US $ 100.00
(e) Infertility Profile (Female)—US $ 90.00

Can be carried out simultaneously with the above Test with no further expenditure of time. Additional Cost: as shown above.

Once all the Reports are ready and gone through by a Panel of Doctors, a further 1 hour Consultation is offered to suggest ways and means to correct and improve upon the deficiencies in these Reports in a short 8 to 12 weeks time. We also offer Root Cause Investigation, Diagnosis and Treatment for all Chronic Health Challenges. All "Mission Impossible" of Medical Science are welcome. Cost US $100.00 per hour per person.

During this Consultation, Future Goals for a Perfect Health and Body are defined and an action plan is custom designed in conjunction with each person's requirement for ways and means to achieve the same. An action plan is drawn up for achieving a State of Perfect Health and Perfect Body in the near future.

The Center will draw up a Protocol of Treatment and an easy to follow Daily Calendar to guide you for a Safe Natural Treatment using only Herbs and Dietary Supplements. No Drugs or Chemicals are used to help you overcome or reduce the severity of any Chronic Health Challenge. Follow-up weekly support by E-mail and Telephone is offered for implementation during your stay in India and for continuation upon your return back to your country. Cost typically varies from US $100.00 to $1,000.00 depending upon the severity of the Chronic Ailments involved and the response of each person concerned.

A Do It Yourself user friendly Detoxification/Rejuvenation Kit is offered for your use after returning back to your country. This comprises of a safe Natural Herbal/Dietary Supplements to be taken orally for improving the functioning of your Colon, Kidneys, Liver, Lungs, Blood and overhauling your entire body to make it run at peak efficiency. This leaves a Healthy Goal on your face which your friends can't help noticing.

Reservation in 4 to 5 Star Hotel/Service Apartment in

Mumbai (Bombay), India. Sight-seeing/shoping in Mumbai during your stay here.

4 to 10 day trips can be arranged to neighbouring towns and cities of your choice—Udaipur, Jaipur, Agra (Taj Mahal), New Delhi.

Relaxation Herbal Body Massages are offered for the treatment of Body Aches, Pains and other problems.

Stay in Ayurvedic Health Resorts in Kerala.

Consultation/Treatment with reputed Doctors for all kinds of Cosmetic work/Plastic Surgery, Dental and Eye (Lasik) Treatment can be arranged. Visit to Optomerist for Eye Glasses can be arranged.

Consultation with Cardiologist for Angiography, Angioplasty and By Pass Surgery can also be arranged.

The Center has Protocol to boost the Immunity of AIDS, Hepatitis and Herpes Patients and to improve the quality of their life and longevity.

General Information for Tourists

Cost of Air Travel from the West Coast to Mumbai, India is roughly US $1400.00 to US $1800.00 per person traveling by Economy Class via the Atlantic on British Airways, Air France, Swiss Airlines, Lufthansa with transit stop in London, Paris, Zurich and Frankfurt respectively. With a quick connection—wait typically 2 to 3 hours.

Cost of Air Travel from the West Coast to Mumbai via the Pacific with transit stop in Hong Kong, Singapore, Seoul is roughly US $ 1200.00 to $1600.00 on Singapore Airlines, Cathy Pacific and Korean Airlines.

Cost of Hotel Rooms in Mumbai (Bombay) as approximately as follows:

4 Star Hotels—$125 to $200 per night for Double Occupancy.
5 Star Hotels—$250 to $450 per night for Double Occupancy.

The Government of India provides Tourist Visa of short duration and a special Medical Tourism Visa (M) of longer duration (up to 1 year) for persons and Visa (MX) for their accompanying spouse coming to India for Medical Treatment.

LIST OF SOME CENTRES OF AYURVEDA AND WELLNESS

Kairali Ayurvedic Health Resort Pvt. Ltd.
(Health Centre and Corporate Office)
120 Andheri Modh, Mehrauli
New Delhi-110 030.
Ph: 011-26802106/26804879
Fax.: 011-26680875/2680
E-mail: kairaliresort@vsnl.com

Kairali Ayurvedic Health Resort
PO-Olassery, Kodumbu,
Palakkad Dist., 678551
Kerala, India.
Tel: 0091-4923-222553, 222623, 224402, 224403, 224404
Fax: 0091-4923-222732
E-mail: kairlpgt@md3.vsnl.net.in
Waterscapes Resort
Kumarakom
Ph: 0481-2525861

Kairali Ayurvedic Health Spa
C-30, Rockland, Panchsheel Enclave
New Delhi-110 017, India
Tel: 0091-11-26491803, 26491804

Kairali Ayurvedic Health Spa
2/40 Central Market
West Punjabi Bagh
New Delhi.
Ph: 011-25160175/76

Kairali Ayurvedic Health Spa
367 Rajita Villa,
6th Road, Chembur
Mumbai-400 071
Ph: 022-25294477/99
E-mail: kairali01@vsnl.net

Kairali Ayurvedic Health Centre
Opposite Khajuraho Airport,
Khajuraho-471 505
Madhya Pradesh, India
Ph: 07686-272219/274757
Email: kairali274@sancharnet.in

Art of Living International Headquarters-Asia
21st km, Kanakapura Road
Udayapura
Bangalore-560082
India
Tel: 91-80-28432273
91-80-28432274
E-mail: ashram@artofliving.org
Website: http://www.artofliving.org

Vipassana International Academy
Dhamma Giri; P.O. Box 6;
Igatpuri-422 403
District Nasik; Maharashtra; India
Ph: [91](02553) 244076, 244086
Fax: [91](02553) 244176
E-Mail: info@giri.dhamma.org

Nashik Vipassana Kendra
Dhamma Nasika; Opp. Water Filtration Plant,
Shivaji Nagar, Satpur, Nashik-422 222; Maharashtra, India
Ph: [91](0253) 561-6242
E-Mail: info@nasika.dhamma.org

Deccan Vipassana Research Centre
Dhammalaya; Near Majle Bus Stand; Hatkangale,
Kolhapur-416 109; Maharashtra; India
Ph: [91](0232) 483-316.
City Office: "Khushbu"; 6, Shivaji Park;
Kolhapur-416 001; Maharashtra; India
Ph: [91](0231) 651-146; Fax: [91](0231) 658-519

Nagpur Vipassana Centre
Dhamma Naga;
Village Mahurjhari,
Near Nagpur-Kalmeshwar Road;
Nagpur, Maharashtra, India.

or

c/o Mr. Goverdhandas Kela
Central Engineering Corporation,
Abhyankar Road, Sitabuldi;
Near Anand Bhandar,
Nagpur-440 012, Maharashtra, India.
Off: [91](0712) 524-685;
Fax: [91](0712) 522-291;
Res: [91](0712) 532-798.

or

Kalyanmitra Charitable Trust
Abhyankar Smaraka Trust Building;
Abhyankar Road; Dhantoli,
Nagpur-440 012; Maharashtra; India
Ph: [91](0712)522-169
E-Mail: dhamma_ngp@sancharnet.in

Khandesh Vipassana Centre
Dhamma Sarovara;
Survey No. 166;
Near Dedargaon Water Purification Plant;
At Post Tikhi, Dhule; Maharashtra; India

or

c/o Sri Prakash Borse
12, Tulsiram Nagar;
Deopur, Dhule-424 002;
Maharashtra; India.
Ph: [91](0256) 222-741;
Office: 222-614.

Pune City Vipassana Centre
Dhammaananda;
Pune City Vipassana Samiti,
Dadawadi, Opp. Nehru Stadium,
Near Anand Mangal Karyalaya,
Pune-411 002; Maharashtra, India.
Ph: [91](020) 446-8903; 446-4243.
E-Mail: info@ananda.dhamma.org

Pune Riverside Vipassana Centre
Dhamma Punna;
Pune Riverside Vipassana Samiti,
2, Vinay Chambers, Vetal Chowk,
971, Senapati Bapat Road,
Pune-411 016; Maharashtra, India.
Ph: [91](0212) 355-472; Fax: [91](0212) 680-558.
E-Mail: mukti@giaspn01.vsnl.net.in

Ajanta International Vipassana Centre
Dhamma Ajanta;
11, Ashok Vihar Society;
Opp. MIDC Office;
Station Road,
Aurangabad-431 005, Maharashtra; India.
Ph: [91](0240) 334-532; 332-324; 484-445.

GUJARAT CENTRES

Dhamma Sindhu;
Village: Bada, District: Kutch,
Gujarat, India-370 475
Ph: [91](2834) 273-303;
Fax:[91](2834) 224-267 and [91](2834) 222-811;
Res.:. [91](2834) 273-304
E-Mail:info@sindhu.dhamma.org

City Contact:
Ishwarlal C. Shah,
K.T. Shah Road, Mandvi,
Kutch Gujarat, India 370 465.

Ph: [91](2834) 223-076 (cloth-shop); 223-406 (Res);
Fax: [91](2834) 224-267; 222-811

Ahmedabad Vipassana Centre
Dhamma Pitha; c/o Sri S.S. Choudhary;
1, Patel Society; Opposite Office Of Police Commissioner; Ahmedabad 380 004; Gujarat; India
Ph: [91](079) 562-4631; 562-4253; 342-2473;
Fax: [91](079) 212-2016.

Rajkot Vipassana Centre
Dhamma Kota; c/o Rajesh Mehta; Bhabah Guest House; Panchnath Road; Rajkot; Gujarat-360 001; India
Ph: [91](0281) 34789/32187

Mehsana Vipassana Centre
Dhamma Divakara;
c/o Mr. Upendra Patel; 18,
Shraddha Complex, 2nd Floor;
Mehsana, Gujarat-384 001; India
Office Ph: [91](02762) 254 634;
Res. Ph: [91](02762) 253 315.

NORTHERN INDIA

Vipassana Centre
Dhamma Thali;
P.O. Box 208;
(Sisodiarani Baug-Galtaji Road);
Jaipur-302 001; Rajasthan; India
Ph: [91](0141) 268-0220, 268-0311;
Fax: [91](0141) 561-283.
E-Mail: info@thali.dhamma.org

Delhi Vipassana Centre
Dhamma Sota;
Vipassana Sadhana Sansthan;
Hemkunt Towers, 16th Floor;
98, Nehru Place;
New Delhi 110 019; India.

Ph: [91](011) 645-2772;
Fax: [91](011) 647-0658.

Kammaspur Vipassana Centre
Dhamma Patthana;
Off Delhi-Ambala National Highway,
Haryana; India

For additional information and registration please contact:

Delhi Vipassana Centre
Dhamma Sota;
Vipassana Sadhana Sansthan;
Hemkunt Towers, 16th Floor;
98, Nehru Place; New Delhi-110 019; India.
Ph: [91](011) 645-2772;
Fax: [91](011) 647-0658

Karnal Vipassana Centre
Dhamma Karunika;
Near Sainik School;
Kunjpura, Karnal-132 001; Haryana; India

For additional information please contact:

Mr. Brij Mohan Verma
5, Shakti Colony, Near SBI;
Karnal; Haryana; India
Ph: [91](0184) 225 0543;
Fax: [91](0184) 225 7543.
E-Mail: bmverma_universe@yahoo.com

Dehradun Vipassana Centre
Dhamma Salila;
c/o Mr T.S. Bhandari;
16, Tagore Villa;
Chakrata Road;
Dehradun-248 001;
Uttaranchal; India
Ph: [91](0135) 2715189 or 2754880;

Fax: [91](0135) 2715580.
E-Mail: assorep@nde.vsnl.net.in

Himachal Vipassana Centre
Dhamma Sikhara;
MacLeodganj;
Dharamsala-176 219;
Dist. Kangra; Himachal Pradesh; India;
Ph: [91](1892) 21-309;
Email: info@sikhara.dhamma.org
Website: http://www.sikhara.dhamma.org

Sarnath Vipassana Centre
Dhamma Cakkaa;
c/o Mr. Parmanand Maheshwari;
"Mangalam",
C27/273, Indian Press Colony;
Madhalla; Varanasi; Uttar Pradesh-221 002; India
Ph: [91](054) 246-644; 344-713.

Jetvan Vipassana Meditation Centre
Dhamma Suvatthi;
Katra By-Pass; Sravasti;
Uttar Pradesh-271 845, India
Tel: [91](05252) 265-439.

Kushinagar Vipassana Centre
Dhamma Vimutti; c/o Dr. V.D. Modi; Arogya Mandir; Gorakhpur; Uttar Pradesh-273 003; India
Ph: [91](0551) 335 805/336 469.

Lucknow Vipassana Centre
Dhamma Lakkhana; Asti Road;
Bakshi ka Talab, Lucknow; Uttar Pradesh; India.
Ph: [91](0522) 250 8525.
E-Mail: dhammalakkhan@rediffmail.com

For additional information please contact:

Mr. Pankaj Jain
A-302, Sterling Appts.,
9, University Road; Lucknow, U.P.; India
Ph: [91](0522) 278 2795.

Hoshiarpur Vipassana Centre
Dhamma Dhaja; Punjab Vipassana Trust;
Anand Public School;
Anandgadh village; Post Melawali;
Dist. Hoshiarpur-146110; Punjab, India.
Tel: 01882-272333, 240202.
E-Mail: dhammadhaja@yahoo.com

CENTRAL INDIA

Balaghat Vipassana Centre
Dhamma Kanana;
Bank of Wainganga; P.O. Garra; Balaghat.

or

c/o Sri Haridas Meshram
G-8, Bagh Colony; Civil Line
Balaghat-481 001; Madhya Pradesh; India.
Ph: [91](076) 322-473; Res. 322-554.

Durg Vipassana Centre
Dhamma Ketu; Village Thanod;
via Anjora, District Durg; Chhattisgarh,
Madhya Pradesh-491 001; India
Ph: (0788) 241-1813.

Contact:
Mr. Sureshchandra Kathane
B-269, Street 5, Smritinagar,
P.O. Nehru Nagar, Bhilai-490 020, M.P.; India.
Ph: (0788) 232-1539 (Res.).

Bophal Vipassana Centre
Dhamma Pala;
c/o Mr. Ashok Kela;
Vipassana Samiti,
E-1/182, Arera Colony;
Bophal; Madhya Pradesh; India
Ph: [91](0755) 563 113; 557-761; 557-762;
Fax: [91](0755) 564 520.
E-Mail: info@pala.dhamma.org

EASTERN INDIA

Calcutta Vipassana Centre
Dhamma Ganga; Bara Mandir Ghat;
Harishchandra Dutta Road;
Panihati (Sodepur);
Dt. 24-Paraganas;
West Bengal-743 176; India.
Ph: [91](033) 553 2855.

or

City Office:
9, Bonfield Lane;
Calcutta-700 001; India.
Ph: [91](033) 242-1767, 242-8043;
Fax: c/o Mr. M. K. Badani [91](033) 225-5174.

Vaishali Vipassana Centre
Dhamma Licchavi;
Atardah (Lalitkunj),
Muzaffarpur, Bihar-842 001; India

or

c/o Rajkumar Goenka
Parijat, Marwari Bazar;
Samastipur; Bihar; India
Ph: [91](0621) 243-403; 243-206.

Bodh Gaya Vipassana Centre
Dhamma Bodhi;
Gaya-Dhoba Road;
Near Magadh University;
Bodhgaya-824 231; Bihar; India

Office:
Shanti Dham
Kankarbagh Road;
Patna-800 020; Bihar; India.
Ph and Fax: [91](0612) 352-874;[91](0631)400-437.

Baracakia Vipassana Centre
Dhamma Upavana
c/o Mr. Ishwarchandra Sinha;
Khabhada Road;
Muzaffarpur-842 001, Bihar, India
Ph: [91](0621) 244-975.

SOUTHERN INDIA

Vipassana International Meditation Centre
Dhamma Khetta;
12.6 km. Nagarjun Sagar Road;
Kusum Nagar Vanasthali Puram;
Hyderabad-500 070; Andhra Pradesh; India
Ph: [91](040) 402-0290; 402-1746; 473-2569;
Fax: [91](040) 461-3941.
E-Mail: info@khetta.dhamma.org
For additional information about Vipassana activities in the Hyderabad area visit the http://www.khetta.dhamma.org/

Nizamabad Vipassana Meditation Centre
Dhamma Nijjhana;
Indhur, Post Pocharam,
Yedpalli Mandal;
District Nizamabad,
Andhra Pradesh-503 186; India
Ph: [91](08462) 273433
E-Mail:dhammanijjhana@yahoo.com

Vijayarayai Vipassana Centre
Dhamma Vijaya;
Vijayarayai, Pedavegi Mandal (Post);
District West Godavari,
Andhra Pradesh-534 475; India.
Ph: [91](08812) 225522

Vipassana Meditation Centre,
Dhamma Setu
533, Pazhan Thandalam Road,
Thiruneermalai Via,
Thirumudivakkam, Chennai-600 044. India
Ph: 44-24780953
Email Id: info@setu.dhamma.org
Website: www.setu.dhamma.org

Bangalore Vipassana Centre
Dhamma Sumana;
c/o Bharat Silks; No. 185,
Above Patel Roadways,
4th cross; Lalbagh Road;
Bangalore; Karnataka-560 027; India.
Ph: [91](080) 2224330; Fax: [91](080) 221-5776
E-Mail:silksb@vsnl.com

or

Shri Chotmal Goenka, Ph: [91](080) 6637173
Shri Jyoti Prakash, Ph: [91](080) 6761646

Ayurvedic Therapies are found in:

Thiruvananthapuram—Shivananda Asharam—www.journeytoindia.com

Kerala—Taj Tamara—-www.ashextourism.com

Agra; Mussoorie—Sansha Healthspa—www.jaypeehotels.com

Conoor—Natural Health Farm—www.ayurveda.org

Mysore—Indus Valley Ayurvdic Centre and Spa—www.ayurindus.com

Travelog—Ayurvda Beach Resort—www.Incredible India.com

Neemrana Hotels—Ayurvedic Rejuvnation www.neemrana.com

Kairali Centres—Kerala; Delhi; Mumbai—www.kairali.com

Rishikesh—Ananda Spa—http://www.anandaspa.com/

Haryana—Yorks health Resort, Nolta—www.saitravels22.com\Yorks.html

Appendix 3

Religious Tourism Centres

Allahabad

Lord Brahma performed the Prakrista Yajna here and that is how Allahabad received its ancient name Prayag. The city is located 135 km west of Varanasi, at the confluence of India's two most important rivers—the Yamuna and Ganges. Allahabad attracts millions of pilgrims every year to the confluence of these rivers where they come to bathe and wash away their sins. You could opt for any of the several pilgrim sites in Allahabad that cater to various faiths. The city plays host to some of the finest Hindu pilgrim sites like: Kumbha Mela: Though held in other parts of India, the Kumbha Mela at Allahabad is the most auspicious and revered one. Held every 12 years the Mela draws about 15 million people from all parts of India and the globe. A huge temporary city is created for the millions of pilgrims that arrive for the most auspicious bathing days. Kumbha Mela is like a "Yogi Convention", where yogis, sadhus (saints), holy people, and pilgrims come from all over India to take a dip in the holy waters. The Naga Babas are the famed ones who are dancing with enthusiasm completely naked. On the most auspicious bathing days there is a big parade, and the bathing order is very strictly observed. The Amavasya (the new moon day) is considered as one of the most auspicious bathing days. So the next time you visit India do visit the Kumbha Mela to wash away your sins and witness a gathering even bigger than the first Woodstock !

If you can't make it for the main event you could always attend the Ardha-mela (half mela), held every 6-years, which draws about 7 million people.

Hanuman Temple

Now here is where Hanuman strikes a unique yet perfect pose. Here Hanuman is in a reclining posture, a few feet below the ground, instead of his usual standing posture. The best part is when the annual floods reach upto his feet and then silently recline back. Do visit the temple to see Hanuman recline in ease.

When in Allahabad you could even visit the Bharadwaja Ashram (mentioned in the Ramayana) and the Sri Rupa Gaudiya Math which are one of the finest Hindu pilgrimage places in India.

Amarnath

This wondrous Cave was chosen by Lord Shiva to narrate the secrets of immortality and creation of the universe to Goddess Parvati (his wife). In the Cave lies the mystical Shiva Lingam which is said to have miraculous powers. The image of Shiva, in the form of a Lingam, is formed naturally of an Ice Stalagmite, which waxes and wanes with the Moon's cycle. When the Shiva Lingam attains its maximum height millions of pilgrims flock the pious temple from various parts of the globe. The cave is about 150 feet high and 90 feet long. Within the cave there are four or five other ice formations that resemble the figures of different gods. Though scheduled between July and August the dates vary every year pertaining to weather conditions and according to Purnima in the month of Shravan.

Getting There

Amarnath is 145 km east of Srinagar in Kashmir and can be accessed by daily flights to Delhi and Srinagar. And if you feel adventurous you could take train from Delhi, Jammu, Mumbai or Kolkata. You could even hit the road with buses to Delhi (14 hr.), Amritsar (5 hr.), and Pathankot (3 hr.).

Badrinath

"There are several sacred shrines in heaven, on earth, and in hell; but there is no shrine like Badrinath."—Skanda Purana

Several venerated pilgrimage sites dot the foothills and the peaks of the Himalayas, but the most noteworthy is Badrinath. The temple of Shri Badrinathji on the banks of the Alaknanda River dates back to the vedic times. Built by the renowned 8th century philosopher and saint, Adi Guru Shankaracharya, the temple is situated at an altitude of 3,133 meters. Also known as 'Vishal Badri', Badrinath is one of the most revered in the Char Dham circuit. The colourful gates welcome you at first and leads you through various statutes of Hindu Gods. But the main attraction is a one meter tall black stone image of Vishnu, as Lord Badri Narayan. The statue depicts Vishnu sitting in meditative posture, rather than his far more typical reclining pose. The best time to visit Badrinath is between June and September. And, don't forget to acrry warm clothes.

The Jolly Grant Airport near Dehradun (317 km from Badrinath) is the best way to get here. Or you could board a train to Rishikesh (297 km) and Kotdwar (327 km).

Bhubaneswar

With 500 temples in-and-around Bhubaneswar it proudly owns the sobriquet of the "Temple Metropolis of India". These temples epitomise a comprehensive history of the Orissan style of temple architecture. Orissa's capital city's history goes back over 2000 years. At one time, the Bindu Sagar tank had over 7000 temples around it. Of these, 500 still survive, all built in the extravagant Orissan style. The Lingaraj, Rajarani, Mukteswar, Brahmeswar and Parasurameswar temples are some of the best specimens of the Orissa Temple Architecture.

Getting There

Bhubaneswar is well conneted by air, rail and roads to various towns and cities in India. If you are coming by air, there are regular Indian Airlines flights connecting Bhubaneswar and major cities of India.

Chidambaram

The southern state of Tamil Nadu is referred to as the cradle of Dravidian culture, an ancient culture distinguished by unique languages and customs. It is a bastion of Hinduism at its most vigorous, whose past endures into the present. And, the Chidambaram temple is the perfect example. Between two rivers in a 40 acre temple-complex lays the temple of Chidambaram, one of the oldest, and most magnificent temples of South India. Shiva Natraja (the Dancing Shiva) stands in his cosmic dance pose in the golden sanctum sanctorum. Flanking the temple are 108 sculptured illustrations of Bharat Natya Shashtra. The Chitsabha, the holiest shrine in the temple, is a wooden structure supported with wooden pillars, with a hut shaped roof. It is in this hall, that the images of Nataraja and Sivakami are housed. Nothing entices more than the four lofty gopurams or towers in the four cardinal directions. Each is a gigantic masterpiece in itself—about 250 feet in height, with seven tiers. Representations of the 108 poses of the classical Bharata Natyam, Hindu mythological images and varied manifestations of Shiva adorn the gopurams.

Dwarka

This ancient sacred city on the edge of the Saurashtra peninsula was once the capital of Lord Krishna's empire. The city gets its name from the Sanskrit word 'Dwar', which translates as "door". You can find references of this splendid city in the Mahabharata, the Harivansha, the Bhagavata Purana, the Skanda Purana, and the Vishnu Purana. Other than being a pilgrimage hub, the city is a centre of archeologists' attraction all over. Its main attraction is the Dwarkadhish Temple which is on of the main "dhams" along with Badrinath, Puri, Rameshwaram. The existing temple is a 15th/16th century structure constructed in Chalukya style.

Getting There

Jamnagar (145 kilometres away) is the nearest airport. You could book train tickets on the Western Railway line. State Transport buses, private buses and taxis and conducted tours run to Dwarka.

Gangotri

Flowing down from the Gangotri Glacier at the foothills

of the Himalayas the Ganga is the holiest of all rivers. Even referred to as the Ganges, the perennial river is held in high regards by the Hindus. The Gangotri Glacier is the source of the Bhagirathi, which joins with Alaknanda (origins nearby), to form Ganga at the craggy, canyon-carved town of Devprayag.

Guruvayour

Located in the Guruvayur town of Trissur district in Kerala the amazing Guruvayur Shri Krishna Temple pays homage to MahaVishnu. The 5,000 years old temple was built by the divine architect Vishwakarma and the idol is made of a rare stone known as Patala Anjana. The temple shot to fame in the 16th century. The temple is the perfect example of Kerala temple architecture. It is built in such a manner that Surya (Sun) himself pays obeisance to Vishnu on Vishu day. You can view the idol from the main entrance itself.

Haridwar

Referred to as Mayapur in ancient Indian scriptures, Haridwar is the most revered temples in India. Millions flock Haridwar with wishes, prayers and chants from various parts of the globe. Haridwar was the spot where the immortal nectar fell when it was carried in a Kumba after the famed churning of the oceans. And that gives all the Hindus enough reason to take a holy dip to attain salvation from their sins of birth. When you are in Haridwar don't forget to attend the dusk arathi performed at Hari-Ki-Pairi. It's a spectacular sight full of sound and colour as the pilgrims float diyas on the Ganges, to commemorate their deceased ancestors. The city is the gateway to three other important pilgrimage destinations: Rishikesh, Badrinath, and Kedarnath. This is the second most holy pilgrimage site after Varanasi for Hindus all over the globe. Haridwar is even the site of the Kumbh Mela, humanity's largest festival.

Kanchipuram

The temple town of Kanchipuram, 64 kms from Chennai, was the ancient capital of the Pallavas. Famous as a city of 1000 temples, it still has 124 shrines. It's the perfect ostentation of Tamil Nadu's magnificent temple architecture. The first temple, dedicated to Shiva, was built in the 7th and 8th century and has paintings on the walls. The temples of Ekambaswara, Kailasanatha, Sri Kamakshi and Varadarajaswamy are also of interest. Kanchipuram, also called Kanjeevaram, is also famous for its silks. The city is situated around 70 km from Chennai in the south Indian state of Tamil Nadu.

Kamakshi Amman Temple

Out of the three main cities where the Goddess Shakti is worshipped, the Kamakshi Amman temple is the prime. The Kamakshi Amman temple is the hub of all religious activities in Kanchipuram. Do visit the Art Gallery showcasing pictures depicting the history of Sri Adishankaracharya and the Shankara Mutt.

Kailashanathar Temple

This is the first of the Pallava's contribution to the rich Tamil Nadu temple architecture. The Lord Shiva temple is the oldest structure in Kanchipuram. Of all the temples in India, no other edifice has been so elaborately filled with all the 64 aspects of Lord Shiva. The annual Shivaratri festival attracts large crowds.

Ekambareshwar Temple

This is the largest of them all. Spanning over 12.14 hectares the 16th century temple is a contribution of the imperial Vijayanagar Empire.

Varadaraja Temple

This Vaishnavite hub is the most celebrated. Located in Vishnu Kanchi or "the Little Kanchi" the temple houses the magnificent Varadaraja Perumal statue in a standing posture. Varadaraja temple with superb art has a magnificent history, which is associated with Sri Ramanuja.

Getting There

A flight to Chennai is the finest option. Or you could take a train for Kanchipuram from Chennai, Chengalpattu,

Tirupati, and Bangalore. The road-trippers could access Kanchipuram from Chennai, which is 75-kms away.

Kedarnath

It is set amidst the stunning mountainscape of the Garhwal Himalayas, the holy Kedarnath temple is at the head of the Mandakini River. Kedar is another name of lord Shiva. The lingam at Kedarnath, unlike its usual form, is pyramidal and is regarded as one of the 12 jyotirlings. As per rituals pilgrims first visit Yamunotri and Gangotri from where they carry holy water to offer abhishekams to the Lord. If you happen to be in Haridwar in the month of June do visit the Badri Kedar festival held in the sacred shrines of Badrinath and Kedarnath. The eight-day long festival acts as a platform for the greatest artists of the country.

Getting There

Kedarnath is 239 km from Dehradun of which the first 225 kms. is by road and the remaining 14 km a trekking route. Rishikesh is the nearest railway station, 221 km from Kedarnath. You get on a pony or hire porters at Gaurikund, from where the 14 km trek to Kedarnath starts.

Madurai

The oldest South Indian city has a lot to offer. From being the cultural centre for Tamilians to being the temple town, Madurai has many faces. But the Meenakshi temple is what attracts millions to this land of harmony. The temples gopurams, rising high above the surrounding countryside, is dedicated to Parvati, the consort of Lord Shiva. Each tower is encrusted with more than a thousand brilliantly painted sculptures depicting an assortment of mythological and auspicious themes. The only hitch being the restriction of non-Hindus into the inner sancta of the temple. The complex itself is a splendid example of the south Indian Dravida architectural idiom.

When in Madurai also visit the Tirumala Nayak Palace, a gracious building in the Indo-saracenic style, famous for the Stuccowork on its domes and arches; the Alagar Hills; and the Tirupara Kundran Rock temple.

Getting There

There are daily flights to and from Tiruchirapalli, Chennai and Bangalore. There are train connections to Madurai from Chennai, which takes eight hours via Trichy and from Rameshwaram, takes six hours. If you approach Madurai from Kerala, some spectacular scenes of the Western Ghats can be viewed.

Mahabalipuram

Mahabalipuram is famous for its' seven pagodas—a group of ancient rock hewn temples on the seashore. They are an excellent example of the Dravidian style of architecture. Mahabalipuram itself is a good example of a temple town, where a multi layered society that preached faith and grew from social harmony developed within the temple precincts.

Getting There

Chennai (58 km) is the nearest airport with both domestic and international terminus. While the nearest railway stations are Chengalpattu (29 km) and Chennai (58 km). You could even board a bus from Pondicherry, Kanchipuram, Chengalpattu or Chennai directly to Mahabalipuram daily.

Mathura

The holy city in Uttar Pradesh is every Hindu pilgrim's fancy. Known as Brajbhoomi, Mathura is the birthplace of Krishna. The city on the banks of the Yamuna River today has little towns and hamlets that are still alive with the Krishna legend and still redolent with the music of his flute. This beautiful city has a plethora of wondrous temples dedicated to Lord Krishna.

Once you are done with all the temples you could visit the Mathura Museum which has the largest collection of redstone sculptures in Asia, depicting many famous Buddha figurines. For now here is a low down on the temples you could visit in Mathura:

Krishna-Balrama Mandir

Established in 1975 by Swami Prabhupada, founder-acharya of the International Society for Krishna Consciousness (ISKON), the temple is Vrindavan's most popular one. Krishna devotees from round the world flock this temple throughout the year. The foreign devotees bring a truly international flavour to this ancient holy city.

Radha Madana-Mohana Temple

This famous temple was established by Srila Sanatana Gosvami and was the first temple to be built in Vrindavana, which at that time was just a forest. The original Deity of Madana-Mohana was taken to Karauli in Rajasthan for safety during the attack on Vrindavana by the soldiers of the fanatical Muslim Emperor, Aurangzeb.

Dwarkadish Temple

The Dwarkadish Temple, built in 1814, is a popular temple in the center of town. This is the most visited temple in the center of town. This is the most visited temple in Mathura. Followers of Vallabhacarya manage this temple. Once you enter this temple from the street, it is fairly interesting architecturally and there is a lot of activity inside. It is located in the eastern part of Mathura, not far from the Yamuna River.

The other temples you could also visit when in Mathura are the Jaipur Temple, Banke-Bihari Temple, Radha Vallabha Temple, Seva Kunja, Radha Damodara Temple, Radharamana Temple, Jugal Kishore Temple, Kesi Ghata, and Rangji Temple.

Getting There

The nearest airport is Kheria, Agra (62 km) or Delhi Airport (155 km). Mathura is on the main lines of the Central and Western Railways and is connected with all the important cities of the state and country such as Delhi, Agra, Mumbai, Jaipur, Gwalior, Kolkata, Hyderabad, Chennai, Lucknow, etc. Mathura is connected to all the major cities, either historical or religious, via the National Highways. It is linked by the regular state bus services of Uttar Pradesh, Madhya Pradesh, Rajasthan and Haryana.

Puri

Washed by the sea and embraced by causarina-fringed beaches, Puri is the holiest place in Orissa and one of the biggest pilgrimage centres in India situated on the shoreline of the Bay of Bengal. Here, the city's activities generally revolve around the Jagannath Temple where devotees visit from far and near. It is said that one obtains 'moksha' from the cycle of birth and rebirth, if one stays here for three days and nights. Most nights, the beaches host colourful markets and the city is abuzz with life. It's possibly one of the very few religious sites, which combines the outdoor pleasures of sea and divine beaches with the religious sentiments of 'darshan'. If you happen to visit Puri in June you can witness the massive rath yatra as the city rejoices in a pompous show. You can even visit the Gundicha Mandir (Temple) and Satyabadi (Sakshigopal) in Mathura.

The best way to move in-and-around is in a cycle rickshaw which is the most popular mode of travel within Puri.

Getting There

The nearest airport is Bhubaneshwar (65 kms). You can get to Puri by rail to other cities in Orissa and the country including Bhubaneshwar and Calcutta.

Pushkar

It is said that while Lord Brahma was passing this spot he dropped a lotus flower From the spots where the petals fell, water sprang out and lakes were formed. That is how Pushkar came into being. The Pulsating beats of vivid images of the Sacred Brahma land, Pushkar brings alive the rich tradition of Rajasthan enhancing the glory of the golden sand. Spectacular Fair Ground in the month of Kartik with bedecked Camels, decorated cattles, adventures competitions, breathtaking events, jostling rustic crowd, meditating sadhus, holy dip, vivid stalls, exotic fair, colourful desert, so typical, so obvious. It can be nothing else but Pushkar Fair.

Getting There

The closest airport is 131 km away in Jaipur. And, the

nearest railway station is Ajmer (10 km) with trains to Jaipur, Delhi, Udaipur, and Ahmedabad.

Rameshwaram

The island of Rameshwaram, spread out over 56 km of gentle sand dunes, embellished with casuarina trees and stark palms, is a sacred place for Hindus since, according to the Ramayana, this is where Rama worshipped Lord Shiva to absolve himself of the sin of killing Ravana. A dip into the sacred waters of the Agnitheertham, which was calmed by Rama, is a must for Hindus.

Rishikesh

The association of five distinct sections—the town, hamlets and settlements—on both sides of the river Ganges is what makes.

- Hrishikesh—the commercial hub.
- Muni-ki-Reti—the sprawling suburb also known as the "sands of the sages".
- Shivananda Nagar—home to the Sivananda Ashram and the Divine Life Society founded by Swami Sivananda.
- Lakshman Jhula—that bridges the void between the temple and its devotees.
- Swarg Ashram—the assorted Ashrams on the east bank.

The Ganga Arati performed at dusk at the Triveni Ghat is a spectacular sight and a must see.

Shirdi

Muslims and Hindus flock this pious destination to get a glimpse of the massive Sai Baba statue. With over 5000 devotees lining up to get a darshan of the magnificent statue which is believed to be miraculous. There have been thousands of stories about the divine healing of ailments without the help of modern science and other myths that have motivated millions to even walk all the way to Shirdi. In his life and teachings he tried to embrace and reconcile both faiths—Hindus and Muslims.

The vast Sai Baba temple in Shirdi is well-maintained by its trustees. The small village has good hotels and lodges available at cheap rates and is well-connected by road to Mumbai, Pune and other places. You could even sit in for one of the food serving session, which is completely free of cost. Thursday's is when Sai Baba gets the whole day with his devotees. It could be a long wait if you plan on visiting the temple on a Thursday.

Getting There

You can take a bus from Mumbai or Pune. It is a straight 6-hour ride from Mumbai by road. The nearest airport is Mumbai.

Sabri Mala

You will see a sudden surge of black clad, bearded men in different parts of India, be it Mumbai or Madurai. Don't worry we are not talking about any cult. These men are Sabri Mala worshippers who believe in months long of penance by sporting uniforms (a black lungi and black shirt), uncut hair and beards and walking barefoot. The Lord Ayyapa's statue is the most revered. From celebrities to the common man, everyone climbs up the treacherous trek straight upto the temple after following the 41-day penance.

Though controversial, young women are still not allowed in the shrine.

Getting There

The airports closest to Sabari Mala are at Thiruvananthpuram (149 km from Erumeli) and Ernakulam/ Cochin (78 km). The nearest train stations are Chengannur (62 km from Erumeli), Thiruvalla and Changanasseri. You can get a bus to Chalakayam, Vandiperiyar or Erumeli—the three starting points for the trek up to Sabari Mala.

Thanjavur

This temple town has the beautiful Chola Temple of Brihadeshwara (a World Culturage Heritage site), capped by a monolithic cupola made of a single granite block weighing 80 tons. It was taken to its' position with the help of a 6 km long ramp, using the same technique as the Egyptians did for building pyramids. Thanjavur is an important center for bronze figure casting, and its bronzes and handicrafts make it one of the highlights of a visit to South India.

Getting There

The nearest airport is at Tiruchi (65 kms east). Next closest airports are at Madurai (200 kms) and Chennai (350 kms). You can get many trains from Tiruchi, Chennai and Nagore to Thanjavur.

Tirupati

The richest, the most crowded and a large collection of human hair. YES! There are millions of devotees who believe in turning bald after every visit to Tirupati. It's an age-old, unquestioned ritual which really works well for the barbers and the temple.

Other than its maverick rituals the temple is renowned for its statue. It is the most venerated Vaishnavite shrine of Lord Venkateswara.

Tirupati was developed mainly by the contributions made by kings during their rule. Almost all the kings from great dynasties of the southern peninsula have paid homage to Lord Sri Venkateswara in this ancient shrine of Tirupati. Situated in the foothills of the Tirumala it still attracts people from various sects, lifestyles, countries and casts. It is the second most visited religious centres in the world following the Vatican. When in Tirupati you could even visit the Sri Kalyana Venkateswaraswami Temple, Sri Venugopalaswami Temple and Srikalahasti.

Getting There

Direct flights to Tirupati are available from Hyderabad and Chennai.

Tirupati is the nearest railway station. OR you could get to Tirupati from Renigunta or Gudur by train, bus, or taxi.

Varanasi

Past and present, eternity and continuity are perfectly

juxtaposed into the communal fabric of this wondrous city. With the Ganges freely flowing by the side, thousands of sadhus, pilgrims from various cultures and lots of milk, Varanasi is heaven on Earth. It is a magnificent city, with myriad attractions, both as an exalted place of pilgrimage and a microcosmic centre of faith. The unique relationship between the sacred river and the city is the essence of Varanasi—the land of sacred light. Life revolves around it right from the break of dawn to dusk.

Pilgrims flock Varanasi to visit the:

- Kashi Vishwanath Temple—dedicated to Lord Shiva and one of the most revered by Hindus.
- Durga Temple—dedicated to Goddess Durga, consort of Lord Shiva.
- Bharat Mata Temple—dedicated to Mother India and is built in the Mahatma Gandhi Kashi Vidyapeeth, which was built by Babu Shiv Prasad Gupt. You could get some patriotic juice right here.

Walk through the busy streets with flowers and fruits lined up for sale. See the boatmen as they wade through the river without a sweat. And the Brahmins performing their religious rituals in a trance. Get into the Varanasi vibe!

Getting There

Varanasi is well connected by air, rail and buses with all the important places of India. It's about 700 kms from Delhi. The airport is about 25 km from the city centre. From ancient times the city was connected to cities like Taxila, Gazipur, Pataliputra, Vaishali, Ayodhya, Gorakhpur, Agra, etc.

Vaishno Devi

Located near the town of Katra, in Udhampur district in the state of Jammu and Kashmir, the Vaishno Devi temple is one of the most revered places of worship in northern India. The journey here takes you through awesome wilderness amidst snow-capped mountains and sprawling forests, to the shrine, sacred and mystical. During the peak season you could hear thousands of pilgrims shouting the phrase "Jai Mata Di". The pilgrims climb up the steep mountain chanting slogans and display the true meaning of the term "religious fervour". When in Vaishno Devi do visit Banganga. It is believed that by taking a bath in Banganga (ban: arrow), a believer of the Mother Goddess can wash away all his sins.

Getting There

The nearest airport from Katra is in Jammu City, 48 kilometers (29.82 miles) away. The nearest railway station is at Udhampur, 25 kilometers (15.5 miles) away. Railway Extension to Katra proper is expected to be operational by 2007

Ajmer, Rajasthan

The lakeside city of Ajmer is located in central Rajasthan and is a hub for both, Hindu and Muslim pilgrims. You can even get to the renowned Pushkar festival from Ajmer. The places to visit in-and-around Ajmer Sharif are Shahjhan's Mosque, the Adhai-din-ka-jhonpra, Taragarh Fort, the Adhal-din-ka-Jhonpra and the Pushkar Lake.

The huge silver doors of the Ajmer Sharif Dargah welcome all its devotees into a domain that has been revered by millions for ages. It is said to be the final resting place for Moinuddin Chishti also known as 'Gharib-Nawaz' (protector of the poor). The Khwaja left for heavenly abode in 1256 AD after a six-day prayer in seclusion and since then this place has been a rage. If you visit Ajmer during the six day feats you are assured of a vibrant Urs (religious fair), loads of kheer (a milky desert) and millions of believers. The shrine is considered to be a place of wish fulfilment for those who pray with devout and pure hearts (even Emperor Akbar has seeked the Dargahs blessings).

Getting There

The nearest airport is Jaipur (130 km away). Ajmer is very well linked by train from the city to other destinations in India, including Delhi, Mumbai and Jaipur. State and interstate roadways buses, RTDC conducted tours and coaches connect Ajmer to most important cities in the region, including Ahmedabad, Jaipur, Udaipur, Jodhpur, Bikaner, Mt. Abu, Jaisalmer.

Mumbai

A few meters away from the hustle-bustle of Mumbai lays the Haji Ali Dargah. Located on an islet off the coast of Worli in Mumbai, the Haji Ali Dargah the structure is a slim solitary minaret. It is linked to the mainland by a tenuous causeway, which is practically not accessible during rough monsoon tides. A marble courtyard contains the central shrine behind the finely sculpted entrance.

Haji Ali is believed to have been a wealthy local businessman who renounced the material world and meditated on a nearby headland following a pilgrimage to Mecca. His casket surprisingly floated back to Mumbai (then Bombay). That is when his devotees built the mosque and the tomb in the early 19th century in his reverence. Sun sets at the oceanfront, with Haji Ali in the backdrop, is a beautiful site. It's the perfect way to romance the sea.

Getting There

The Chatrapati Shivaji International Airport in Mumbai is obviously the nearest airport. You can take a local train to Mumbai Central or Mahalakshmi station and walk it down to Haji Ali from either. Haji Ali is a main stop for many of the buses linking to the various parts of Mumbai, Mumbai and Delhi.

Delhi

Standing on 260 pillars and supported by 15 domes, the Jama Masjid is one of the architectural wonders of Shah Jahan's era. Formally referred to as the Masjid-i-Jahan Numa, it is built in yellow sandstone and combines the best of Hindu and Muslim styles of architecture. Masjid-i-Jahan Numa means "the mosque commanding a view of the world", which it really is. Located in the centre of the old city the Mosque can house twenty-five thousand worshippers. The Mosque is the largest in India and flocked by people from varied parts of the globe. The gargantuan Buland Darwaza is the perfect display of 16th century architecture. Built in 1575 it celebrates Akbar's successful Gujarat campaign. The majestic Mosque is capacious and a reminiscent of the glorious Mughal era.

Getting There

The nearest airport is obviously Delhi. You could take a cab or a bus to Jama Masjid.

Shimla

Overlooking the ridge this is Shimla's renowned landmarks. The stained glass windows, the cruciform design and the ingenious architecture—everything freely blends into one seamless form. The Church is the second oldest church of Northern India. Visit the Sunday morning sermons in English after which you could wander around the magnificent Church. The Church compliments the beauty of Shimla.

Nashik

The small yet buzzing town Nashik is normally flocked in the month of February by millions of pilgrims. Their destination—the Infant Jesus Shrine. The supposedly miraculous Church has long queues of devotees from various parts of India with candles, flowers and rosaries in hand. This small Church houses the idol of Infant Jesus which is matchless.

Velankani

Pilgrims from far across pay their ode to the famed Our Lady of Health Church in Velankani. The so-called Mecca of Christians is also colloquially referred to as the 'Sacred Arogya Matha Church'. The small Church plays host to thousands of pilgrims in the month of February. The seamless architecture and sky-reaching towers are a sight. Don't miss out on the museum that displays the offerings made by those who were cured of their disease. Located in Nagapattinam, the Church houses a beautiful

Goan Churches

Goa is not all about its beaches. The real Goa is in its less-popular interiors where you could discover its rich and true cultural heritage and religious roots. The influence of 450 years of Portuguese rule is evident in Goan life. Goa Velha or Old Goa was once the Portuguese empires capital and has the finest most comprehensive group churches and cathedrals built during 16th to 17th century AD. Though aged by time, the churches and cathedrals still have an undying charm that attracts tourists and pilgrims from various parts of the globe.

The Basilica of Bom Jesus

The world-renowned church is known for housing the mausoleum of Saint Francis Xavier. The intricate designs and finely carved embellishments are matchless and are a perfect display of Renaissance architecture at its best. Every aspect of the church is well-thought—from the confession box to the exquisitely carved stone doorway. Sculptor Giovanni Batista Foggini designed the tomb of St. Francis Xavier, which is the main attraction. The church construction begun in 1594 and went on till 1689.

Se Cathedral

Everything at Se Cathedral is large. The Se Cathedral has the largest altar and the largest bell. It took 80 long years to build it. And, the Se Cathedral is the largest church in Asia. The Portugese wanted a grand, plush church that promulgated the wealth, power and prosperity of its empire. With 15 altars, 8 chapels, huge pillars.

Church of Lady of Rosary

Royally perched on the Holy Hill is the Church of Lady of Rosary. One of the oldest churches in Goa it was built in 1544 and took 6 years to complete. The Manueline style of architecture dominates the church interiors along with Gothic elements. It was here that St. Francis Xavier taught Catechism and spread the word of Christianity. The main attraction is the glorious feast in the month of November.

The Church and Convent of St. Francis of Assisi, Chapel of St. Catherine, and Church of St. Augustine are the other churches that are a must see when in Goa.

Come and discover the pious side of Goa !

Anandpur Sahib

Historians and specialists in Eastern religions generally believe that Sikhism is a syncretistic religion, originally related to the Bhakti movement within Hinduism and the Sufi branch of Islam, to which many independent beliefs and practices were added. Keeping that argument open we move on to our Sikh pilgrimage destination—Anandpur Sahib. From Chandigarh, barely 75 km up the highway towards Dharamsala and Manali, lies Anandpur Sahib, the impressive gurudwara that is one of the holiest Sikh shrines.

The holy City of Bliss is located on the lower spurs of the Himalaya surrounded by picturesque natural scenery, with the river Satluj forming a shimmering and shiny blue border on the south-west barely four miles away. This shrine consecrates the memory of an earlier visit of Guru Gobind Singh to the place in course of his return from Kurukshetra. This Shrine ranks second (after the Golden Temple) in every Sikhs pilgrimage itinerary.

Getting There

The nearest airport is Chandigarh (75 km away), while the nearest railhead is Nangal. If you plan on taking the road you couls always start hitchhiking Chandigarh (75 km away).

Amritsar

Amritsar is one of the most ancient and legendary sites in the Punjab. This pious city plays host to millions. The origin of the place where the Sri Hari Mandir stands is shrouded in mystery. Here lies the famed Temple which ranks high in Sikh pilgrims.

The Golden Temple

Every Sikhs goal is to build a close, loving relationship with God. And in the process the Golden Temple is the prime pilgrimage spot. The glorious temple has seen it all, from controversies to varied pilgrims. Also referred to as Harimandir the temple is a symbol of freedom and spiritual independence. Millions come to the Temple from all over the world to enjoy its environs and offer their prayers.

This place of peace and calm is brilliantly orchestrated around a small lake. The 16th century temple was re-built in the 1760s after the Afghan attack. All the gold and exquisite marble work were conducted under the patronage of Ranjit Singh, Maharaja of the Sikh Kingdom of the Punjab. There are four doors to enter the Harimandir and anyone who wants to enter may do so, irrespective of religion, colour, creed or sex. The Akal Takht (Eternal Throne) is part of the Golden Temple complex and is situated on the other end of the causeway connected to the Harmandir Sahib. Akal Takht symbolizes the dispensing of justice and temporal activity. From the Harimandir to the Akal Takht, the varied architectural influences are spun out into a splendourous unison.

If you happen to be in Amritsar in the month of April you could witness the Baisakhi celebration with fervour in Harimandir Sahib.

Getting There

Amritsar is 234 km from Chandigarh and 445 km from Delhi. The station is situated in the northern part of the city and is connected to Delhi, Kolkata and Mumbai.

Uttar Pradesh

Shri Guru Nanak Dev Ji, (1469-1538) born in the Punjab area of what is now Pakistan was the founder of the religion. He preached the brotherhood of humanity. He has been revered and remembered by the millions of Sikhs all over the world through various landmarks. And the Hemkund Sahib is every pilgrims fancy.

Set at an altitude of 4329 m above sea level, Hemkund Sahib is one pilgrim destination on every Sikhs list. The Gurudwara is on the banks of the glacial Hemkund Lake surrounded by seven peaks. It's an awsome sight. The uphill trek starts from Gobindghat, which is about 275 km from Rishikesh. You really have to be good shape to do this trek. The 10,000 ft hike uphill from Gobindghat is through cliffs, pine forests.

Getting There

The nearest airport is Jolly Grant (307 kms) and railhead is Rishikesh (293 km). By road Hemkund Saheb is 5 Km from Ghangharia, which is approachable on foot from Govindghat which is connected by road with Rishikesh, Kotdwara, Dehradun, Haridwar, Nainital, Ranikhet and other important hill stations of Garhwal and Kumaon Hills.

Hastinapur

Situated at a distance of 37 kilometers from Meerut and 120 Kms from Delhi, Hastinapur is of great relevance to Jains and tops their pilgrimage itinerary. According to the Jain traditions and history, many Tirthankars, Chakravartis, Great Sadhus, the Omniscient souls, ascetics, Shravakas and Shravikas are associated with to this ancient land. This is the place where Aadi Teerthankar Prabhu Adinathji concluded fasted for 400 days by drinking sugarcane juice. And people come here from far, far away to celebrate the Parma ceremony with sugarcane juice. The reddish colour Shri Shantinath Bhagwan idol in the Padmasan Mudra is the main attraction. People flock the place from varied parts of the world to get a glimpse of the idols.

The Archaeological Department is taking great interest in this city due its Hindu and Jain roots. With all the cultural influences and tradition Hastinapur is the perfect place to study Jaina cosmology and cosmography.

Palitana

Gujarat is also a major centre for the Jains, and some of its most interesting sights are Jain temple centers. The Jains have five separate hill locations for their holiest clusters of temples and Shatrunjaya Hill in Palitana is considered the most important among them. 50 km South-West of Bhavnagar city, Palitana houses perhaps the largest cluster of Jain temples anywhere. From the base to the peak of the Shatrunjaya Hill, where the Palitana temples are located, there are in all 863 temples. Simply heaven for Jains!

Palitana was the capital of a princely state of the Gohil Rajput clan and now is one of the greatest tourist attractions in Gujarat for foreign tourists. The entire summit of majestic mount Shatrunjaya is crowned with about 900 temples, each rivalling the other for beauty and magnificence. The temples are exquisitely carved in marble, veritable prayers in stone. To an observer, these appear to be ivory miniatures when seen from a distance. The most important temple is that of the first teerthankara, Shri Adishwar. The entire collection of Temples in one glance is impressive.

The only hitch is that you can't sleep in the temple area (not even the priests).

Bhavnagar

Bhavnagar, the nearest airport lies at a distance of 51 kilometer from Palitana, but the most convenient airport is Ahmedabad as it is connected through regular flights to many important cities of the country like Mumbai and Delhi. Palitana is a small railway station and has connection only with Bhavnagar. Most of the trains stop at Sihor, which is connected to Ahmedabad and Gandhinagar. There are hourly buses for Bhavnagar from Palitana. Regular buses are also available for Ahmedabad, Talaja, Una, and Diu. The total journey time to Una or Diu is around 6 hours as the roads are not in a good condition. Taxis are also available on hire for Palitana from Bhavnagar. The bus stand is situated 800 meters away from the Palitana railway station.

Ahmedabad

In the year 1411, when Sultan Ahmed Shah built a city on the banks of River Sabarmati, little did he know that, 550 years later, his Ahmedabad would be known as the 'Manchester of the East'. Right in the heart of Ahmedabad is the Magen Abraham Synagogue. The name commemorates the founder of the prayer hall, Dr. Abraham Erulkar. This Synagogue is well maintained, and looks after the religious welfare of the Bene Israels in the city and the surrounding.

Getting There

Ahmedabad is well connected by air, road and rail to all major cities.

Rajgir

The meandering river Banganga and five hills ensconce picturesque Rajgir, ancient Rajagriha (literally, the abode of kings). During the lifetime of the Buddha this was the capital of the powerful Magadhan kingdom, ruled by the virtuous King Bimbisara. The surrounding hills and caves were home to many spiritual teachers, and like many others in search of Truth, the former Prince Siddhartha came to this city to seek the path of salvation after renouncing his royal heritage. Later, as The Buddha, he often visited Rajagriha to retreat at the Jivakamaravana monsastery, and preach and meditate on the Gridhakuta Hill, where he delivered the Lotus Sutra (which promises salvation for all beings) and the Prajnaparamita or Perfection of Wisdom Sutra. Rajagriha sank into oblivion when the Magadha monarchs decided to move their capital to Pataliputra (modern Patna).

Rajgir is also sacred to Jains as Lord Mahavira, the 24 th Tirthankara, studied and mediated here. Rajgir is connected to Patna, Kolkata and Delhi. Visit the Vishwa Shanti Stupa—built by the Nipponza Myohoji sect of Japan it stands on the summit of the hill where Buddha preached and meditated.

Rumtek and Pemagyantse

Nestled in the lap of the Himalayas, the North Eastern Indian state of Sikkim is famous for its gompas and their fascinating monastic ceremonies.

Rumtek is the seat of His Holiness, the XVIth Gyawla Karmapa, the head of the Karma Kagyu Order of Tibetan Buddhism. On the 28th and 29th day of the tenth lunar month (July) the cham dance is performed by monks wearing grotesque masks and colourful dresses, culminating in a ritual dismembering of an effigy symbolising evil.

The monastery at Pemagyantse, at an altitude of 2085 meters, is where the arrow shot by Padmasambhava (Guru Rinpoche) looking for a place to meditate, landed. On its top floor, the monastery houses a wooden, intricately crafted structure, depicting Guru Rinpoche's abode. The annual cham festival is held in February.

Tabo Monastery

Set in the magnificently isolated Spiti valley in Himachal Pradesh, Tabo is more than 1000 years old, making it the oldest continuously functioning Buddhist enclave in India. The 9 temples here, known for their murals and life-size statues, make Tabo one of the most significant art collections of the Tibetan Buddhist world. A small community of monks resides here.

Sankeshwar

Dedicated to Sri Sankeshwar, the 23rd Teerthankara, this 25-year old temple is a well-known Jain pilgrim centre. With 52 idols standing tall this temple was built in the year 1155 on the banks of the Rupen River. Till 1760 the temple was renovated, destroyed and again restored. Since then, this vast and beautiful temple with a 52 idols and passage for going round it stands there. The architecture is modern yet enticing. The idol of Bhagawan Bhidbhanjan Parshvanath is in small temple to the right of the chief idol and the idol of Bhagawan Ajitanatha is in the small temple to the left of the main idol. During the Diwali days, thousand of pilgrims come here to observe a two-day long fast.

Getting There

The nearest railway station of Harij is at a distance of 10 kilometers and Viramgam is at a distance of 62 kilometers. Bus service and private vehicles are available. Boarding and lodging facilities are available at this place.

Ranakpur

Visual wonders in amber stone. That is the best way to describe the Jain temples of Ranakpur. Ranakpur is amongst the five holiest places of the Jain community and exceptional in beauty. Constructed in the AD 1439, in the rule of the gifted monarch Rana Kumbha, the temples are located in the mountain ranges of Pali District. If you are driving down you could view the heart capturing views. The Ranakpur Jain Temple were built during the reign of the liberal and gifted monarch in the 15th century. Spread across 48,000 sq ft, four subsidiary shrines, twenty-four pillared halls, 1444 columns and millions of pilgrimages make up Ranakpur Temple. From the huge bell to the motifs, everything is detailed out with perfection.

Getting There

Pali district 39 kms away from the Phalna and Udaipur railway station.

Patna

Today the capital of the state of Bihar, it was known as Pataligram in the days the Buddha visited it. Situated on the banks of the Ganga, it was a thriving township during the Buddha's lifetime, with the river traffic providing endless trade opportunities. The Magadha monarchs moved their capital here (from neighbouring Rajgir) in the 6th century BC, and that saw Pataligram blossoming into Pataliputra, which reached its zenith under two major dynasties, the Mauryas and Guptas. During the reign of Emperor Ashoka, it was the focus from which the Buddha's message of peace and non-violence, compassion and love, was spread far and wide. The third Buddhist Council was held here.

Patna is well connected by air, rail and road to Calcutta, Delhi, Mumbai and Varanasi. Visit the Patna Museum, established by the British in 1917, to house more than 50,000 rare and valuable antiquities and art objects, including narrative panels and stone sculptures of the Buddha and Bodhisattva figures. The most prized exhibit here is the Holy Relic Casket containing the sacred ashes of the Buddha, unearthed in Vaishali.

Kochi

Known as the "Queen of Arbian Sea", the flourishing city of Kochi plays hosts to the finest Jewish Synagogue in India. Before the mass immigration of the Jews to Israel (in the early 1950s) they lived quite comfortably for well over 1000 years in Kerala. The Synagogue in Mattancherry is reminiscent of the Jewish settlements. Built in 1568 A.D. the synagogue has scrolls of Old Testament and a number of copper plates inscribed in the Hebrew Script preserved till date. It's the perfect testimony for the communal harmony in the state for centuries. The 18th century clock tower is an enticing sight. You can visit the synagogue from 10 am to 12 noon and 3 pm to 5 pm on all days except Saturdays and Jewish holidays.

Getting There

Kochi is north of Trivandrum (218 km) and south of Kozhikode (223 km).

Pune

The small and cozy town of Pune plays host to thousands of Jewish pilgrims. And Why? Cause Pune is home to the Ohel David Synagogue. With an uncommon sobriquet like "Lal Dewil" the Ohel David Synagogue was built by David Sassoon in 1863 in Poona. This well known Pune landmark is an aesthetic wonder. Everything about this Synagogue is special—the clock tower, the 90 foot spire, the bell, the stained glass or the architecturally brilliant interiors. David Sassoon rests in peace in a fine mausoleum in the synagogue.

Getting There

Mumbai is the nearest airport. Pune is a 2-and-a-half hour drive from Mumbai. You get many buses from Mumbai or even catch a train to Pune.

Sarnath

Sarnath, only 10 kms from Varanasi, the holy city of the Hindus, is where the Buddha founded the Sangha with his five old companions as his first disciples. It was in the Deer Park at Sarnath that the Buddha gave his first significant sermons on the Middle Way, the Four Noble Truths and the Eightfold Path. Sarnath gained eminence during the reign of Emperor Ashoka. However in the 12th century both Varanasi and Sarnath faced the onslaught of Muslim invasion. After Qutbuddin Aibak's attack in 1194, the thriving monastery in the Sarnath lay in ruins, and the few monks who survived, fled. Sarnath never rose again. Its ruins still carry the presence of the Great Teacher.

Amravati

Kushinagar, or Kushinara as the capital of the Malla republic was then known, is where, the Buddha chose to make his Mahaparinirvana, or final exit from earth. He was 80. It was here, while entombing the relics of the Buddha, that the architectural form of the stupa was created. Today, Kushinagar is identified with the modern village of Kasia, 51 kms from Gorakhpur city, in eastern Uttar Pradesh. Visit the Mahaparinirvana temple (which enshrines a giant 6 metre long statue of the Buddha in the reclining position), Rambhar Stupa (built at the spot where the Buddha is believed to have been cremated), and Mathakuar shrine (built on the spot where the Buddha delivered his last sermon).

Ladakh

The once independent kingdom of Ladakh, in the state of Jammu and Kashmir, is a land of passes, a high-altitude desert. Ladakh has a number of palaces and ancient Buddhist hilltop monasteries, including the ones at Hemis (which has the largest tangkha in India), Stok (with a collection of rare paintings), Spituk (with a collection of ancient masks), Shankar (with innumerable statues of pure gold), Thikse (one of the finest examples of Ladakhi architecture) and Alchi (with thousands of miniature pictures of the Buddha). The region is one of the best living traditions of Tibetan Buddhism in the world today.

Nagarjunakonda

One of India's richest Buddhist sites, and perhaps the least known, Nagarjunakonda, named after the monk who founded Mahayana Buddhism, now lies almost entirely under the Nagarjunasagar Dam, touted as the world's largest masonry weir. About 1700 years ago, the lush jungles here sheltered a flourishing city, Vijayapuri, the capital of the Ikshvaku kingdom and a major centre of Buddhist learning. Numerous monasteries dotted the region. There was also a Buddhist university. The excavated remains of Buddhist civilisation found at the site have been meticulously reconstructed and carefully preserved at Nagarjunakonda, a unique island museum situated on top of a hill which rises from the middle of the Nagarjuna lake. Buddhist Vihara, the island museum houses a stupendous collection of relics of Buddhist art and culture. Famous exhibits include a small tooth and an earring believed to have belonged to the Buddha.

Appendix 4

GLOBALIZATION AND MEDICAL TOURISM

I. Identification

1. Issue

Globalization has caused many countries to reevaluate their economical strengths and weaknesses, as well as reassess what products or services in which nations can benefit. One such product and service that has emerged over the past decade is medical tourism. Medical tourism involves the practice of citizens exercising their personal healthcare choices in less restrictive areas. It is the traveling by candidate service recipients from one institution, jurisdiction or country where treatment is not available to another institution, jurisdiction or country where they can obtain the kind of medical procedures and innovative treatments they desire. Despite the less restrictive policies that encourage this business, these services often can also be offered as a lower-cost and more-timely option.

Because of the nature of this practice and its policies, this phenomenon has only occurred in certain, specific areas around the world. These regions and nations have attractive policies in place and have implemented unique marketing strategies that encourage the medical tourism business. This industry has demonstrated significant impact on these nations' economic health. Unfortunately, other nations, like the United States, have not been as successful in attracting the medical tourism business. Therefore, the issue is to more thoroughly understand, through the analysis of other country's experiences, policies and marketing strategies, why the United States should take advantage of the opportunity to further participate in this emerging industry.

2. Description

Medical tourism is a universal term that encompasses several specialty markets. Included in these specialty markets are health tourism, reproductive tourism, suicide tourism, as well as other niche business opportunities. Tourism, in the sense of this emerging market, is basically traveling from a place where treatment is not available, because of the prevailing rules, to a place where it is available. These rules are not necessarily laws but may also be the personal and moral convictions of the healthcare provider, institutional policy guidelines, and recommendations by committees. Thus, policy, in some fashion, is the driver of this industry.

Medical tourism is also the most common practice carried out all over world. However, there are other specialty markets within medical tourism that are also emerging as significant businesses. Health tourism is travel in a recuperative climate with natural therapeutic resources. The health tourism business is more specifically known for offering yoga, massage, traditional ayurvedic medicine and spa resorts. Reproductive tourism is the practice of consumers exercising their personal reproductive choices in less restrictive areas by traveling to another jurisdiction or country where the desired medically assisted reproduction procedures and treatments can be obtained. Suicide tourism is a very small branch of medical tourism yet its presence is still notable. This practice, much more so than the others, is tightly structured by policy.

Once consumers commit to travel for their desired medical treatment, often consumers will also take the opportunity to be a tourist in the visiting country and enjoy what it has to offer. Thus, consumers may combine their holiday and medical care into one venture. Medical tourism is comprised of three basic aspects: hospital/health services, hotels and travel/leisure. Thus, with attractive policies and/ or the correct marketing strategies, this emerging industry can have significant opportunity for economic growth and infrastructure development for participating nations.

3. Related Cases

As noted, medical tourism is the universal practice with

numerous specialty markets within this business. Because this in an emerging industry, extensive research for any particular country or on any individual branch of medical tourism, its policies and marketing strategies are not available. Therefore, all areas comprising medical tourism for many of the participating geographical regions or nations will be addressed. In summary, this case study will address a broad overview of the industry.

II. Policy Impacts

5. Social

The policy behind medical tourism has two distinct functions. In the case of those countries benefiting from medical tourism, standing policy allows for the nation to promote this business to consumers who are willing to travel and have the ability to pay. In essence, policy allows consumers new and different options for their healthcare needs. Medical tourism policy offers consumers choices. Secondly, this policy can also be enacted to protect the nation and its consumers. In the healthcare field, ensuring necessary and quality service is of the utmost importance. Therefore, policy, in the medical tourism sense, protects the rights of its participants while also giving consumers more opportunity and choices in their healthcare.

6. Environmental

While medical tourism focuses on fulfilling healthcare choices, traveling to a different country or state is also necessary. This is the basic premise behind medical tourism. Thus, by traveling to another geographical area, it is promoting tourism to location. Tourism is being used as a means for providing capital for development and preservation of these geographical areas.

7. Economic

Medical tourism has had significant economic impacts on particular geographical regions and nations. The goal of this industry is to provide economic stimulus to the geographical areas, often developing nations. The objective of this business is to increase jobs, income, and quality of life of the participating nations of medical tourism. This business also promotes infrastructure development to support the industry.

8. Other

Since this is an emerging, competitive industry, countries seek education, advanced skills and training to benefit from this profitable business. Therefore, medical tourism, and the policies around it, has encouraged participants to receive continued education and training. Additionally, this business also requires the use of advanced technology, and this, in turn, encourages participating countries to gain more exposure to these various technologies.

9. Suggested Interventions

While there are several specialty markets of medical tourism that are very controversial, specifically reproductive and suicide tourism, countries are reconsidering and/or analyzing their standing policies. There are consumers who take advantage of these opportunities, as well as opposition from non-market groups who have forced possible policy reform. Thus, these nations must continue to analyze and revise their policies in order to protect the practice of medical tourism and its consumers.

III. Legal Clusters

10. Disclosure and Status/Policy Issue

While there is no main policy issue, policy, or less restrictive policy, is the backbone of this industry. Most often, consumers are willing to travel to receive medical procedures in a geographical location that maintains policies that are less prohibitive than their current location's policies. There are other factors, too, that encourage medical tourism, like time and money. However, if policy is not in place to encourage this business, regions or countries would not be able to participate and benefit from this industry. Additionally, because of their particular standing policies, nations are better able to market themselves to new consumers globally.

11. Forum and Scope/Existing Policy Framework

International

The concept of medical tourism is primarily to encourage travel by consumers globally. Therefore, most countries enact a policy framework that is attractive to worldwide consumers on the basis that if they are willing to travel and pay the necessary fee, consumers are able to receive the healthcare practice they desire.

National

Medical tourism does not require a consumer to have to cross-national borders. Often, medical tourism is evident from state to state or jurisdiction to jurisdiction. In this case, policy encourages consumers to travel from one area to another area where policy is more attractive or less restrictive. This type of medical tourism that markets this practice is more often seen in the specialty market of reproductive tourism.

Regional

Although countries do not tend to formulate policies based on regional expectations, there are certain geographical areas that do benefit more from the medical tourism industry. Southeast Asia has marketed itself as the primary geographical area to cater to medical tourism consumers. Since this has become a competitive business, countries in this geographical area continue to analyze and reform their policies to encourage this practice and rise above their competitors. Additionally, as this industry continues to emerge, this similar phenomenon is becoming more apparent in the European Union as well.

12. Decision Breadth/Stakeholders/Policy Actors

Policy is often shaped by numerous actors. The government plays are large role in outlining medical tourism policy in its nation. However, there are other actors that can affect policy. Healthcare providers, institutions, special committees, advisory boards, associations, as well as numerous other players, can all impact policy guidelines.

On the tourism aspect of this industry, there are also other actors that can also influence policy. Businesses, recreational organizations, as well other associations and groups can impact policy guidelines that encourage medical tourism.

13. Legal Standing/Legal Regulatory Framework/Suggested Policy Interventions

Although there is no documented legal regulatory framework for the medical tourism industry, there is always a legal liability concern when dealing with the healthcare industry. The healthcare industry is a much regulated business entwined with liability issues. Therefore, countries enact policies that address this concern on an individual basis. Because some countries are willing to take on more risk with healthcare liability, they have been able to emerge as leaders in this industry. Other countries, like the United States, have not been able to benefit as greatly from medical tourism because of increased legal liability and policy.

IV. Trade Clusters

14. Type of Measure

Research states that the economic profit that the medical tourism industry contributes to the nation's gross domestic product (GDP) is the measure of success. This financial revenue can be calculated by healthcare earnings, as well as the profits from tourism related activities. Besides the monetary value that is calculated, countries can measure the affects of this industry by the increase in number of tourists, as well as the number of new jobs. Together, countries are able to determine the many influences that the medical tourism industry has on its economy.

15. Relation of Trade Measure to Environmental/Tourism Impacts

Directly Related to Product

The revenue generated from the consumers traveling to the country for their healthcare needs will go towards building the nation's healthcare system and tourism infrastructure.

Indirectly Related to Product

Because medical tourism crosses many different types of business sectors, the revenue generated will also indirectly support these other sectors indirectly as well. While this practice will primarily benefit the healthcare and lodging industries, the service and recreational industries will also profit from this business.

Not Related to Product

The result of the medical tourism industry is far-reaching. Not only will it benefit many different business sectors directly and indirectly, medical tourism can provide an increase in a nation's overall economic health. Revenue generation will increase the GDP. This resultant growth will encourage development of the nation's infrastructure and its people's quality of life.

Related to Process

Revenue generation from this business will hopefully encourage the further development of the infrastructure that is required to carry out the medical tourism product. Development of the healthcare system, as well as the travel and tourism infrastructure, will benefit the nation and its people on the whole.

16. Trade Product Identification/Trade and Services

The medical tourism product generally provides numerous types of services. First and foremost, medical tourism is providing a consumer with the healthcare service that they need or desire. In addition, this type of business also offers the consumer the lodging services that they require to participate in this process. Often consumers will also take part in some leisure, recreational or sightseeing activities while visiting the country. Therefore, the tourism industry may also be providing a service to these consumers as well.

17. Economic Data

The medical tourism industry can be a product for any country. However, numerous nations have significantly benefited from this business more than others. The country's that have demonstrated the most significant gains are noted below:

- Medical tourism has contributed approximately $25 million per year to Cuba's economic status.
- India has seen a 27 percent increase in tourists while medical tourism, itself, has demonstrated a 20 percent growth. Additionally, India has attracted 150,000 medical tourists in 2003. By 2012, medical tourism is expected to bring an additional $1.1-2.2 billion in annual revenue.
- In 2002, Thailand treated more than 600,000 tourists that generated approximately $503 million in revenues.
- In 2000, Singapore attracted more than 150,000 tourists for medical care which added 0.19 percent to its GDP. By 2012, this island is expected to treat more than 1 million tourists. This figure will complement a 3 percent market share for healthcare services, generate some $3 billion in revenue, add 1 percent to the GDP and lead to some 13,000 new jobs

18. Impact of Trade Restriction

Because the basis of this industry requires consumers to travel for their healthcare needs, trade restrictions on travel would impact its capabilities. Among the two most problematic restrictions would be on visa issuing and International Travel Bans to specific regions or countries. Thus, if the consumers are unable to travel to the desired country, the product and service cannot be sold.

19. Industry Sector

As suggested previously, the primary industry sector for medical tourism includes: the healthcare industry, as well as the international travel and tourism industry. The secondary industry sectors would include: service, information technology and communication industries.

20. Exporters and Importers

In the medical tourism industry, the export is the consumer. Because the consumer comes into the country for their healthcare needs, they provide foreign currency to the economy. In the end, they leave the country with the desired medical care. It is the hope that there are no real imports and that all of the goods and services are provided domestically.

V. Macro/Environment Cluster/Tourism Policy Clusters

21. Environmental Problem Type/Environmental Aspects

Although the main focus of the medical tourism product is the healthcare service provided, countries are also encouraging consumers to be tourists. As a tourist, they are enjoying the beauty and recreation of the area. The hope is that some of the revenues from these activities will go into developing the environmental infrastructure, as well as conservation and preservation.

22. Resource Impact and Effect

This type of practice does not really require any substantial amount of environmental resources. Therefore, there are no major impacts or effects of the medical tourism business on a nation's environmental resources.

23. Urgency and Policy Review

On the whole, medical tourism is still in an emergent state. Therefore, this practice has not necessitated any type of real urgency. However, most of the countries participating in this business have launched a global advertising and marketing campaign to varying extents. Each country has unique marketing strategies that target specific markets. Additionally, because each country seeks growth, each has their own unique policies that allow for the attraction of these consumer markets.

24. Substitutes and Alternative Policies

The most common alternative to receiving healthcare in one's desired country is obtaining one's healthcare needs in a competitive country. Therefore, countries attempt to make their policies as attractive and simplified as possible to attract the consumer. If not, consumers may find a different country with less restrictive policies to provide them their desired care.

VI. Other Factors

25. *Culture*

Because this industry is carried out in many different countries around the world with various languages and practices, culture can play a significant role in this business. Nations must be cognizant of culture when marketing to specific target markets. Additionally, consumers must appreciate culture and traditions that may affect their foreign healthcare experience. Because many of the countries providing this service are developing countries, culture can be very different and varied. All participants in this business must understand and appreciate that culture can play a significant role in the medical tourism process.

26. *Trans-boundary Issues*

For medical tourism on a whole, overwhelming trans-boundary issues are not present. However, there are two specific markets within medical tourism, reproductive and suicide tourism, which do present trans-boundary challenges. With reproductive tourism, often consumers travel to another jurisdiction to receive a service that cannot be provided at home. Abortions and decisions surrounding *in vitro* fertilization can be two specific practices that can present challenges to the consumer. This is true for suicide tourism as well. There are issues surrounding the rights of the individual accompanying the consumer. Some countries view this as assistance, which often is prohibited. Therefore, although medical tourism does not present too many trans-boundary issues, specific markets can present challenges and should be more closely analyzed.

27. *Rights*

For the most part, medical tourism is not affected by one's rights. However, when dealing with reproductive and suicide tourism, a consumer's rights must be considered. Consumers have rights. However, they may be affected by receiving treatment in a foreign country or upon returning to their home country. Consumers must consider their rights, and they make seek treatment in alternative locations if a different area's policies better serve a patient's rights. This could be true for practices or procedures such as abortions, *in vitro* fertilization, as well as euthanasia. Thus, consumer's rights may play a part in decisions made for the medical tourism product.

28. Policy Implications

Many nations around the world, particularly developing countries, have taken advantage of the benefits of medical tourism. This emerging industry can provide significant economic stimulus for a nation's revenue growth and financial health. It can also stimulate infrastructure development and improve the quality of life of the nation's people. However, nations must position themselves correctly to reap this profit.

Countries must establish attractive policies that encourage medical tourism practice in their country as well as attract consumers to participate in this phenomenon. Nation's often demonstrate less restrictive policies than its neighbours and competitors.

Once a nation has policies in place, they must correctly market themselves. Countries use different and unique marketing strategies, such as lower-cost, more-timely, higher-quality, to promote their services to their target market. Thus, this industry has demonstrated significant impact on the nation's economic health, however less-restrictive and attractive policies must be in place first. Countries must also market themselves properly to continually enjoy the benefits of this emerging business.

APPENDIX 5

MEDICAL TOURISM BLOG

Tuesday, August 21, 2007

1. Interview with Karen Timmons, President and CEO—JCI

Couple of weeks back, we interviewed Brian Gooch, JCI consultant, who explained how he helps international hospitals plan and prepare for JCI accreditation. Today, we bring you Karen H. Timmons, President and Chief Executive Officer of Joint Commission Resources, Inc. (JCR) and Joint Commission International (JCI). Under her leadership, JCI is developing an international collaborative network to improve patient safety. Ms. Timmons is also the primary liaison with the World Health Organization (WHO) and is a past board member and Treasurer for the International Society of Quality Assurance (ISQua).

Question: ISO also concentrates on organization-related standards. How does JCI add to that, specifically in terms of standards related to patients, and their safety?

Karen Timmons: We believe that JCI's combination of patient-and organization-centered standards helps assure that all aspects of a patient's journey through a healthcare organization are as safe and of favourable quality as possible. JCI's standards also account for proper education, not only of caregivers, but of the patients they treat and the too-often-forgotten patients' families. Accreditation is a risk-reduction activity. By compliance with standards, organizations are in fact performing to "evidence-based" practices and have a greater likelihood of good outcomes, with less risk to patients.

Patient-focused standards are included in seven chapters of our current hospital standards manual: "Access to Care and Continuity of Care"; "Patient and Family Rights"; "Assessment of Patients"; "Care of Patients"; "Anesthesia and Surgical Care"; "Medication Management and Use"; and "Patient and Family Education". Healthcare Organization Management Standards are covered in six chapters: "Quality Improvement and Patient Safety"; "Prevention and Control of Infections"; "Governance, Leadership, and Direction"; "Facility Management and Safety"; "Staff Qualifications and Education"; and "Management of Communication and Information".

Question: JCI is a subsidiary of the Joint Commission, which accredits U.S. Hospitals. What are the differences in the standards for U.S. hospitals and those outside? Is the bar set lower, or do you need to take into consideration other factors?

Karen Timmons: With the release of the 3rd edition of the JCI Hospital Standards in July 2007 (effective from 1 January 2008), our most comprehensive and stringent to date, JCI's standards are different from, but comparable to, Joint Commission standards. Our standards account for countries' and regions' specific legal, religious, and cultural factors, whereas The Joint Commission's standards reference United States federal requirements (such as the National Fire Protection Associations and others). We consider JCI's standards to be optimal, achievable criteria for organizations dedicated to improving the quality of patient care, ensuring a safe environment, and continually working to reduce risks to patients and staff.

Question: JCI accreditation is purely voluntary and there are currently approximately 130 hospitals which are JCI accredited. Do you think that this is limiting the impact that you are having on improving standards of hospitals worldwide? Do you think hospitals which cater to international patients need a little prodding to get themselves accredited?

Karen Timmons: JCI's accreditation process is indeed voluntary. We launched JCI's international accreditation program in 1999 in response to the increasing global demand for valid external evaluation of healthcare quality and safety.

To date, more than 130 organizations have achieved JCI accreditation and the numbers are growing at a rate that exceeds our forecasts. JCI standards are viewed as the international healthcare standards and their impact is significant and lasting.

Additionally, JCI has working public-private partnerships with a number of Ministries of Health and other governmental and non-governmental agencies across the globe in which JCI standards are serving as the foundation for national accreditation programs. The most recent example of this type of arrangement is our agreement with the People's Republic of China's Ministry of Health, in which JCI is assisting the Ministry in improving the safety and quality of patient care through a series of initiatives in Chinese hospitals, clinics, laboratories, and other healthcare settings. JCI is helping create strategies to further strengthen qualifications and training of hospital staff, as well as collaborating with medical facilities, research institutes, and non-governmental organizations to establish standards-based guidelines for blood safety, medication management and information management.

Question: I understand you review accreditations once in three years. What happens if a hospital adds a new specialty in between, with new staff and new equipment? Do you have agreements in place to make it necessary for the hospitals to either stick to the standards, or request an emergency review of the new facilities?

Karen Timmons: We require that organizations notify us in writing within 30 days of any significant changes to their organization or facility during the course of their 3-year accredited status. If and when that happens, JCI schedules what we call an "extension survey"-a survey that makes certain that this new "extension" of an organization's service meets JCI standards.

Question: I take it that JCI accreditation involves implementing changes in the way that the hospitals and their staff treat and manage patients, in addition to infrastructural requirements. Do you provide them with any help for that, or just explain the requirements?

Karen Timmons: When an organization approaches JCI about accreditation, they are given the following:

(a) One of our brochures, describing JCI accreditation process.
(b) A list of for-purchase publications and education conferences, including the JCI accreditation manuals and other accreditation—or patient safety-related publications, audio conferences, etc.
(c) Web links, including a link to the most recent JCI standards applicable to their organization.

If an organization requests more technical assistance, we provide it by giving the organization a phone number to contact the international consulting division of Joint Commission Resources. We do that because of our self-imposed "firewall" between JCI's accreditation and consulting; accreditation cannot and will not know which organizations seek or use JCI consultants and JCI consultants do not know an organization's accreditation status prior to a public announcement is made. That division works completely independently of JCI's accreditation operations; neither organization is aware of the other's clientele (until an organization is publicly acknowledged as accredited). Although consultants may assist an organization with preparing for JCI accreditation, consultation in itself is by no means a required or even recommended step in the accreditation process.

Question: What information about an accredited hospital can a prospective patient expect to get from JCI? You must be collecting a lot of data from each hospital on a regular basis. So if someone contacts JCI regarding a particular hospital, what would you be saying to them?

Karen Timmons: We envision a time when JCI will provide an international service similar to The Joint Commission's Quality Check Web Portal (http://www.qualitycheck.org/), a wide-ranging guide to the 15,000

Joint Commission-accredited healthcare organizations and programs in the United States. As JCI continues to grow, we see that sort of quality-monitoring service as a patient-centric priority. Today, though, we are able to tell prospective patients who contact JCI whether or not a healthcare organization is accredited or not.

Question: Are you seeing an improvement recently in the numbers of hospitals applying for JCI accreditation? If so, why?

Karen Timmons: As I described earlier, we have seen an upswing in interest in JCI accreditation, and we believe that the surge in interest is an indication that our message is being heard by a larger audience. Eight years into its existence, JCI is becoming more widely known around the world as an accreditor of choice. We believe our patient-centric focus is a big part of the growing acceptance of JCI everywhere, in addition to the growing consensus across borders that there is a business case for patient safety. More and more, patients are taking control over their searches for quality healthcare, and the stamp of approval that JCI accreditation provides is becoming a "gold standard" for knowledgeable patients and care givers alike.

Question: Does JCI get involved in partnerships or collaborations? Do you have any programs other than accreditation which deal with improving healthcare and patient safety?

Karen Timmons: JCI has several patient-safety collaborations separate from its accreditation activities, including the following:

WHO Collaborating Centre for Patient Safety: Since its launch in August 2005, the World Health Organization (WHO) Collaborating Centre for Patient Safety has been building an international network to identify, evaluate, adapt and disseminate patient safety solutions worldwide. A WHO collaborating centre is "a national institution designated by the Director-General of the World Health Organization to form part of an international collaborative network carrying out activities in support of WHO's mandate for international health work and its programme priorities." This specific Collaborating Centre, a cooperative endeavor of WHO, JCI, and The Joint Commission, is operationalized by The Joint Commission International Center for Patient Safety (see below) through the establishment of a collaborative network of leaders in developing, transitional, and developed countries, who are helping to identify healthcare safety needs and match these with known best practices and solutions. Specific projects of the Collaborating Centre include the following:

Patient Safety Solutions: Announced in May 2007, the basic purpose of the Patient Safety Solutions is to guide the redesign of care processes to prevent inevitable human errors from actually reaching patients. The Solutions include any system design or intervention that has demonstrated the ability to prevent or mitigate patient harm stemming from healthcare processes. Solutions disseminated by the Collaborating Centre are evidence-based, presented in a standard format, and will be updated at regular intervals. The inaugural Patient Safety Solutions address the following issues:

- Look-alike, sound-alike medication names
- Correct patient identification
- Hand-over communications
- Correct procedure at the correct body site
- Control of concentrated electrolyte solutions
- Medication accuracy
- Catheter and tubing misconnections
- Needle reuse and injection device safety
- Hand hygiene

Additional solutions for 2008 release are currently under development.

High 5s: Drawn from a broader set of patient safety solutions, the overall goal of the initiative is to achieve significant, sustained, and measurable reduction or elimination of five highly prevalent patient safety problems in selected hospitals in each country over a five-year period (hence "High 5s"). The High 5s build on the partnership established by the Commonwealth Fund with Australia, Canada, New Zealand, the United Kingdom, and the United

States, and the more recent expansion of this international program to include Germany and the Netherlands. These solutions are the following:

- Prevention of patient care hand-over errors
- Prevention of wrong-site, wrong-procedure, wrong-person surgical errors
- Prevention of continuity of medication errors
- Prevention of high concentration drug errors
- Promotion of effective hand hygiene practices

In March 2005, The Joint Commission and JCR announced the establishment of the Joint Commission International Center for Patient Safety, a virtual organization which leverages the expertise, resources, and knowledge of the Joint Commission and JCR toward its mission of continuously improving patient safety in all healthcare settings. The Center does the following:

- Collaborates with other leading patient safety organizations around the globe to achieve its goals, including the identification, development and sharing of patient safety solutions.
- Serves as a credible source of valid and meaningful information and education about patient safety.
- Engages patients, families, practitioners, and providers in improving patient safety.
- Advocates for public policy that promotes patient safety.
- Conducts research related to patient safety.

The Center's Web site (http://www.jcipatientsafety.org) features a variety of quality and safety links and resources, including the following:

- Patient Safety Practices (PSP)—nearly 1,000 links to patient safety publications and Web sites, with tips, tools, and resources for addressing patient safety and quality issues.

- Patient Safety Goals—both the National and International Patient Safety Goals are listed, with links to articles and other publications offering compliance tips and other related research.
- Complementary Patient Safety Resources—abstracts of current literature on patient safety, a sample outline for a patient safety plan, and selected bibliography medical error disclosure.
- Web Site Links for Healthcare Professionals, Providers, Patients, and Families—a directory of online quality and safety resources.
- Sentinel Event Alerts—a Joint Commission publication identifying specific sentinel events, describing their common underlying causes, and suggesting preventive steps for the future.
- Patient Safety Link—a monthly electronic newsletter, available at no cost to subscribers.

Why Singapore?

Question: Dr. Yap, you are the Director of Healthcare Services with the Singapore Tourism Board. I hope that is correct. So are your duties, and those of your office, tilted more towards healthcare or tourism? Or are you specifically handling medical tourism?

Dr. Yap: Yes, the designation is correct.

First and foremost, STB's focus goes beyond mere "medical tourism". We prefer to call it Medical Travel. While many do go on "medical holidays" where healthcare offerings are combined with leisure activities, a great many others travel solely for healthcare. Therefore, what STB takes care of are medical travelers.

Unlike our major competitors, Singapore has an unusual reason for being in the medical travel industry. While the revenue from international patients is naturally welcome in a country that has had to rely on international trade for its national survival, the reality is that Singapore would make more money investing its resources in other directions. However, the national imperative to make and maintain Singapore as an international medical hub arises from the need to look after its own citizens and residents.

Through the decades of strong economic growth, Singapore has invested in its own healthcare system and created one of the best healthcare systems in the world. Singapore sent its doctors overseas to train in the best international centers. These doctors eventually return to upgrade and improve local healthcare services to be on par with where they had trained. All the major healthcare networks are JCI-accredited and Singapore accounts for some one-third of all JCI-accredited healthcare facilities in Asia.

However, with a small population of only 4.5 million residents, Singapore finds it increasingly difficult to sustain the many subspecialties, to maintain the many high-end services and to afford the technology. Thus, the effort to draw international patients is to maintain a critical mass of patients. Ironically, and unlike other countries, Singapore seeks foreign patients in order to serve local patients.

The Singapore Tourism Board (STB) plays an instrumental role to develop and maintain Singapore as a medical hub, not only for international patients, but for medical conferences and training, healthcare consultancy, regional and international headquarters of healthcare organisations, manufacturing of pharmaceuticals and medical devices, etc. STB's main role is in international marketing and the development of people-oriented services for medical travelers.

Question: What advantages does Singapore hold, for a medical tourist, as compared to countries like Thailand or India?

Dr. Yap: There are several reasons why medical travelers choose Singapore as their choice healthcare destination.

The first and foremost reason is simply that, it is Singapore. Singapore is known for its excellence, efficiency and effectiveness. Having the best international airport, the best airline, and the busiest port in the world, these accolades are evidence of Singapore's world-class standards and achievements.

The clinical services in Singapore emphasize excellence, safety and trustworthiness, with internationally accredited facilities and renowned physicians trained in the best centers in the world. In 2000, the World Health Organization ranked

Singapore's healthcare system as the sixth best in the world and the best in Asia, and Singapore accounts for one-third of all JCI-accredited facilities in Asia. Beyond international certifications, the quality of healthcare is also seen in published clinical indicators. Many healthcare institutions in Singapore publish their success rates on their corporate websites, and these rates are comparable to, if not exceeding, international standards.

Singapore is a true multi-faceted regional medical hub, not only for patients' services but also as a meeting place for medical professionals for conferences and training, as a base for healthcare consultancy and operations management, and as the centre for research and clinical trials.

Cost is an important consideration for many international patients. For instance, an angioplasty costs approximately US $57,000-83,000 for an uninsured patient in the United States, whereas in Singapore, it costs only US $13,000, similar to the costs at other major Asian medical travel destinations. So even after factoring in travel and accommodation expenses of the patient and their accompanying persons, the cost savings are still considerable. On top of the affordability, patients in Singapore are assured of world-class treatment and high clinical outcomes.

Finally, Singapore is an international city which welcomes people of all cultures. The Singapore Changi International Airport is connected to some 180 cities in the world, making it highly accessible. Transport and accessibility within the country is equally easy and convenient. English is the first language of education and business. The people in Singapore enjoy high security and low crime. As Singapore is a multi-racial and multi-culturally accommodating city, patients of all race and creed will not find it difficult to meet people in Singapore who speak their language or share their religion.

Ultimately, the medical traveler seeks peace of mind. They do not want to go where there are uncertainties about the quality of care or the safety of the blood, rumors of wars and bombs, government or social unrest, natural disasters, or any concerns about safety for themselves and their families. Singapore is one destination where medical travelers will have no such fears, where they can enjoy peace of mind when their health really matters.

Question: Approximately how many international patients does Singapore receive annually, from which parts of the world, and what are the most sought after treatments by these patients? How much growth is Singapore expecting in this area in the next year and beyond?

Dr. Yap: Based on exit surveys conducted of international patients, out of the nearly 10 million visitors to Singapore in 2006, approximately 410,000 or four percent travelled specifically for healthcare. These patients did not come alone. Approximately 89,000 persons accompanied them on their visits. Another 56,000 received healthcare incidentally when on visits for other purposes. In total, some 555,000 international visitors to Singapore in 2006 were involved in some aspect of medical travel.

The majority of our medical travelers come from the established markets of Indonesia, Malaysia and Brunei, but the list of countries that patients now come from have gone up tremendously in the past half-decade. Singapore continues to be a favoured destination for our established markets. Readers Digest in a 25,000-reader survey found that their readers ranked Singapore only after USA as most favoured healthcare destination, even ahead of Europe. Consider how the number of healthcare visitors grew from 320,000 in 2004 to 410,000 in 2006, a 28% increase. Some of that increase is accounted by gradual increases in numbers from the relatively stable, established markets, but the remainder is from the rapidly growing markets in ASEAN, the Middle-East, South Asia, Russia, etc.

Singapore offers a wide spectrum of healthcare services ranging from health screening and cosmetic surgery to complex specialty care such as ophthalmology, orthopedic surgery, cardiology, cardiothoracic surgery, obstetrics and

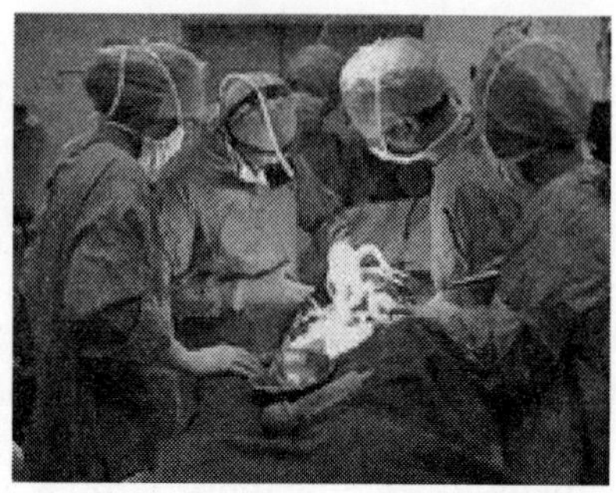

gynecology, neurology, neurosurgery and oncology amongst others.

Categorically, international patients come to Singapore for four main types of healthcare. They come for essential healthcare where the care is not available in their own country, affordable healthcare where the care is available but not affordable, quality healthcare where the care available locally is or is perceived to be of inferior quality, and premium healthcare where traveling for healthcare is seen as a luxury and adds prestige to the traveling person.

The most significant reason for patients coming to Singapore from the surrounding regions such as Indonesia, Malaysia, Indo-China and India, is for quality healthcare. Many also come for essential healthcare, in particular, complex heart, brain, lung, liver and orthopedic surgeries, organ transplantations, as well as cancer care where their home countries just do not have a similarly high level of medical sophistication, whereas patients from the United Kingdom come to Singapore to avoid long waiting times for surgeries like hip replacements.

For visitors from the United States who usually come to Singapore for orthopedic surgeries and cardiology, the biggest motivation is the cost savings for high quality healthcare, as patients can receive US-standard healthcare from JCI-accredited healthcare facilities and internationally known doctors at a fifth of the price back home or less.

In total, some 555,000 international visitors to Singapore in 2006 were involved in some aspect of medical travel. Thus, medical travel is a very big market. Singapore hopes to attract at least 1 million medical travelers to Singapore every year starting from 2012.

Question: The Singapore Government seems to be much more involved in promoting medical tourism and getting the various agencies to coordinate in order to provide a better experience for visiting patients. Is this a conscious effort, or is it just the way you do things?

Dr. Yap: While many other countries and regions announce their plans to "go into medical tourism", Singapore has been quietly doing it all along. The "Whole of Government" approach to supporting Singapore's international medical travel industry is evident in the SingaporeMedicine initiative.

Singapore Medicine is a multi-agency government-industry partnership to develop and maintain Singapore as a medical hub and international patient destination. It is led by the Ministry of Health, and supported by three government agencies: the Economic Development Board which develops industry capabilities, the International Enterprise Singapore which fosters regionalization by Singapore's local healthcare players, and the Singapore Tourism Board which manages international marketing and associated people-oriented services.

The government agencies work with the local and international healthcare and medical travel industries to ensure that patients are well taken care of. Where there are issues affecting other government agencies (e.g. visas), there is a government-wide consensus and effort to balance the different needs to achieve the best solutions.

Most important of all, as mentioned in Q1, the main motivation behind the government supporting medical travel is that Singapore needs to have patient volumes to maintain the clinical subspecialty expertise, and to gain economies of scale for its technology.

So yes, it is a conscious effort by the government to ultimately provide and sustain the level of clinical expertise and medical care that Singaporeans have since become used to.

Question: We recently interviewed Dr. Milica Bookman, who is doing research on the effect of medical tourism on developing countries. Not to say that Singapore is a developing country, but is medical tourism having any effec' on healthcare you offer to your own citizens? If so, could y' elaborate on that?

Dr. Yap: As emphasized in Q1, Singapore needs foreign patients in order to serve its own patients.

Question: Please tell us a bit more about Singapore medicine (Singaporemedicine.com), its mission and activities.

Dr. Yap: Activities undertaken by SingaporeMedicine partners include: Media familiarization trips for international journalists.

Participation in healthcare conferences and tradeshows in key and emerging overseas markets such as Indonesia, Malaysia, India, Bangladesh, the Middle East, Russia, and more recently, the United States.

Intensified market development, business development and product development programmes by the Singapore healthcare providers through the support of Singapore Medicine.

Singapore Medicine is also working closely with medical institutions to improve international patient support through the provision of international patient liaison services, translation and interpretation services as well as foreign language signages to meet the diverse needs of foreign patients.

Question: We're seeing some employers and insurers showing interest in medical tourism in the US. What do you think about medical tourism as an industry? What's the potential? What changes do you see in the near future?

Dr. Yap: The Medical Tourism market is currently valued at US $20 billion annually. Some of these dollars is perhaps hype but the market is obviously significant whatever the actual numbers. These numbers are expected to double by 2010.

The world has flattened for many industries like manufacturing and software engineering, where many companies have gone to China and India respectively. We expect to see the flattening of the world (as in Thomas Friedman's book) finally reach the healthcare world. Today people in many countries and regions find that the healthcare in their own locality is not accessible, affordable, adequate or acceptable. With the relative ease and low costs of travel today, patients will travel in search•of better healthcare.

The medical travel industry has grown in several waves. Initially, there was the local/proximate movements of people to nearby countries for better healthcare, for example, Singapore has been serving the peoples of Indonesia, Malaysia, Brunei and the rest of the ASEAN region long before the term "medical tourism" was ever coined. The people started moving farther afield when they found that they, as consumers, had the ability to choose, which was when individual, often uninsured, Americans started looking to Asia for lower cost healthcare.

The next wave is waiting, when corporate entities realise that, just they can source worldwide for manpower and means of production, they can also start looking overseas for healthcare for their manpower. When corporations, for example in the US and the developed world, started sending their staff around the world for the best and the most affordable healthcare, then truly the world would be flat indeed.

Question: The main worry about medical tourism is that there's no legal recourse in case things go wrong when you opt for surgery abroad. There is realistically very little chance of a successful and timely malpractice suit in most countries promoting medical tourism. What is the status of Singapore, in this regard?

Dr. Yap: Patients travelling for healthcare should by and large be seeking reliable and safe healthcare, and legal proceedings should ideally be a low probability event. Given the excellent clinical outcomes and assured quality of healthcare in Singapore, the chances of patients having to seek legal recourse are significantly lower as compared to other healthcare destinations. However, medicine being what it is, it is not possible to rule out completely the possibility of mishaps and other untoward events. Legal suits related to healthcare services delivered in Singapore would generally be contested in Singaporean law courts. The legal system in Singapore is well known for its impartiality and reliability. In 2004, the Political and Economic Risks Consultancy (PERC) rated Singapore's judicial system as the best in Asia, ahead of

Hong Kong and Japan. It also ranked Singapore as the top in consistency of application of laws. In addition, Singapore's legal system has been praised by the International Monetary Fund and the Economic Intelligence Unit. Therefore, the medical traveler can be assured of fairness in the rare event that legal action is appropriate.

That was Dr. Jason Yap, Director, Healthcare Services, STB. The main advantage Singapore has is that things work efficiently, and on time. A medical tourist in Singapore gets the same, if not better, level of care, at a fraction of the price, has legal recourse which is fair and quick, and best of all, you have the option of recuperating with a great post surgical vacation in Singapore. And an indicator of their efficiency is the fact that the SingaporeMedicine website can be accessed in five languages—English, Chinese, Arabic, Indonesian and Vietnamese. That shows how consumer friendly they are, and how far they are willing to go to attract and satisfy medical tourists. Stay tuned for more interviews.

Thursday, August 16, 2007

Bargain Surgery in Thailand!

"The Chaophya hospital is one of five hospitals in Thailand and in Singapore offering stem cell therapy for end-stage heart disease. Thailand is also a destination for medical tourists with a very different agenda from those of Dr. Supachai's patients: it is one of the world's leading centers for sex reassignment surgery. The boom in medical tourism in recent years has spawned the growth of a new travel market, with specialized agencies ready to serve their clients' clinical and travel needs, whether they're Americans seeking cosmetic surgery, or Canadians who don't want to wait up to a year for a government-funded hip replacement."

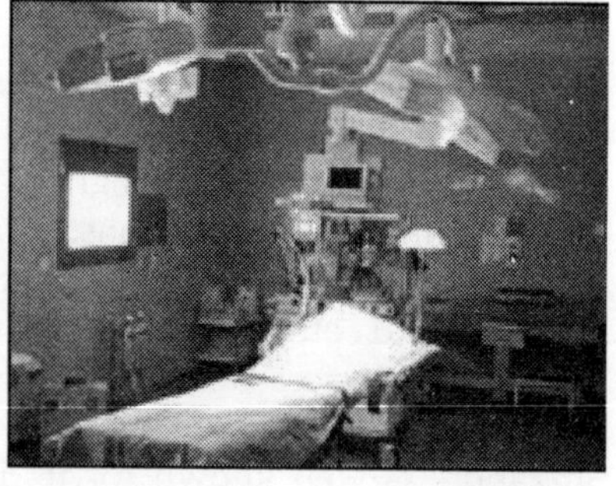

Medical tourism is an increasingly attractive option for any kind of medical treatment or surgery which is not immediately available or is unaffordable locally. And unless employers and health plans start considering medical tourism as an option, the slow bleed of patients going abroad, without any kind of safety net will continue.

Dentists in eastern Europe were the first to attract British patients for teeth whitening and other cosmetic work. But now plastic surgeons are following suit—offering bargain breast implants and other procedures."

Richard Slater lives at a nursing home in Mexico, comfortably settled into his own cottage surrounded by purple bougainvillea and pomegranate trees. . . . He gets 24-hour nursing care and three meals a day, cooked in a homey kitchen and served in a sun-washed dining room. For this, Slater pays just $550 a month, less than one-tenth of the going rate back home in Las Vegas. For an additional $140 a year, he gets complete medical coverage from the Mexican government, including all his medicine and insulin for his

diabetes. "This would all cost me a fortune in the United States," said Slater, a 65-year-old retired headwaiter. "I'm real happy with the place." Um...Maybe the Mexicans should build a border fence to prevent all those seniors from the United States sneaking across the border into Mexico, trying to escape the squalor and poverty at home and enjoy the good times in Mexico. . . .

Appendix 6

BEDSIDE INDIA

By Bruce Stokes

The most striking aspect of Fortis Healthcare's Rajan Dhall Hospital may be what it lacks. Rajan Dhall, located in the middle-class Vasant Kunj neighbourhood of south New Delhi, doesn't smell like a hospital. Absent is the scent of disinfectant and disease that is so pervasive in most medical centers. And the dreary claustrophobia felt in so many institutional settings built for function rather than for human beings is not present, either; the hospital's soft-green walls and oddly angled corridors lighten the mood. Finally, the red-sari-clad attendants walking the halls bear no resemblance to Ken Kesey's infamous Miss Ratched.

This reassuring first impression is by design. Jasbir Grewal, Fortis's vice president for operations, worked in East Asia for the Hilton hotel chain for years. He knows that initial experiences matter to people, be they overnight lodgers or sick patients. "We are a hotel delivering clinical medical excellence," Grewal said, reflecting Fortis's ambition to provide first-class, private health care for India's burgeoning middle class and for a growing number of foreigners.

This reporter spent six hours being poked and prodded during a comprehensive executive-fitness checkup at Rajan Dhall, and the experience confirmed that Fortis provides world-class medical services with a hotelier's touch, and at cut-rate prices.

On the hospital's spacious lower floor, a dozen examination rooms for outpatients surround a well-appointed waiting area. The decor and atmosphere is more airport business lounge than public health clinic. Gracious aides usher patients from test to test. Hurry-up-and-wait brusqueness is kept to a minimum, reflecting a finely tuned patient flow. Medical technicians are courteous but definitely on a schedule, juggling multiple procedures. Yet the final interview with a doctor to review the results, the interaction that is undoubtedly the most important to the patient, is unhurried and complete, taking a full half hour. Many of the tests performed—an echocardiogram, a stress test, a lung-function test, and an ultrasound of internal organs—would never be part of a basic annual physical in the United States. In America such examinations simply cost too much. Here the total bill was $125. A comparable battery of tests in Washington would cost at least $4000, a difference that would have more than covered the entire cost of a trip to India.

The number of foreigners who come to India each year for such checkups, or for more-extensive surgical procedures, is not huge: fewer than 200,000 a year, and these visits generate about $300 million in revenue for Indian hospitals. That amount, however could grow to $2 billion a year by 2012, according to an estimate by the management consulting firm McKinsey & Co. In the $800 billion Indian economy, $2 billion is small change. But to put that sum in perspective, it is more than the Indian auto parts industry earned from exports in 2005.

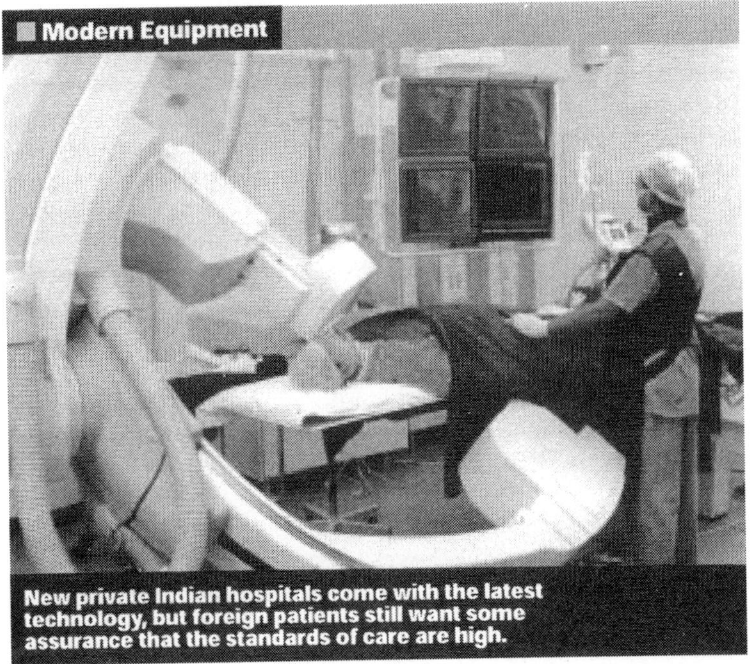

New private Indian hospitals come with the latest technology, but foreign patients still want some assurance that the standards of care are high.

New Hospital

The 120-bed Rajan Dhall Hospital, named for an Indian fighter pilot, will eventually to 200 beds. It has three deluxe suites often used by foreigners.

India has high hopes for medical tourism. Currently, most such visits are by patients who somehow find their own way here for treatment; it is a hit-or-miss interaction. In the future, Indian health care providers, such as Fortis, foresee medical tourism becoming a much-higher-volume business, in which patients' insurance companies steer them to India because of the nation's reputation for low-cost, high-quality elective surgery. In this way. India hopes to capitalize on its pool of skilled, English-speaking doctors and nurses to better integrate its economy into the global market and to diversify its service exports, now heavily dependent on software and call centers. (When India treats a foreigner in one of its hospitals, it is, on the country's balance sheet, an "export" of services.) "India will become the global health care hub," predicted Harpal Singh, Fortis's chairman.

Most of India's foreign patients do not come from the United States. And the outsourcing of large numbers of American medical procedures to India is still some time off.. The subcontinent is too far away, too exotic, and too poor for all but the most adventurous or the most cash-strapped Americans. India still lacks brand-name hospitals and easy physician follow-up. And if something were to go wrong, a patient would stand little chance of successfully suing.

But as Americans scramble to pay runaway health care bills. India promises to draw more and more cost-conscious patients from overseas. The financial savings for foreigners are so compelling that it is only a matter of time before private U.S. insurers and the corporations that foot many of the health insurance bills of their American employees offer treatment options in India.

Private-sector Challenge

Health care is the largest service industry in India in terms of revenue and the second largest, after education, in terms of jobs, employing more than 4 million people. Yet overall, India's health care system is in shambles—overstretched and underfinanced. India spends only 4.8 percent of its gross national product on medical care, less than China and far less than the United States. For every 10,000 patients, India has only six physicians, eight nurses, and nine hospital beds. That is 64 percent fewer doctors, 17 percent fewer nurses, and 64 percent fewer hospital beds per capita than in China.

Private upscale hospitals such as the Fortis facility are the exception in India, not the rule. They are primarily an outlet for the well-to-do and for foreigners who can afford to travel here—a thin veneer on top of a vast table of underserved patients.

Improving the availability of health care for all parts of India's society is a staggering challenge. The World Health Organization estimates that India needs to add 80,000 hospital beds a year over the next five years; McKinsey, in turn, says that India must invest at least $77.9 billion in health care by 2012 to meet expected demand.

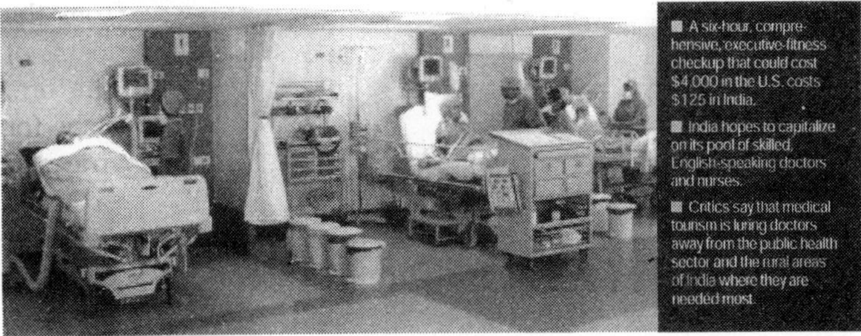

Competing priorities to build roads and schools put such investment in health care beyond the Indian government's means. As a result, McKinsey estimates that 89 percent of new capital spending for health care will have to come from the private sector.

Fortis Healthcare

India's private hospitals already provide more than half of the country's hospital beds. But for-profit facilities are often little more than private clinics, with four in five having fewer than 30 beds. Recent economic good times and the prospect that private-hospital revenue could double by 2012 have triggered a boom in the consolidation and expansion of the private health care business in India, and many large, modern, highly efficient facilities such as Rajan Dhall are under construction. "We are redefining the parameters and raising the benchmarks," Singh said.

Rajan Dhall, named after an Indian fighter pilot killed in the country's 1971 war with Pakistan, opened in July. The sleek, low-rise, 120-bed facility, which will eventually grow to 200 beds, has three deluxe suites—often used by foreigners—where family members can stay with patients. It also has a luxurious presidential suite. With 80 doctors on staff and scores of consultants, the hospital specializes in cardiac care, joint replacements, diabetes, and renal and respiratory diseases.

Rajan Dhall is one of the newest links in a chain of hospitals either owned or managed by Fortis Healthcare, a company established in 1996 by the family that started Ranbaxy Laboratories, India's largest pharmaceutical maker (see NJ, 4/16/05, p. 1146). Fortis, the second largest of India's private health care providers, opened its first facility in 2001 and now has a network of 12 hospitals with 1580 beds across north India. Fortis also has three facilities under construction, one each in Jaipur, Gurgaon, and New Delhi, and it hopes to run at least 40 hospitals nationwide by 2010.

About 3 percent of Rajan Dhall's patients are foreigners, many of them expatriates living in New Delhi. Overall, about 6 percent of Fortis's patient load is from abroad, and its number of non-Indian patients could reach 2,000 this year. Most come from Asia and the Middle East, with Europe and the United States accounting for only about one in 10. Cosmetic surgery is Fortis's big draw: It attracts about 50 percent of its foreign patients. An additional 20 percent come from abroad for gall bladder operations and treatment of kidney stones. About 30 percent of foreigners seek out Fortis for more-serious procedures, including heart surgery and knee replacement.

Lower Costs

The worldwide market for medical tourism is estimated at $40 billion; India's share is less than 1 percent. By 2012, the total market could be $100 billion, and India's share could be 2 to 3 percent, according to a McKinsey estimate. To realize that target, Fortis and its competitors are positioning themselves to provide more high-end procedures, leaving nip-and-tuck plastic surgery to Thailand and Singapore, the current destinations of choice for many medical tourists.

On price, India's competitive advantage is formidable. A knee replacement at Fortis costs a patient a third of what it would in the United States, a liver transplant is a quarter of the cost, and a bone marrow transplant is a tenth of the American price.

Lower labour costs are responsible for much of these savings. Fortis estimates that it pays its doctors as much as 40 percent less than what comparable physicians earn in the United States, even though many of the Indian doctors have been trained in American medical schools. Fortis can attract foreign-trained doctors because India's cost of living is so low that physicians earning smaller salaries can still afford drivers, servants, and big houses. And for Indian physicians trained abroad, family ties obviously beckon. The reduced threat of malpractice lawsuits is also a factor.

Moreover, Fortis pays its nurses between $2,100 and $10,000 a year, while the median annual salary for a hospital nurse in the United States is $53,000. But Fortis says that its real labor savings are achieved in the maintenance and administration of its facilities, thanks to the relatively low cost of Indian carpenters, plumbers, and receptionists, who are part of India's abundant supply of semiskilled labour.

Another plus is Fortis's focus on efficiency. "We have to make a profit," Grewal said. "So we run this like a business. It is no different from when I ran a hotel."

His boss, Singh, who came from the auto industry, added, "If you get good process, you get good outcomes. To do a dozen knees a day, you have to have the process down. Even in the laundry, if you get good process, you get clean sheets."

Despite these competitive advantages. Fortis is moving cautiously into medical tourism. "We don't want to be overly aggressive," said Sudarshan Mazumdar, the company's director of marketing. "We have to hit the low-hanging fruit, those with no or limited insurance, or those who want procedures not covered by insurance. We don't want to push the service until we can meet people's needs. The patient has to be comfortable about coming here. One negative experience would spoil the image of the company and India as a health care destination."

As a result, Singh said, "we don't anticipate more than 10 percent of total revenue from overseas patients."

Grim India

Singh's circumspection reflects the daunting reality that foreign patients face when seeking care in India.

New Delhi is a 17-hour flight from the East Coast of the United States. Fortis does pick-up overseas patients on arrival, but travelers first must navigate the capital's teeming, antiquated airport (thankfully, soon to be replaced). Then it's a stomach-churning, disregard-that-truck-that-almost-clipped-you trip into town on traffic-choked highways, past

Improving health care in India for all parts of society is a staggering challenge. The World Health Organization estimates that India needs to add 80,000 hospital beds a year over the next five years.

depressing street scenes of appalling poverty and human deprivation. It's enough to make many Americans wonder what they have gotten themselves into.

"Once the numbers are big enough, we could go to charter flights" to make the long trip from North America more tolerable, Fortis's Mazumdar said. For now, Fortis is pushing the Indian government to allow it to pick up patients directly from the tarmac to ease the transition. The hospital that Fortis is building in Gurgaon, a facility adjacent to the airport, will cater to foreigners, enabling them to avoid many of the hassles of daily Indian life.

But before patients come from abroad in great numbers, they must trust the care they will receive here. The Joint Commission International, which is affiliated with the group that accredits U.S. hospitals, has given its approval to fewer than 100 facilities outside of the United States. The commission is now reviewing two of Fortis's facilities for possible accreditation.

It is hard for potential patients to get quality-of-care data on any hospital, much less an Indian one. Data on the complication rates for heart surgery or knee replacement, for example, would help consumers pick and choose between Indian hospitals. But internationally comparable measurements of outcomes at various hospitals simply don't exist. Indian health care centers, like most American hospitals, do not publish such information.

Although sketchy, existing evidence seems to be supportive of the Indians. In testimony before the Senate Select Committee on Aging last year, Dr. Arnold Milstein, medical director of the consulting firm Pacific Business Group on Health, said, "The low gross mortality rates" in Indian hospitals for coronary bypass surgery suggest that any American quality advantage on that particular procedure "may be negligible."

Quality Reassurance

To really be comfortable in an Indian setting, Americans may insist on some reassurance of quality, perhaps through Indian hospitals partnering with a major American hospital, for example. A patient might feel more confident having knee-replacement surgery in India if it were done at a Johns Hopkins/Fortis affiliate. Such partnerships would also give patients access to follow-up at a U.S-based institution if complications developed.

Any such partnerships would make the economics of surgery in India less attractive because the savings from outsourcing such procedures would have to be shared with the American affiliate. But that may be the price of attracting a larger number of foreign patients. "We would be more than pleased to encourage joint ventures," Singh said.

Liability is another issue. Americans cherish the right to sue doctors if something goes wrong with a medical procedure. Currently, foreign patients must sign a consent form agreeing that their only legal recourse in case of a botched operation is through the Indian court system, which is excruciatingly slow and not nearly as friendly to medical malpractice suits as are courts in the United States. Fortis says that no international patient has ever sued it. But to reassure skittish patients worried about malpractice, U.S. insurance companies may need to offer coverage that would recompense victims of poor treatment without their having to fight their case in an Indian court.

The biggest impediment to medical tourism in India may prove to be opposition from domestic public health care providers. "In this country," Fortis's Grewal said, "hospitals are considered a socialized thing, so you aren't supposed to make money in health care."

In décor and atmosphere, Rajan Dhall Hospital's waiting area is more airport business lounge than public health clinic.

Proponents of private-sector medicine in India contend that medical tourism creates career opportunities and generates revenues to pay the salaries that entice world-class Indian-born physicians to return home from abroad, reversing a decades-long medical brain drain. Indian critics counter that medical tourism is luring doctors away from the rural areas where they are most needed and is tempting physicians to leave the already understaffed public health care sector. Both effects undermine medical treatment for all Indians, the critics say. Until the Indian government spends adequate amounts on public health care for its own people, this opposition will remain.

The U.S. Implications

The migration of elective surgery from the United States to foreign locales such as India may be inevitable, given the unsustainable rise in the cost of American medical care.

The average U.S. family's out-of-pocket spending on health care, excluding payment of health insurance premiums, rose nearly twice as fast as family income between 1996 and

2002, according to an analysis by the Commonwealth Fund, a private foundation that conducts research on the health care system. A recent study by McKinsey concluded that even after adjusting U.S. spending to account for higher average incomes, Americans still spend $1,645 more per capita per year on health care than consumers in other industrial nations.

Many Americans are open to the idea of traveling overseas to save on expenses. Some 61 percent of those without health insurance and 40 percent with insurance said they would be willing to travel 10,000 miles if they could save more than $5,000 on elective surgery, according to a May 2006 poll by *Time* magazine. "People are willing to travel if the value proposition—the quality of care, timeliness, and the cost—is strong," said Fortis's Singh.

Beautification

50%

of foreign patients who come to India's Fortis hospitals are there for cosmetic surgery.

Comparing labor costs at U.S. hospitals with those at hospitals in other industrial economies, McKinsey estimates that the United States has $54 billion in excess costs, even after factoring in Americans' greater wealth. U.S. hospitals also bear $87 billion in excess costs for operational and support functions compared with other countries. This fat makes American medical centers particularly vulnerable to lower-cost foreign competition.

Physicians in the United States are similarly exposed. They earn significantly more than Indian doctors, and more than their counterparts in other industrial countries relative to per capita incomes in those economies. As concerns about liability and India's quality of care are addressed, American physicians may find their patients deciding that the premium they pay U.S. doctors is not worth it.

A key question for the United States is how strongly American hospitals and doctors may push back if they see a sudden and steady exodus of profitable elective surgery to foreign shores.

Opposition from those with a vested interest in the status quo could be ferocious, if the reaction of other sectors of the American economy to their first competition from abroad is any guide. So a protectionist backlash to medical tourism from the politically potent American Medical Association and the American Hospital Association may be unavoidable.

Indian hospitals have a clear economic advantage in exporting their health care services, an edge that gives India a leg up in its growing global competition with China. If India can offer its world-class medical services to more foreigners, the nation's overall economy—and, ultimately, Indians themselves—will benefit. It is the kind of economic win-win that trade is supposed to bring to all. But because it involves the sensitive health care sector—a point of pride for many countries—and questions of life and death, the globalization of this service is likely to be more of a long-term investment than a short-term payoff.

The author a staff correspondent for National Journal, is also a journalism fellow with the German Marshall Fund of the United States, which supported research for this article. He can be reached at bstokes@nationaljournal.com.

Bibliography

American Autoimmune and Related Diseases Association 2006, Accessed on 12/2006-2/19/2006 at: http://www.aarda.org

Provides research information, statistics, NIH and legislative updates.

Angrosino, Michael, 1986, Health and Illness in Sociocultural Perspective in A Health Practitioner's Guide to the Social and Behavioural Sciences. Pp. 53-64. Auburn Press.

Chrisler, Joan C. and O'hea, Erin L., 2000, Gender, Culture, and Autoimmune Disorders in Handbook of Gender, Culture and Health. Richard M. Eisler and Michael Hersen, Pp. 321-42. First Edition. Mahwah: Lawrence Erlbaum Associates, Inc.

Farquhar, Judith, 1996, Knowing Practice: The Clinical Encounter of Chinese Medicine (Studies in and belief graphic Imagination). First Edition. Boulder, CO: Westview Press

Hadady, Letha, 1996, Asian Health Secrets: The Complete Guide to Asian Herbal Medicine. First Edition. New York: Three Rivers Press

Han, Henry, Miller, Glenn E, Deville, Nancy, 2003, Ancient Herbs, Modern Medicine. First Edition. New York: Bantam Books Ming, Dr. 2006 The Huai Hua Red Cross Hospital Accessed on 12/2006-2/19/2006 at: <http://www.tcmtreatment.com/hospital.htm>

McCurdy, David W., 1995, Using Anthropology in Conformity and Conflict: Readings in Cultural Anthropology. James Spradley and David W. McCurdy, eds., Pp. 415-27. Eleventh edition. Boston: Allyn and Bacon.

Penn, Nolan E., Kramer, Joyce, Skinner, John F., Velasquez, Roberto J., Yee, Barbara, W.K., Arellano, Letticia M., Williams, Joyce P. 2000 Health Practices and Healthcare Systems Among Cultural Groups in Handbook of Gender, Culture and Health. Richard M. Eisler and Michael Hersen. Pp. 105-138. First Edition. Mahwah: Lawrence Erlbaum Associates, Inc.

World Health Organization, 1978, The Promotion and Development of Traditional Medicine 2001 Traditional Medicine: Growing Needs and Potential.

———, 2006, Accessed on: 12/2005-2/19/2006 at: <http://www.who.int>

———, 2006, Traditional Medicine: Definitions.

———, 2006, Traditional Chinese Medicine Could Make "Health for One" True (Jia) (WHO Traditional Terms 2006, *et. al*).

J. Guest, "High Rate Robbery," Consumer Reports 67, No. 10 (2002): 7.

E. Warren and A.W. Tyagi, The Two-Income Trap (New York: Basic Books, 2003).

U.S. Bureau of the Census, Statistical Abstract of the United States, 1982-83 (Washington: U.S. Department of Commerce, 1983); and Administrative Office of the U.S. Courts, "Record Breaking Bankruptcy Filings Reported in Calendar Year 2001," Press Release (Washington: Administrative Office, 19 February, 2002).

See M.B. Jacoby, T.A. Sullivan, and E. Warren, "Rethinking the Debates over Healthcare Financing: Evidence from the Bankruptcy Courts," *New York University Law Review,* 76 (2001): 375-418.

S. Fay, E. Hurst, and M.J. White, "The Household Bankruptcy Decision," *American Economic Review,* 92, No. 3 (2002): 706-711.

E.M. Kennedy, In Critical Condition: The Crisis in America's Healthcare (New York: Simon and Schuster, 1972).

P.F. Short and J.S. Banthin, "New Estimates of the Underinsured Younger than Sixty-five Years," *Journal of the American Medical Association,* 274, No. 16 (1995): 1302-06.

M. Merlis, Family Out-of-Pocket Spending for Health Services (New York: Commonwealth Fund, June 2002).

E.J. Emanuel *et al.*, "Understanding Economic and Other Burdens of Terminal Illness: The Experience of Patients and Their Caregivers," *Annals of Internal Medicine,* 132, No. 6 (2000): 451-59.

Access Project, The Consequences of Medical Debt: Evidence from Three Communities, February 2003, www.accessproject.org/downloads/med_ consequences.pdf (13 December 2004).

NPR/Kaiser Family Foundation/Kennedy School of Government, "National Survey on Healthcare (chartpack)," June 2002, www.kff.org/kaiserpolls/upload/14064_1.pdf (27 January 2005); J.H. May and P.J. Cunningham, Tough Trade-Offs: Medical Bills, Family Finances, and Access to Care (Washington: Center for Studying Health System Change, June 2004); and S.R. Collins et al., The Affordability Crisis in U.S. Healthcare: Findings from the Commonwealth Fund Biennial Health Insurance Survey (New York: Commonwealth Fund, March 2004).

Uncontrolled gambling is classified as a psychiatric disorder in the Diagnostic and Statistical Manual of Mental Disorders, Fourth Edition (DSM-IV) and contributed to about 1 percent of the bankruptcies.

E. Flynn et al., "Bankruptcy by the Numbers," ABI Journal, 20, No. 10 (2002): 28-29; 21, No. 3 (2002): 22, 49; and 20, no. 8 (2001): 20.

The New Bankruptcy Epidemic (Hackettstown, N.J.: SMR, 2001), 127. A high incidence of collection agency calls was reported in NPR/Kaiser et al., "National Survey on Healthcare"; May et al., Tough Trade-Offs; and Collins et al., The Affordability Crisis.

Statistical Abstract of the United States: 1986 (Washington: GPO, 1985). The estimate that 8 percent of these were medical is from T.A. Sullivan, E. Warren, and J.L. Westbrook, The Fragile Middle Class: Americans in Debt (New Haven, Conn.: Yale University Press, 2000).

Administrative Office of the U.S. Courts, "Bankruptcy Cases Continue to Break Federal Court Case Records: Total

Bankruptcy Filings and Non-Business Filings Hit Highs," Press Release, 18 August 2003, www.uscourts.gov/Press_Releases/603b.pdf(13 December 2004).

J.S. Ziegel, "A Canadian Perspective," Texas Law Review, 79, No. 5 (2001): 241-56.

Rome/Vatican City (Clermont-Ferrand, France: Michelin Travel Publications, 2001).

American Medical Association Online, "Physicians react to projected Medicare physician payment cuts". 16 March 2006, 11 September, 2006. http://www.ama-assn.org/ama/pub/category/16122.html

Barmeyer, Robert A. Personal Interview. 12 September, 2006, Cannon, Michael, F. and Michael, D. Tanner.

Greenberg, Brad A. "Have Ailment, Will Travel", The Los Angeles Daily News, 7 August 2006, 8 September 2006, www.planethospital.com.

Healthcare Tourist.com. "The Process". 7 November 2006.www.healthcaretourist.com/main.php?page=process

Kasturi Dewi, K., "Hospitals set fees for health tourism", The Star, 28 Oct. 2003, The Association of Private Hospitals of Malaysia, http://www.hospitals-malaysia.org/

Kher, Unmesh, "Outsourcing Your Heart", Time.com., 21 May 2006, 6 September 2006. http://www.time.com/time/magazine/article/0,9171,1196429,00.html

Lancaster, John, "Surgeries, Side Trips for Medical Tourists", The Washington Post Online, 21 October 2004, 7 September 2006, www.washingtonpost.com

Marcelo, Ray, "India Fosters Growing Medical Tourism Sector", The Financial Times, 2 July 2003, 8 September 2006, http://yaleglobal.yale.edu/display.article?id=2016.

"NBC News", NBC, 20 February 2006, 11 September 2006, www.planethospital.com

Thai Websites, "Healthcare in Thailand" 7 November 2006 www.thaiwebsites.com/healthcare.asp

Todd, Stephen, "Medical Tourism Saves You Money, But Which One Is Best?", Ezine Articles.com., 7 September 2006, http://ezinearticles.com/.

Uretsky, Samuel D, "The 'Thailand Tuck'", MedHunters.com. 9 May 2005, 10 September 2006, http://www.medhunters.com/articles/medicalTourism.html

U.S. Census Bureau, "Poverty: Health Insurance Coverage in the United States", 13 October 2004, 11 September 2006, http://factfinder.census.gov/jsp/saff/SAFFInfo.jsp?_pageId=tp8_poverty

Wikipedia: the free encyclopedia, "Healthcare System", 11 Sept. 2006, www.wikipedia.org

Wikipedia: The free encyclopedia, "Medical Tourism", 11 Sept. 2006, www.wikipedia.org

1. Lancaster, "Surgeries, Side trips for Medical Tourists".
2. "Medical Tourism", Wikipedia.org
3. Uretsky, "The Thailand Tuck".
4. Kasturi Dewi, "Hospitals set fees for health tourism".
5. Kher, "Outsourcing Your Heart".
6. Kher, "Outsourcing Your Heart".
7. Lancaster, "Surgeries, Side trips for Medical Tourists".
8. Kher, "Outsourcing Your Heart".
9. Kher, "Outsourcing Your Heart".
10. Lancaster, "Surgeries, Side trips".
11. Lancaster, "Surgeries, side trips for medical tourists".
12. Kher, "Outsourcing Your Heart".
13. "NBC News".
14. Lancaster, "Surgeries, side trips for medical tourists".
15. Lancaster, "Surgeries, side trips for medical tourists".
16. Marcelo, "India fosters. . .".
17. Uretsky, "The 'Thailand Tuck'".
18. Robert Barmeyer, Personal Interview.
19. Kher, "Outsourcing Your Heart".
20. Kher, "Outsourcing Your Heart".
21. Uretsky,"The 'Thailand Tuck'".
22. *Ibid*.
23. Uretsky, "The 'Thailand Tuck'". . .
24. Lancaster, "Surgeries, Side trips. . ."
25. Todd, "Medical tourism saves. . ."
26. *Ibid*.
27. Uretsky, "The 'Thailand Tuck'".
28. Kher, "Outsourcing Your Heart".

29. U.S. Census Bureau.
30. Lancaster, "Surgeries, Side trips. . ."
31. Marcelo, "India fosters Medical tourism".
32. *Ibid*.
33. Lancaster, "Surgeries, Side trips. . .".
34. Kher, "Outsourcing Your Heart".
35. Cannon pg. 27.
36. Robert Barmeyer, Personal Interview.
37. Cannon pg. 139.
38. Thai Websites, "Healthcare in Thailand", 7 November 2006.
39. Healthcare Tourist.com. "The Process", 7 November 2006.

Marcelo, Ray, "India Fosters Growing Medical Tourism Sector", *The Financial Times,* 2 July 2003, 8 September 2006. http://yaleglobal.yale.edu/display.article?id=2016.

"NBC News", NBC, 20 February 2006, 11 September 2006, www.planethospital.com Thai Websites. "Healthcare in Thailand" 7 November 2006, www.thaiwebsites.com/healthcare.asp

Todd, Stephen, "Medical Tourism Saves You Money, But Which One Is Best?", Ezine Articles.com. 7 September 2006, http://ezinearticles.com/

Uretsky, Samuel D., "The 'Thailand Tuck'", MedHunters.com. 9 May 2005, 10 September 2006, http://www.medhunters.com/articles/medicalTourism.html

U.S. Census Bureau, "Poverty: Health Insurance Coverage in the United States". 13 October 2004. 11 September 2006, http://factfinder,census,gov/jsp/saff/SAFFInfo,jsp?_pageId=tp8_poverty

Wikipedia: the free encyclopedia, "Healthcare System", 11 Sept. 2006, www.wikipedia.org

Wikipedia: The free encyclopedia, "Medical Tourism", 11 Sept. 2006, www.wikipedia.org

Aaron, Henry J., William B. Schwartz, and Melissa Cox, Can we say no? the challenge of rationing healthcare, Brooklings Institution Press: Washington, 2005.

Cogan, John F., R. Glenn Hubbard, and Daniel P. Kessler, Healthy, Wealthy, and Wise: five steps to a better healthcare system, AEI Press: Washington, 2005.

Richmond, Julius B., and Rashi Fein, The Healthcare Mess: how we got into it and what it will take to get out, Harvard University Press: Cambridge, 2005.

The White House Domestic Policy Council, Health Security: the President's Report to the American People, October 1993.

Index

AAPI (American Association of Physician of Indian Origin), 99
Abhyanga, 189
Abnormal Uterine Bleeding, 149
Acupressure, 193
Acupuncture, 193
Advent Medical Services, 37, 89
Agarwal Vasan's Eye Hospital, 90
Aguada Beach, 14
AHLL (Apollo Health and Lifestyle Ltd.), 92
All India Institute of Medical Sciences, 76
Amarnath, 10
Ancient Civilization, 6
Angioplasty, 133
Apollo Cancer Hospital, 88
Apollo Hospitals Group, 88, 91
Aromatherapy, 194
Art of Living Course, 203
Asian Heart Institute, 76
Asia;
 Private Sector is Leading the Growth, 49
 Growth of the Medical Tourism Industry, 49
Aulia, Nizamuddin, 10
Axillary Breast Augmentation, 147
Ayurveda;
 Benefits, 185

Back-end Rule Setting, 85
Badrinath, 10
Bangla Sahib, 10
Beauty Care, 198
Benefits in India;
 Cost Benefit, 77
 Timeliness, 77
B.M. Birla Heart Research Centre, 76, 88
BMC (Bangkok Hospital Medical Centre), 59
Body Lift;
 Alternatives, 145
Bodhgaya, 10
Bone Marrow Transplant, 127
Brachioplasty;
 Benefits, 143
Brajbhoomi, 10
Breach Candy Hospital, 76
Breast Implant, 146
Breast Reduction, 148
British Patients, 169
Buddha, Gautama, 6
Bumrungrad *vs.* Bangkok Hospital, 56

CAM (Complementary and Alternative Medicine), 67
Cardiac Care, 128
Cardiac Catheterization, 132
Care and Cure Medi-Tours, 89
Central Body Lift, 143
Chakra Therapy, 195
Char Dham Yatra, 9
Chattris, 13
Choornaswedan, 189
Chisti, Moinuddin, 10
Christian Medical College, 76, 88
Common Surgical Interventions, 127
Coronary Angioplasty;
 Risks, 134
 Benefits, 133
 Alternatives, 132
Coronary Stenting;
 Benefits, 134-35

CT Angiography, 132
Cutting-edge Vacations, 159

Dental Care Packages, 39
Destination Banglore/Chandigarh, 85
De-Stressing, 73
Dhanyavaad, 118
Dialysis, 136
Drug Eluting Coronary Stenting;
  Benefits, 135
DSA (Digital Subtraction Angiography), 132

Eco-Tourism, 12
EHIRC (Escort Heart Institute and Research Centre), 96
Escorts Hospital and Research Centre, 89
Executive Health Check-up, 151
Extension of Visa, 22
Eye Care, 40

Fasting, 141
Feast and Festivals, 18
Foreign Medical Tourists, 114, 168

Gandusa, 191
Gangotri, 10
Gem Therapy, 193
Global Healthcare Bazaar, 113
Globalization and Medical Tourism, 284
Golden Temple, 10
Government and Private Care;
  Synergy, 74
Government Corporate Sector, 33
Grewal's Eye Institute, 90
Grim India, 319
Gynecology, 136

Health-Building, 73
Healthcare Business Services;
  Claim Adjudication, 84
  Network Intelligence, 85
Healthcare;
  Opportunities, 217
Healthcare Services and Medical Tourism, 206
Healthcare System, 176
Health Tourism, 25

Hinduja Hospital, 89
Homoeopathy, 196
Hospital Beds, 218

Incredible India Compaign, 4
India and US;
  Procedure Charges, 42
India as a Health Tourism Destination;
  Realities, 72
India;
  Facilities Available, 41
  United Health Group, 83
  Moving Ahead, 35
Indian Doctors;
  How can you Trust?, 158
Indian Medicine;
  Traditional Form, 185
India's Healthcare Industry, 207
India's Medical Tourism, 38
Indraprastha Medical Corporation, 89
Ind-US Health, 37
Industry's Best Practices, 50
Infra-mammary Breast Augmentation, 146
Inspiration Kerala, 89
Institute Cardiovascular Disease, 89
Insurance Muddle, 179
International Affiliations, 93
Interventional Cardiology, 128

Jaslok Hospital, 76
JCAHO (Joint Council on Accreditation of Healthcare Organisations), 180
JCI (Joint Commission International), 121
Joint Replacement Surgery, 137

Karnapooranam, 191
Kashaya Vasti, 190
Kaval, 190
Kayakalpa Chikitsa, 197
Kedarnath, 10
Kerala;
  God's Own Paradise, 183
  Pioneer State, 184
Kidney Transplant, 136
Kovai Medical Centre and Hospital Ltd., 103

Landscapes;
Variety, 10
Languages, Cultures and Dances, 19
LASIK (Laser Assisted Stromal Insitu Keratomileusis), 40
Longfield Management, 90
Lower Body Lift, 143
Lotus Temple, 10

Magnet Therapy, 195
Mahaveer Jayanthi, 18
Manipal Heart Foundation, 76
Marma Chikitsa, 191
Massage;
Oil and Herbs, 185
Medical and Surgical Excellence;
India's Islands, 87
Medical Equipment, 219
Medical Tourism;
Need, 31
Scope, 31
Selling Points, 109
Problems, 216
Medical Tourism as a Distortion of Priorities, 214
Medical Tourism Blog, 295
Medical Tourism Boom, 67
Medical Tourism in India;
How to Promote?, 108
Medical Visa, 26
MediEscapes India, 89
Member Benefit Analysis, 85
Member Benefit Creation, 85
MLC (Multileaf Collimator), 100
MRA (Magnetic Resonance Angiography), 132
MTC (Maharashtra Medical Tourism Council), 123

NABH (National Accreditation Board for Hospitals and Healthcare Providers), 80
Naga Hills, 11
Nalanda, 10
Nankana Sahib, 10
Nasyam, 191
National Health Policy, 109
Naturopathy, 192
Natya Shastra, 20
NCAER (National Council for Applied Economic Research), 9
Nehru Hospital, 89
Neuro Surgeon's Delight, 177
Neurosurgery, 138
NHS (National Health Service), 29
Njavarakizhi, 192
NM Excellence, 97
Non-Medical Services, 51

Optional Services, 82
Osteoporosis, 137

Panchkarma, 198
PATA (Pacific Asia Travel Association), 3
Patna Sahib, 10
PD Hinduja National Hospital, 98
Peri-areolar Breast Augmentation, 146
Philippines Faith Healers, 69
PHP (Preventive Healthcare Programme), 38
Pizhichil, 190
Plastic Surgery, 142
Pragati Maidan, 24
Pranayama, 187
Prerana Healthcare Services, 89
Preventive Healthcare, 140
PTA (Percutaneous Transluminal Angioplasty), 129
Procedure, 130

Quality Healthcare, 77
Quest Med Tourism, 78

Rajasthan Enterprise, 125
Rameshwaram, 10
Rasayana Chikitsa, 197
REIKI, 196
Refractive Surgery, 139
Religious Tourism, 8
Religious Tourism Centres, 256
Religious Tourism *v.* Medical Tourism, 124
Reproductive Tourism, 176
Rivers;
Ganges, 11

Sahaj Dental Clinic, 89

Sarvanga Dhara, 190
Satellite Centres, 103
Sea Resorts, 14
Service Providers, 156
Shirodhara, 189
Siddha, 200
Sirovasti, 190
Sisganj Gurudwara, 10
SLE (Systematic Lupus Erythematosis), 67
Snehapanam, 190
Spinal Fusion Surgery;
Treatment, 115
Spiritual Healing, 202
Sudarshan Kriya, 204
Sweda Karma, 198

Takra Dhara, 189
Tata Memorial Cancer Hospital, 88
TAT (Tourism Authority of Thailand), 55
TCM (Traditional Chinese Medicine), 50, 67
TCS (Tata Consultancy Service), 95
Technological Sophistication, 77
Tibetan, 201
Tooth Tourism, 126
Top Ten Medical Tourism, 52
Tourism;
Perspectives, 1
Trauma Surgery, 138
Trehan, Naresh, 80
Tummy Tuck, 149
Twain, Mark, 4

Umblical Breast Augmentation, 147
Unani, 199
Unethical Practices, 216
Urology, 139

Vaishno Devi, 9
Validity of Visa, 27
Vdvarthanam, 191
Villas and Palaces, 17
Vindya Mountain, 11
Vipassana Meditation, 204
Visa to Attendant, 27

What is Body Lift?, 143
What is Coronary Angiography?, 131
What is Medical Tourism?, 29
WHO (World Health Organisation), 216
World-class Treatment in India, 153
Cost Savings, 154

Yamunotri, 10
Yoga, 187